MW00442468

Mountaineering in
ANTARCTICA

Cover image: against a backdrop of the dramatic Fenris Mountains, expedition skiers
Alex Lowe, Conrad Anker and Jon Krakauer approach a climb in Queen Maud Land.

MOUNTAINEERING IN ANTARCTICA
Climbing in the Frozen South
Damien Gildea

© Damien Gildea, 2010
First published in 2010 by Éditions Nevicata, Brussels, Belgium.

ISBN 978-2-87523-006-5
Dépôt légal: novembre 2010
D/2010/9594/4
© Éditions Nevicata, 2010

A French version of this book is published simultaneously by Éditions Nevicata
under the title 'Les Montagnes de l'Antarctique' (ISBN 978-2-87523-000-3).

Climbing, skiing and mountaineering are inherently dangerous activities.
The author and publishers shall accept no liability whatsoever for any loss,
injury or inconvenience resulting from the use of this book.

Éditions Nevicata
42, avenue du Général de Gaulle
1050 Brussels
Belgium
info@editionsnevicata.be
www.editionsnevicata.be

Mountaineering in
ANTARCTICA
Climbing in the Frozen South

Damien Gildea

ÉDITIONS
NEVICATA

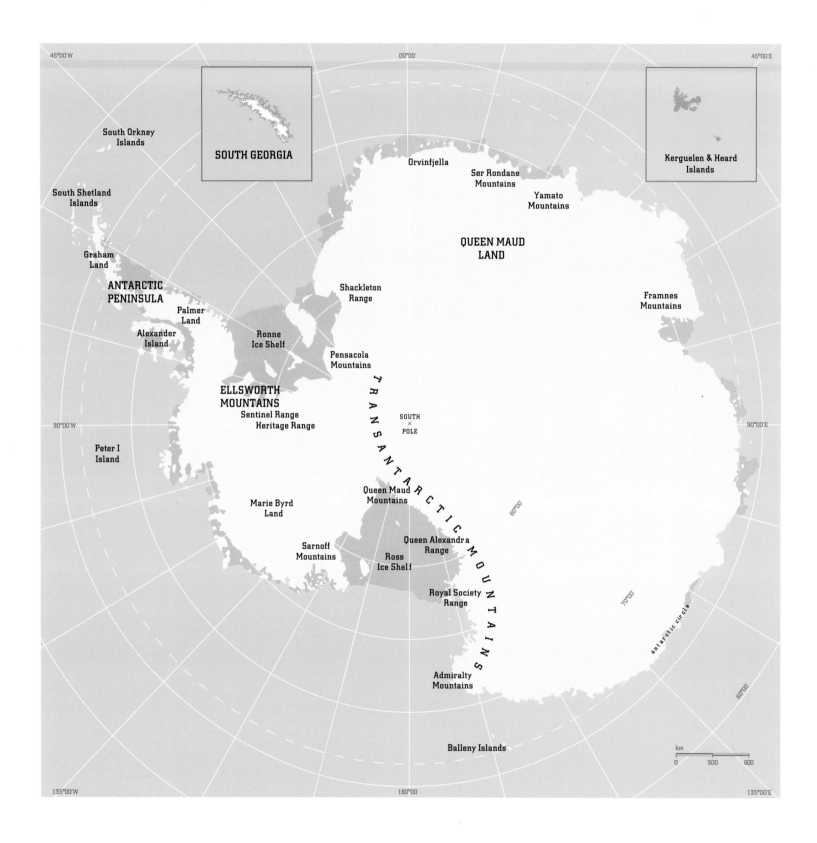

South Orkney
Islands

SOUTH GEORGIA

Kerguelen & Heard
Islands

South Shetland
Islands

Orvinfjella

Sør Rondane
Mountains

Yamato
Mountains

QUEEN MAUD
LAND

Graham
Land

ANTARCTIC
PENINSULA

Palmer
Land

Shackleton
Range

Framnes
Mountains

Alexander
Island

Ronne
Ice Shelf

Pensacola
Mountains

ELLSWORTH
MOUNTAINS

Sentinel Range

Heritage Range

SOUTH
×
POLE

90°00'W

90°00'E

Peter I
Island

Marie Byrd
Land

Queen Maud
Mountains

80°00'

Sarnoff
Mountains

Queen Alexandra
Range

Ross
Ice Shelf

70°00'

Royal Society
Range

antarctic circle

Admiralty
Mountains

60°00'

Balleny Islands

TRANSANTARCTIC MOUNTAINS

45°00'W

00°00'

45°00'E

135°00'W

180°00'

135°00'E

km

0   300   600

Contents

Introduction   7

(1) ELLSWORTH MOUNTAINS   11

    Sentinel Range   11

    Heritage Range   43

(2) ANTARCTIC PENINSULA   47

    South Orkney Islands   51

    South Shetland Islands   52

    Graham Land   58

    Alexander Island   93

    Palmer Land   95

(3) QUEEN MAUD LAND   99

(4) TRANSANTARCTIC MOUNTAINS   127

(5) SOUTH GEORGIA   147

(6) OTHER AREAS   167

    Kerguelen Islands   167

    Heard Island   173

    Framnes Mountains   177

    Marie Byrd Land   178

    Remote Antarctic Islands   180

Antarctic 4000 m Mountains   182

Antarctic Feature Names   183

Index   184

Acknowledgements   191

Introduction

Climbing in Antarctica is a special experience that never fails to affect those fortunate enough to do it. For most of Antarctica's human history this experience was restricted to those who worked as part of national government Antarctic programs, requiring great financial and logistical efforts. Visitors – and in Antarctica we are *all* visitors – were a small cog in a vast scientific and political machine. The scope and quality of work done by these programs has been incredible and continues to be so, providing us with critical insights into not only Antarctica but also our world as a whole. However, in purely mountaineering terms, the activity of such operations was understandably limited. Mountaineering merely enabled scientific work, with recreational climbing discouraged and usually unrecorded. In the following pages I hope to preserve at least some of those ascents, as often they have proven to be more significant to those involved than the official scientific record may indicate, and they are part of the rich human history of Antarctica that should be recorded for all to enjoy.

In general the earliest climbs were done on the Antarctic Peninsula, as it was the most accessible part of the continent and it remains popular to this day, the mountains set against the sea as beautiful as ever. As human activity spread to other parts of the land, scientific stations were established and they became bases for exploring any nearby mountains, most notably the vast Transantarctic Mountains from Scott and McMurdo bases on Ross Island. However, with the advent of private travel to inland Antarctica in the 1980s, other areas became popular solely for their value as climbing objectives. Thus the continent's highest mountain, Mount Vinson in the Sentinel Range, has become a commercially viable destination on an annual basis and the stunning rock towers of Queen Maud Land are visited with some regularity. But other areas also contain interesting peaks, particularly the southern Transantarctics – home to Antarctica's highest unclimbed mountains – and the relatively unexplored ranges of Alexander Island, too far down the Peninsula to sail to, not popular enough to fly to. Scattered around the continent are other worthwhile objectives, such as the big rock walls in the Ohio Ranges and Sarnoff Mountains, the remote peaks of Mac Robertson Land and, of course, the storm-swept giants rising out of the sea on South Georgia.

STEPHEN CHAPLIN CLIMBS HIGH ON THE WEST FACE OF MOUNT CRADDOCK, Sentinel Range, Ellsworth Mountains. Beneath, the Bender Glacier drains south into the larger Nimitz Glacier, beyond which are the smaller peaks of the Bastien Range.

No one mountain or route in Antarctica could be said to be anything greater – higher, longer, harder, steeper – than some other route or mountain on another continent. The location is the difference. There is only one Antarctica. Climbing in Antarctica is the closest that most of us will get to climbing on another planet – *on* Earth, but not *of* Earth. To walk the Vinson summit plateau is to tiptoe across the roof of a great ship adrift in an endless white sea, suspended above every other thing on the continent. You cannot walk out to a village or road, as in the Himalaya or Alaska. You can never walk home.

It would be wrong to discuss the future of the continent for Science only in the loose, emotional language of modern environmentalism, or through the selfish justifications of adventurers and sportsmen. But just as Antarctica should not be a political fiefdom for diplomats, it is more than just a giant laboratory and requires more than just science programs to ensure a safe future. We should *all* care about Antarctica; it is too important not to.

JED BROWN ON AN UNNAMED SUMMIT ABOVE THE EMBREE GLACIER. Behind is the dangerous northeast face of Mount Anderson, Sentinel Range, Ellsworth Mountains.

8

CLIMBERS AT THEIR BASE CAMP
in the Orvinfjella Range, Queen Maud Land.

Climbing in Antarctica is not essential to humanity: it is a luxury. It is also a way in which we can see, understand and connect with a continent that is so important to the rest of the world. By opening up both the history and future of these faraway Antarctic mountains to a wider audience I hope that more people will come to love this place and hence care more about it.

Antarctica presents us with a challenge: to interact more responsibly with the natural environment of which we are all a part, not above. We must not damage that on which we rely for our survival, we have to make use of it without destroying it, and to share it without conflict. Our choice defines us, as will our stewardship of Antarctica.

Climbing, at its best, is about desire, passion, partnership, integrity, commitment, excellence and joy. Antarctica deserves no less.

1. Sentinel Range
2. Heritage Range

ELLSWORTH
MOUNTAINS

The Ellsworth Mountains are comprised of two main ranges: the high Sentinel Range in the north and the lower Heritage Range in the south, with the two separated by the Minnesota Glacier that runs from west to east.

SENTINEL RANGE

The Sentinels stretch for almost 200 km like a long, jagged spine, with numerous rocky ridges shooting out to the side and sweeping down to the ice, unusually uniform in their appearance and spacing. In between these ridges lie many couloirs and big, mixed faces, some rising over 2000 m above the flat ice stretching out east and west.

At 4892 m, Mount Vinson[1] is the highest peak in Antarctica and the highest point of the Vinson Massif. A great white bulk of terrain around 15 km long by 15 km wide, it is situated roughly midway along the Sentinel Range, at the southern end of the highest section. The Massif is crowned with numerous small peaks situated around a high, windswept plateau of bare ice, from which several long ridges drop down to the surrounding glaciers. As is so often the case in other ranges around the world, the highest mountain has some relatively gentle slopes, but Vinson also has steeper faces and narrow ridges that provide more challenging climbing. North of Vinson, once Mount Shinn is passed, the range narrows dramatically to the sharp crests of Epperly, Tyree and Shear and generally stays that way until its far northern end, past Long Gables and Anderson. South of the Vinson Massif and joined to it by a high col, is the Craddock Massif, a smaller and steeper ridge-like massif containing several high points. Yet the southern end of the Craddock Massif provides a dramatic end to the high Sentinels, as once Craddock's south face drops to the Severinghaus Glacier there is nothing higher than 4000 m along a line from here all the way to the South Pole.

[1] Until August 18th 2006 there was no such thing as 'Mount Vinson', despite the claims of numerous commercial websites, magazine articles and expedition merchandise to the contrary. Frustrated with the proliferation of this misnomer, Damien Gildea suggested to the United States Geological Survey Advisory Committee on Antarctic Names (USGS ACAN) in March 2006 that the name 'Mount Vinson' be added to denote the highest point of the existing Vinson Massif and the peak that all successful Vinson mountaineers climb. This was officially approved in 2006. Hence, Mount Vinson is the highest summit of the Vinson Massif.

DAMIEN GILDEA
near the summit of Mount Anderson.

Sentinel Range

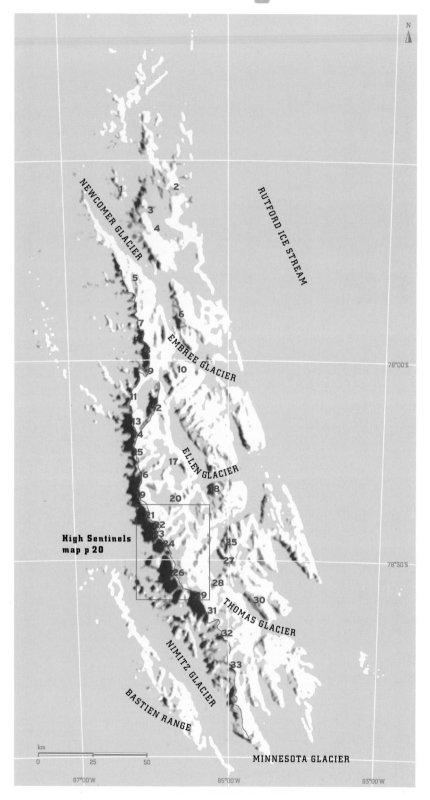

Newcomer Glacier

Rutford Ice Stream

Embree Glacier

Ellen Glacier

High Sentinels
map p 20

Thomas Glacier

Nimitz Glacier

Bastien Range

Minnesota Glacier

78°00'S

78°30'S

87°00'W

85°00'W

83°00'W

km
0   25   50

1. **Mount Wyatt Earp** 2370 m
2. **Mount Morgensen** 2790 m
3. **Mount Ulmer** 2775 m
4. **Mount Washburn** 2727 m
5. **Mount Crawford** 2637 m
6. **Mount Malone** 2460 m
7. **Mount Sharp** 3359 m
8. **Mount Dalrymple** 3600 m
9. **Mount Goldthwait** 3813 m
10. **Mount Schmid** 2430 m
11. **Mount Hale** 3546 m
12. **Mount Press** 3760 m
13. **Mount Bentley** 4137 m
14. **Mount Anderson** 4144 m
15. **Long Gables** 4059 m
16. **Mount Giovinetto** 4074 m
17. **Mount Jumper** 2890 m
18. **Mount Levack** 2751 m
19. **Mount Ostenso** 4085 m
20. **Mount Bearskin** 2850 m
21. **Mount Gardner** 4573 m
22. **Mount Tyree** 4852 m
23. **Mount Epperly** 4508 m
24. **Mount Shinn** 4660 m
25. **Mount Waldron** 3217 m
26. **Mount Vinson** 4892 m
27. **Mount Tuck** 3588 m
28. **Mount Mohl** 3604 m
29. **Mount Rutford** 4477 m
30. **Mount Benson** 2184 m
31. **Mount Craddock** 4368 m
32. **Mount Allen** 3248 m
33. **Mount Southwick** 3087 m

FINDING 'VINSON'

It may seem hard to believe now, but Antarctica's highest mountains were almost completely unknown until the 1950s. In 1935 the American aviator Lincoln Ellsworth had flown over the range that was later to bear his name but it was almost totally obscured by cloud. Only a small peak at one end was visible, so he had no idea that the continent's highest peaks lay right beneath him. He named the 2775 m high peak after his wife, Mary Louise Ulmer, although now it is known simply as Mount Ulmer.

Up until 1959 the exact location of the continent's highest point was unknown, but it had already been provisionally named 'Vinson', after Carl G. Vinson, Senator for the US state of Georgia, who had long been a strong supporter of US Antarctic operations. Even as late as 1959, however, there was some speculation that this 'Vinson' may actually lie in the area of the big volcanos in Marie Byrd Land, rather than further east in Ellsworth Land[2]. This speculation is believed to have originated from a flight by Richard Byrd and Paul Siple, during the 1946-47 season of Operation Highjump, when they reported seeing rocky mountain features above their plane flying at around 3000 m. Siple and others on the plane estimated that the top of the 'mountain' must be over 5000 m. It is now believed that this was a mistake caused by the angle of the plane flying past one of the bigger peaks of the Executive Committee Range (even though these peaks had been known by Byrd since 1934) and possibly exacerbated by previous flights that had already mistaken Mount Sidley for the elusive 'Vinson'. The USAF had even published a chart that showed a big 'peak' around 77°S 124°W that people thought was either 'Vinson' or 'Nimitz', another feature whose existence had yet to be proven.

This ambiguity persisted for years, but by the late 1950s the US had begun mapping Antarctica and traverse parties set out to find and map these mythical mountains. In 1959 one such party found 'Nimitz', as the expedition leader, Scottish climber John Pirrit, later wrote:

'... according to the map, Vinson should be on our left towering about 14,000ft above the snow level... no sign of anything, must have passed over the spot where Mount Nimitz supposed to

2   Pirrit, John, *Across West Antarctica*, John Smith, Glasgow, 1967.

LOOKING SOUTH FROM THE SUMMIT OF MOUNT BENTLEY.
The obvious large rocky face left of centre is the north face of Mount Tyree with the summit of Mount Shinn visible to the left. Right of Tyree is the summit of Mount Gardner.

be... nothing.... mountains ahead must be peaks of the Executive Committee Range.'

Pirrit then climbed to around 3650 m on one of these peaks, later shown to be Mount Sidley, which at 4285 m is the highest of the Executive Committee Range, as well as summiting and surveying three smaller peaks to the north. But still no 'Vinson'.

However, in January 1958 a USN flight from Byrd Station had sighted high mountains further east in Ellsworth Land[3]. During the 1958-59 season another traverse party driving Tucker Sno-Cats headed in this direction and found a great mountain massif, which when surveyed seemed to be higher at its highest point than anything else yet seen in Antarctica. At last, Vinson had been found. One of the members of that traverse was a young glaciologist named Bill Long, who would return seven years later to stand on that highest point. More scientific parties visited the area in the early 1960s and even made a few minor ascents. The first mountain climbed in the range was Mount Wyatt Earp (2370 m) in December 1961 by US geologists Trevor Bastien and John Splettstoesser, who had climbed the lower Howard Nunataks (c.1800 m) the week before. In the 1963-64 season a team from the University of Minnesota conducted work in the area and one member, a young geologist and keen climber named John Evans, was even offered a helicopter ride to the summit of Vinson, which he declined. Evans, like Long, was destined to return.

POLITICS & PLANS

Now that Vinson had been confirmed as Antarctica's highest mountain, interest in climbing it naturally began to grow. This was particularly so in the United States, where two separate groups of experienced climbers, one based on the east coast and the other based in the Pacific northwest, had been making informal plans to attempt Vinson. Yet they had met with no success, particularly with regard to the main obstacle: the huge logistical effort to access inland Antarctica. The US Antarctic authorities had already established what would become a permanent policy stance: their facilities, personnel and logistical capabilities were for science, not sport. However, a rogue element was set to force their hand.

[3] Ibidem.

In 1962, Woodrow Wilson Sayre, a well-connected New Englander and grandson of former US President Woodrow Wilson, made a daring lightweight attempt on Mount Everest. Gaining a permit for the nearby Gyachung Kang (7952 m), Wilson and his three team mates gained the Nepal-Tibet border pass of the Nup La with the help of Sherpas, but then diverted back down east into the western arm of the Rongbuk Glacier. Travelling light and relaying loads, they reached the main Rongbuk and turned into the eastern arm, gaining the old pre-WWII advance base camp of the British expeditions to the north ridge. They were defeated at the North Col and returned unscathed back the way they had come. Their adventure was understandably frowned upon in Nepal and caused something of a diplomatic incident that threatened the upcoming 1963 American Everest Expedition, which would eventually go on to make the first ascent of Everest's difficult west ridge. Sayre's raid, later recounted in the book *Four Against Everest*, was temporarily covered up by the authorities, but not forgotten. Now, a couple of years later, Sayre was making plans for Vinson and was even reported to have hired a pilot and plane to fly there. The US government heard of the plans and decided to step in, to pre-empt the situation and repel Sayre and any others that they now realised may try to do something similar. In fact the famous Austrian climber Heinrich Harrer also planned a Vinson expedition and even enquired as to the possibility of obtaining logistical help when he visited the McMurdo base as a guest in 1961.

The authorities approached the American Alpine Club with a proposal to support a team of American climbers to climb Vinson and contact was made with the two groups who had already shown interest. To avoid potential conflict it was decided to choose a leader from outside these two groups and so Nicholas Clinch was approached. Clinch, a lawyer from California, had already led two major American mountaineering expeditions with great success. In 1958 he led a team to attempt the 8068 m high Gasherbrum I (Hidden Peak) in the Karakoram range, Pakistan. The expedition put Andy Kaufmann and Pete Schoening on the summit, which was the first American ascent of an 8000 m peak and eventually the only 8000er to have had its first ascent by Americans. In 1960 Clinch returned to Pakistan, leading a team on the first ascent of Masherbrum (7821 m), the twenty-second highest mountain in the world.

The US authorities were open about wanting to 'spoil the prize', as Clinch later put it, so that no one else would want to go to Antarctica for Vinson. In fact, on seeing photos of the highly impressive-looking Tyree and realising climbers would find it irresistible, one senior Navy official suggested that the team should climb it as well, just to be sure! As it transpired, in addition to their summit success, the resulting expedition could also be seen as successful, as no non-government climbers tried to set foot on Vinson for nearly 17 years.

Despite the scientific visits made to the lower Sentinels in the early 1960s, Vinson as a climbing objective in 1966 was a complete unknown. In contrast, by 1966 all of Asia's fourteen 8000 m peaks had been climbed. In fact, Mount Everest had been climbed by 24 people, from five expeditions, via three different routes. More people had stood atop Everest than had even set foot in the Sentinel Range.

1966 - THE FIRST ASCENT

Clinch's team was strong and experienced. John Evans had already visited the Sentinel Range as a geologist in 1961-62 with a team from the University of Minnesota, but he is probably better known for making the first ascent of the stupendous Hummingbird Ridge on Canada's highest peak, Mount Logan (5959 m), in 1965. Evans made an early ascent of The Nose on Yosemite's El Capitan and would later go on major expeditions to the southwest face of Everest in 1971 and the ill-fated 1976 expedition to Nanda Devi (7816 m), as well as pioneering a route on the west face of Alaska's beautiful Mount Huntington (3731 m). The glaciologist Bill Long, then living

ONE OF THE PENNANTS OF THE 1966-67 AMERICAN ANTARCTIC MOUNTAINEERING EXPEDITION.
This pennant was left on the summit of Mount Gardner in January 1967 and retrieved by Mugs Stump in 1989.

and teaching in Alaska, had also worked in Antarctica and had been in the Vinson area. In 1958 he made the first ascent of Mount Glossopteris (2865 m) in the remote Ohio Range, and the leaf fossils found there helped strengthen the case for the theories of tectonic plates, continental drift and the existence of the supercontinent Gondwana. Brian Marts – at 23 the team's youngest member – and Barry Corbet were both professional climbing guides, and Corbet had been on the famous 1963 American Everest Expedition that made the first ascent of the mountain's west ridge. Peter Schoening from Seattle was already famous in the climbing world, not only for his first ascent of Hidden Peak and a new route on Mount Logan, but for saving four of his team mates on K2 (8611 m) in 1954 when he held their fall with just an ice axe belay. Sam Silverstein, the team doctor, and Charles Hollister had been on the 1954 first ascent of the huge southeast spur of Mount McKinley (6194 m) in Alaska, while Eiichi Fukushima and Richard Wahlstrom were climbing instructors at the University of Washington in Seattle.

They all flew to Christchurch, New Zealand, from where the United States bases its Antarctic program with flights to the McMurdo base on Ross Island and onward to the South Pole. In Christchurch the team obtained all their expedition food, greatly assisted by Norman Hardie, the climber who made the first ascent of the world's third highest mountain Kangchenjunga (8586 m) in 1955 and who had been a former leader of the NZ Scott Base on Ross Island. After a brief stop at McMurdo the team flew straight to the range but could not land due to poor visibility, so diverted to Byrd Station where they waited for 10 hours. On December 8th they eventually landed a ski-equipped LC-130 on the flat ice around 20 km west of the main peaks. From here they used a snowmobile to carry their supplies closer to the mountain, though they were forced to do a short stint of manhauling as the fuel for the machines, dropped on a previous flight, could not initially be located.

Sam Silverstein had identified a narrow gap in the ridge that runs down southwest from Mount Shinn as a possible entry point to the actual slopes of Vinson itself. The climbers soon reached this gap, naming it 'Sam's Col', and fixed ropes up it to carry loads to the next stage. Crossing the basin of the upper Branscomb Glacier beyond, the team ascended the headwall to what is now Goodge Col and set a camp. Setting off on December 18th Barry Corbet, John Evans, Bill Long and Pete Schoening soon reached the summit, where they took photographs with the flags of the 12 original signatories of the Antarctic Treaty arranged in a circle. The rest

‹ **PETE SCHOENING AND JOHN EVANS**
on the summit of Mount Vinson,
December 18th 1966.

› **BARRY CORBET**
on the summit of Mount Tyree,
Antarctica's second-highest mountain,
January 5th 1967.

‹ **BARRY CORBET** high on the northwest ridge of Mount Tyree during the first ascent.

› **BRIAN MARTS** climbing high on the northwest ridge of Long Gables during the first ascent, January 1967.

of the team would summit Vinson over the next two days. The prize had been spoiled! In the few days before Christmas the team then turned to the nearby Mount Shinn, again summiting in three groups over three days.

The whole group then moved north and started up the obvious couloir at the northern end of Mount Gardner's long west face. Fixing ropes in the couloir, they placed a camp on a rocky platform near the top, before traversing along and across the vast undulating plateau to set a camp at around 4100 m on the upper eastern side of Gardner. From here Evans and Marts summited first, on New Year's Eve, followed by all the others except Corbet. However, the great challenge of Tyree looms to the north above this high camp, a steep rocky pyramid separated from Gardner by a narrow ridge. Many in the team were intimidated by the thought of attempting Tyree, so it was never a sure thing. They realised they would need a forward camp closer to Tyree itself, which meant finding a way from high on Gardner down and onto the ridge leading to Tyree. The first attempt ended in Evans and Corbet dangling out of a bottomless gully high over the huge east face. The eventual route went almost to the summit of Gardner but then dropped off down the upper east face to the snowy slopes on the east side of the ridge. This was fixed with ropes and Fukushima, Long and Marts helped set and supply a camp to launch Corbet and Evans onto Tyree. Again, an initial attempt failed, when they tried to follow the crest of the ridge from their camp along to Tyree. They then realised they could move along the snow under the ridge and gain a small couloir that cut back up onto Tyree's northwest ridge where it starts to rise. Following this they gained the ridge but actually climbed for much of the time on the upper west face where the climbing was never difficult but challenging and very exposed. On January 5th 1967 Corbet and Evans reached the summit of Tyree, the grand prize and far and away the hardest climb in Antarctica up to that time. The pair retraced their route down the ridge, unroping for much of it, and reached their camp after a momentous 22 hours. On the way back over Gardner they even diverted to allow Corbet to stand on Gardner's summit, the only member not to have done so by then.

Less than a week later the whole team was once again travelling north along the flat ice to squeeze a couple more climbs in before they left, thinking they would never get the chance to return. Two attempts were made on the long west ridge of Long Gables before a third saw them finally reach the summit. Fukushima, Long, Marts and Schoening climbed the ridge and traversed onto the upper north face to circle around to the summit, a long single push giving sustained and exposed climbing second only to Tyree in difficulty. At the same time, Hollister and Silverstein, who had been about to attempt Mount Giovinetto, joined Evans and Wahlstrom to make the first ascent of Mount Ostenso, climbing the moderate snow slope on the northwest side to reach an airy whipped-cream summit.

So ended one of the most successful mountaineering expeditions of all time. A single team had arrived in an unknown range, climbing not only the highest mountain on the continent, with all members summiting, but also reaching the summits of the second, third and fourth highest peaks as well, with a couple of other high summits thrown in for good measure. It was an incredible achievement. Corbet and Evans became the first people to climb Antarctica's three highest mountains, a feat not equalled for over two decades, when they were eventually climbed again by Conrad Anker.

1979 - A STOLEN SUMMIT & THE MYSTERY FLAG

Vinson Massif was not visited again for 13 years, when a US scientific party led by Professor Campbell Craddock based itself to the south of the range, on the Minnesota Glacier. The party also included three international guests: geologists Peter von Gizycki and Werner Buggisch from West Germany, and Victor Samsonov from the Soviet Union. These three needed to do field-work low on the mountain and were instructed not to go for the summit. Yet after being dropped by helicopter at a base west of 'Sam's Col', they could not resist the urge to climb Antarctica's highest peak and reached the summit on December 22nd 1979, by the route of first ascent. Samsonov rammed his ski pole into the snow on the summit – it remained there until 2007 – and tied a small, red USSR flag to it. A US survey team far out on the ice to the southeast could actually make out the flag with their instruments, and in so doing were fortuitously able to produce a

IN DECEMBER 2006 FOR THE 40TH ANNIVERSARY OF VINSON'S FIRST ASCENT Eiichi Fukushima, John Evans, Sam Silverstein and Brian Marts returned to Vinson Base Camp.

19

**GERMAN SCIENTIST AND CLIMBER
PETER VON GIZYCKI**
with the State Flag of Alaska that he found
on the summit of Vinson in 1979.

more accurate height for Vinson than had been previously calculated. Thus the height of Vinson was adjusted from 5140 m down to 4897 m, though the older figure erroneously appeared on some maps for years afterwards. The unauthorised ascent of Vinson caused some controversy within the US program.

As a sidenote, the three also made an error that would be repeated occasionally in following years. Ascending the shallow valley up to the main summit, they initially thought a similar peak to the east of Vinson was actually the main summit. However, upon reaching its top they saw the higher peak to the west and, realising their error, moved across to climb the true high point. In fact, the 1966 Vinson first ascent team had wondered if they were actually on the highest point and several of them secretly feared for years – unnecessarily of course – that they had made a giant mistake! This peak was erroneously climbed in 1989 and then deliberately climbed again in 1992. The latter team of Britons thought they had made a first ascent and named it 'Kershaw Peak', after Giles Kershaw, who had been killed not long before in a gyrocopter accident on the Antarctic Peninsula. However, as Kershaw already had a feature named after him, the USGS rejected it and adopted the British climbers' second suggestion, Sublime Peak, which is now the official name.

On the summit von Gizycki found a blue flag, half-covered in snow. Though ripped and somewhat faded, a few stars could be made out, leading the trio to believe they had found the Australian flag left on the summit by the 1966 first ascent team, who had left a flag of each of the 12 member nations of the Antarctic Treaty at that time. Some years later von Gizycki was in contact with John Evans and mentioned the flag. Seeing a photo of it, Evans did not think it was the flag they had left on the summit. On reviewing his June 1967 *National Geographic* von Gizycki realised that his flag was indeed noticeably larger than the 12 national flags left in a circle by the Americans.

So who had left the flag? Had an Australian climber secretly ascended Vinson in the years between 1967 and 1979? Such an outlandish feat seemed the only possible answer, and caused numerous discussions amongst those involved. In an attempt to solve the mystery of the flag, Damien Gildea travelled to Germany in February 2003 to interview Peter von Gizycki and photograph the flag in more detail, and he also corresponded further with Evans and others. Then, in 2004, Evans mentioned the flag to Bill Long, the other geologist on the first ascent of Vinson. Long remembered that he had in fact taken, and planted on the summit, an extra, more personal flag. It was this flag, and only this flag, that had survived 13 years on the roof of Antarctica: the state flag of Alaska.

1983 – VINSON AS THE SEVENTH SUMMIT

The next person to touch Samsonov's ski pole was the famous British climber Chris Bonington. He had been invited on a bold expedition organised by the wealthy US pair of Dick Bass and Frank Wells, who had embarked on an odyssey to climb the highest point on each continent. The challenge would become known as the Seven Summits and revolutionised private travel to Antarctica. Bass and Wells chartered a DC-6 and the experienced British polar pilot Giles Kershaw to fly them, Bonington, Rick Ridgeway, Steve Marts and two Japanese climbers to Vinson from Punta Arenas, Chile, via the Antarctic Peninsula and using fuel caches placed with assistance from the Chilean government. Legendary Italian mountaineer Reinhold Messner had wanted to join the group but Bass and Wells refused, as it would have led to Messner becoming the first person to complete the Seven Summits.

The Bass and Wells group used the same route as the 1966 and 1979 ascents, but on the first attempt, on November 23rd, all except Bonington were turned back by high winds and the brutal cold. Bass, Wells, Ridgeway and Marts summited a week later. This was the first time Vinson

High Sentinels

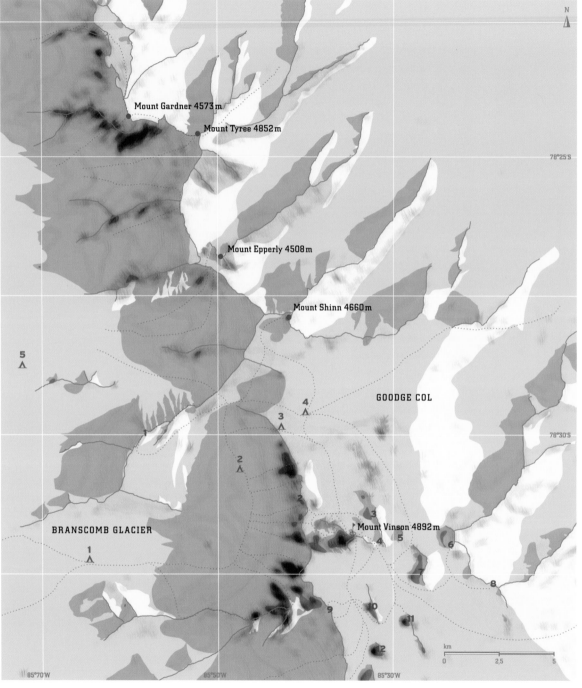

1. **Knutzen Peak** 3373 m
2. **Branscomb Peak** 4520 m
3. **4753 m**
4. **Sublime Peak** 4865 m
5. **Corbet Peak** 4822 m
6. **Schoening Peak** 4743 m
7. **Clinch Peak** 4841 m
8. **Marts Peak** 4551 m
9. **Silverstein Peak** 4790 m
10. **Hollister Peak** 4729 m
11. **Wahlstrom Peak** 4677 m
12. **Fukushima Peak** 4634 m

1. **Vinson Base Camp** 2100 m
2. **Low Camp** 2800 m
3. **High Camp** 3775 m
4. **Shinn Camp** 3700 m
5. **Old Vinson Base Camp** (1966–1993)

Main routes
....

Mount Gardner 4573 m
Mount Tyree 4852 m
Mount Epperly 4508 m
Mount Shinn 4660 m
GOODGE COL
BRANSCOMB GLACIER
Mount Vinson 4892 m

78°25'S
78°30'S
85°70'W
85°50'W
85°30'W

km
0   2,5   5

THE WEST FACE OF MOUNT VINSON
above the Branscomb Glacier.

had been climbed as one of the Seven Summits and the first time it had been climbed without government assistance south of the Peninsula.

1985 - ADVENTURE NETWORK INTERNATIONAL

Through 1984 and 1985 Canadian climber Pat Morrow was planning to climb Vinson to complete his own version of the Seven Summits quest, which included Carstenz Pyramid (4884 m) in Indonesia's West Papua province (formerly Irian Jaya) instead of the much lower and easier Kosciuszko (2228 m) in Australia. Morrow brought together people from various areas to form the expedition team, but an attempt in 1984 via Ushuaia failed due to engine trouble. However, in late 1985 Giles Kershaw once again flew down the Peninsula from Chile and they reached the mountain. This required no small amount of political negociation and diplomacy with the Chilean authorities, but the resulting relationships formed the basis for operations that last to this day.

Morrow was on the flight and his November 19th summit of Vinson made him the first person to do the 'Carstenz set' of the Seven Summits. The Canadian-resident British climber Martyn Williams was also there and with Morrow he made the first ski descent of Vinson. Morrow, Williams and Kershaw would continue the operation for several years, taking climbers to Vinson and other adventurers to inland Antarctica under the name Adventure Network International (ANI). Also on that flight was US businessman Steve Fossett, who would go on to break world ballooning records but tragically died during a routine plane flight in 2007. Part of the deal with the Chilean authorities, who consider the Ellsworths to be in their sovereign territory as part of their Antarctic claim, was that the expedition must include a Chilean national. Hence a young climber from Santiago joined the team. Alejo Contreras went on to make numerous ascents of Vinson over the following years as a guide and has worked in support for many other major Antarctic expeditions since then. A month later a second flight went in, carrying some of ANI's first 'celebrity' clients: the outdoor entrepreneurs Yvon Chouinard and Doug Tompkins, as well as Gerry Roach and Glen Porzak. Roach became the second person to do the 'Kosciuszko set', with Porzak not far behind.

From the 1986-87 season the number of clients grew, most of them in the process of completing the Seven Summits, a concept that was then considered relatively new and adventurous. Others came simply to experience a new adventure, taking advantage of these new logistics that opened up a part of the planet that had before seemed almost impossibly inaccessible. Messner finally reached his seventh summit in 1986, and in 1988 the American guides Phil Ershler and Vern Tejas began guiding clients up Vinson, a job they continue to do independently some 20 years later.

THE HUGE SOUTHWEST FACE OF MOUNT EPPERLY showing the 1994 Loretan route of first ascent (left) and the 2007 Gildea-Rada line *The Fifth Element* (right).

Vinson Records

First Ascent: Barry Corbet, John Evans, Bill Long, Pete Schoening (USA) Dec 18th 1966

First Solo Ascent: Vern Tejas (USA) 1988 – 1966 Route

First New Route[1]: Rudi Lang (GER) 1991 – West Face Ice Stream Left – *Rudi's Runway*

First Ski Descent: Pat Morrow & Martyn Williams (CAN) 1985

First Snowboard Descent: Stephen Koch (USA) 1999

First Paraglider Descent: Vern Tejas (USA) 1988

First Female Ascent: Lisa Densmore (USA) 1988

First Female Solo Ascent: Heather Morning (UK) Jan 2004

First Complete Female Ski Descent[2]: Kit DesLauriers (USA) Nov 2005

Youngest Summiter: John Strange (USA) – 12 years old – Dec 2004

Most Ascents: 26 by Dave Hahn (USA) as of 2010

Fastest Ascent: Conrad Anker (USA) – 9 hours 10 minutes return – 1998

Note:

[1] At least one variant to the 1966 route was climbed before this date. It passed between the upper Branscomb Glacier and a high camp and was similar to the current normal route. There are also rumours of an ascent of a new route on the west face by Mugs Stump in the 1988-89 season.

[2] After her solo ascent in January 2004, Heather Morning descended all but a very short section at the top of the headwall beneath Goodge Col on skis.

1989 - MUGS, TYREE & GARDNER

Non-ANI visitors to the range were rare even by this time, but geologists Ed Stump (US) and Paul Fitzgerald (NZ) had work to do in the area. Their field assistants were Ed's brother Mugs, already one of America's finest alpinists, and the New Zealand guide Rob Hall. All made an ascent of Vinson and Hall even soloed a route on the south face of Shinn above Goodge Col. Ed Stump left the team early with minor frostbite, but the rest remained, at one point using their snowmobiles to help rescue stricken ANI climbers on Vinson. However Mugs, against the very specific policies of his employment with the National Science Foundation (NSF), could not resist testing his skills on the huge faces above their base camp. The team had discussed the impressive 2000 m high southwest face of Mount Gardner and it was up this that Mugs first launched. Joining two shallow couloirs, broken by a short rock section, Mugs reached the summit – the first person to do so for nearly 23 years – where he found a pennant left by the first ascent team in 1967. Days later he repeated the style, but on the bigger west face of Mount Tyree, climbing the giant mixed face for over 2300 m of vertical gain. Mugs descended the original 1967 Corbet-Evans route along the northwest ridge and continued down over Gardner in a total time of around 12 hours! In the land of massive logistics and the safety first principle, Mugs had epitomised the Alpine ideal of doing more with less, but took it to an extreme degree and with great élan. The NSF was not happy with the relatively minor publicity these climbs received. Yet there was no doubt that Mugs had single-handedly raised the bar of Antarctic alpinism to a level that would not be equalled for nearly a decade; if in fact it has been equalled at all, given the boldness and style he showed at the time. Two years later Mugs was killed in a crevasse fall whilst guiding on Mount McKinley.

THE 1990s

This decade saw a huge growth in the number of guided groups climbing Vinson, but only occasional ascents of other peaks. German climber Rudiger Lang was the first to climb one of the 'ice stream' routes on Vinson's west face, taking the most direct line up the left side of the main stream in January 1991, a route now known as *Rudi's Runway*. In December 1992 Conrad Anker and Jay Smith arrived on the Gildea Glacier – which was then unnamed and untrodden – guiding several clients up the first ascent of Vinson's south face, stopping just short of the main summit but naming the route *From The Heart*. Anker and Smith then crossed into the Bender and Severinghaus Glaciers to attempt the huge south face of Mount Craddock (4368 m) but retreated due to avalanche danger. Returning to the Gildea Glacier the pair bagged the first ascent of Craddock, via a spur on the west side. Craddock was thought at the time to be the sixth highest mountain in Antarctica, based on an inaccurate height of 4650 m accompanying it on the USGS map. This was the first expedition to the Sentinels for Anker, but he would go on to become one of the most significant figures in the history of climbing in the range. Also in this group were another two Americans, Robert Anderson and Joseph Blackburn. Anderson soloed the first ascents of both a new route on Vinson's south face and a second route up the southwest ridge, both done in long single pushes.

The 1993-94 season saw Jay Smith return to Vinson. With his then-wife Jo, he made the first ascent of the right-hand ice stream that comes down from Silverstein Peak, naming the route *Heavenly Father*. A month later Jay soloed the first route to breach the main west face of Vinson. *Linear Accelerator* took an obvious straight couloir in the centre of the face and exited at the top just north of Branscomb Peak.

Though it towered over the old site of Vinson BC, Mount Epperly was one of the highest unclimbed mountains in Antarctica and also one of the steepest. In November 1994 the Swiss alpinist Erhard Loretan climbed on Vinson and Shinn, then descended to the basin beneath Epperly. After one aborted attempt Loretan soloed the stunning narrow ice gully that splits the south face, finding it more difficult than he expected, with loose overhanging rock at the top of the couloir. The next month a Spanish expedition climbed two lines beneath Silverstein Peak. One finished at the small rock promontory west of the peak, a point they named 'Pico Principe de Asturias' after their home province. The same team attempted the first ascent of Silverstein itself, which was then unnamed and referred to by them as 'Monte España'. They took the broad couloir to the right of the 1993 Smith route but retreated well short of the summit. The team also made an ascent of the small rocky summit on the western bank of the Branscomb, naming it 'Pico Jaca'. This peak gives a fantastic view of the west side of the Vinson Massif, but had been climbed numerous times before and was re-named Knutzen Peak by the USGS in 2006.

The 1995-96 season turned out to be both productive and dramatic. On December 29th Loretan returned to repeat the Epperly climb for a film shot by Romolo Nottaris. After this he headed north, alone again, and made the first ascent of the high peak immediately south of Mount Tyree. The peak is just over 4500 m high and has a big west face, much like all the big Sentinels nearby, but Loretan raced up a narrow couloir that ascends almost the entire height of the face reaching the ridge just to the south of the summit. Some commentators named this summit 'Peak Loretan' though Erhard never suggested the name himself. December 1995 was also notable because the first climbers visited the Patton Glacier on the east side of the range. Rob Hall and Ralf Dujmovits had considered attempting Tyree from this side, but felt the conditions were not safe. Instead they guided clients up two smaller virgin peaks nearby, Mount Bearskin (2850 m) and Mount Jumper (2890 m).

But the season ended in dramatic fashion. On January 11th the French husband-and-wife team of Erik Decamp and Catherine Destivelle bypassed Vinson completely and flew north. They made the first ascent of Mount Viets (c.3700 m), a small pyramidal peak just north of Mount

CLIMBERS HIGH ON THE SOUTHWEST FACE ROUTE OF MOUNT SHINN, Antarctica's third-highest mountain. The route continues up through the gap in the seracs above.

Vinson Routes

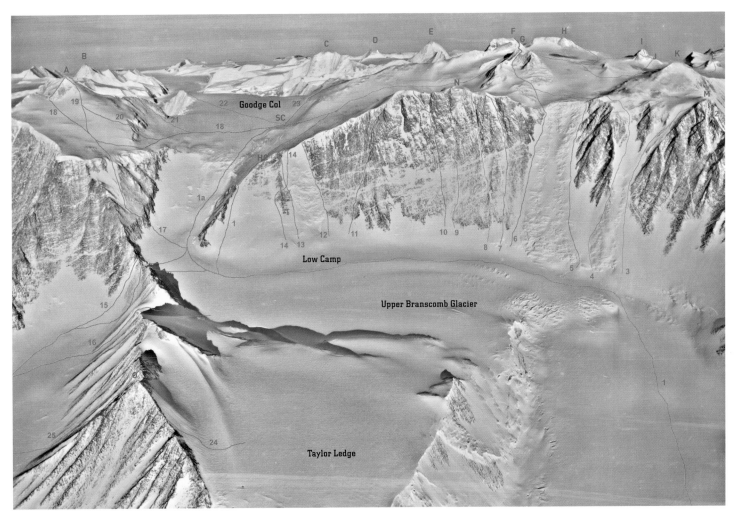

Goodge Col
Low Camp
Upper Branscomb Glacier
Taylor Ledge

A. Mount Shinn 4660 m	**1. Vinson Normal Route** 2007	**15. Vinson Original Route** 1966-1993 (variants to col)
B. Mount Farrell	**1a. Headwall Route** 1966-2007	**16. Dave Hahn** - mid-1990s
C. Mount Waldron 3217 m	**2. Vinson West Ridge** - Anker 1997	**17. Sol de Media Noche** - Paz Ibarra/Rada 2006
D. Mount Havener	**3. Asturias Route** - Alvarez/Huez 1997	**18. Shinn Normal Route** - Corbet/Hollister/
E. Mount Tuck 3588 m	**4. Heavenly Father** - Smith/Bentley 1993	Silverstein/Wahlstrom 1966
F. Schoening Peak 4743 m	**5. Ice Stream Right Side** - Anker 1998	**19. Shinn Southwest Face** - first ascent unknown
G. Mount Vinson 4892 m	**6. Rudi's Runway** - Lang 1991	**20. Chouinard Route** - Chouinard 1985
H. Clinch Peak 4841 m	**7. Banana Friendship Gully** - Vidal 2004	**21. Shinn Southeast Ridge** - Monteath/Mortimer 1988
I. Wahlstrom Peak 4677 m	**8. Purple Haze** - Morton/Passey 2005	**22. Route across Goodge Col to Point 3692 m**
J. Hollister Peak 4729 m	**9. Conjugant Gradients** - Brown 2006	**23. Hubert Route** - Garcia/Hubert/Joris 2003
K. Silverstein Peak 4790 m	**10. Linear Accelerator** - Smith 1993	**24. Knutzen Peak Normal Route** - first ascent unknown
L. Fukushima Peak 4634 m	**11. Chilena-Slovak Route** - Paz Ibarra/Tyrril 2007	**25. Knutzen Peak North Face** - first ascent unknown
M. Asturias Peak	**12. Smith descent route from (10)**	(Paz Ibarra/Tyrril 2007?)
N. Branscomb Peak 4520 m	**13. Gildea** 2006	**HC High Camp** from 2007 - present
O. Knutzen Peak 3373 m	**14. Ruta Galfrio** - Lagos/Vidal 2004	**SC Shinn Camp** - formerly High Camp until 2007

1997 – Triumph & Tragedy, the GMHM Expedition

MOUNT TYREE FROM THE PATTON GLACIER.
Left to right: the unclimbed east ridge, the French 1997 *Grand Couloir* route, the unclimbed northeast ridge,
the unclimbed north face and, on the right-hand skyline, the 1967 northwest ridge route taken by Corbet and Evans
on the first ascent, having traversed from Mount Gardner.

In late 1997 an expert team met with both triumph and tragedy. The climbing team from the French Groupe Militaire de Haute Montagne (GMHM) comprised Bernard Virelaude, Antoine Cayrol, Jean-Marc Gryzka and was led by Antoine de Choudens. Though relatively unknown, de Choudens was one of the strongest alpinists in the world at the time. A combination of physical strength and great endurance, with top-level technical ability and adaptability to altitude, had got him up WI7 ice routes, A4 aid and F7a rock climbs in the Alps. His list of notable achievements also included a Baffin Island big wall in 2001 and hard climbs in the Himalaya, including the east ridge of Shivling in 1999, Nilgiri NE (6750 m) in 2000, a solo summit of China's elusive Minya Konka (aka. Gongga Shan, 7556 m) and a hard new route on Arwa Tower (6352 m) in 2002, and an almost-free 2003 ascent of Nameless Tower (6286 m) in the Karakoram. He was the first – and to this day the only – person to have achieved the combination of an ascent of Everest without supplementary oxygen (via the north ridge in 1997) and unsupported ski journeys to both the North and the South Poles. Virelaude and Cayrol had been with him to both Poles, making them an unusually strong and experienced team. A separate team of three GMHM members – Thierry Bolo, François Bernard and Laurent Miston – were to ski to Vinson from Patriot Hills. GMHM expeditions are funded by the French government as training exercises and often include specific medical and equipment tests.

The climbing team flew straight to the Patton Glacier on the east side of Mount Tyree at the start of November and wasted no time in making the first ascent of the stunning pyramid of Evans Peak (3950 m)*. They found the climb up the 1700 m south ridge to be similar in difficulty to the Hörnli Ridge on the Matterhorn and took only nine and a half hours for the ascent. Three days later, on November 14th, they all climbed a smaller peak to the east of Evans, then made the first ascent of Mount Shear (4050 m), one of the steepest peaks in the range. Virelaude and de Choudens raced up the north face, taking longer to descend the northeast ridge, for a total outing of 23 hours. Gryzka

and Cayrol had attempted to climb the ridge but turned around after dropping an ice axe. Though a commercially guided team had visited the Patton Glacier in 1995 they had not attempted Tyree, and climbed the smaller peaks of Mount Jumper (2890 m) and Mount Bearskin (2850 m). So Tyree had lain inviolate for nearly nine years, since Stump's solo. On November 19th de Choudens and Cayrol set off up Tyree's most obvious weakness, the east couloir. Climbing on mostly steep snow for over 2300 m of vertical gain, they reached the prized summit and descended the same way. Also on the 19th, having a somewhat less strenuous day, Virelaude and Gryzka had made the second ascent of Mount Bearskin, noting the appearance of strange 'tracks' in the icy slopes.

The team now had to sledge back to Vinson BC and elected to go north to cross the range. They skied down the Patton then turned north, crossing two low east-west ridges before turning west, crossing the steep col between Giovinetto and Viets. The crossing involved more than 200 m of ascent over rock on the eastern side, necessitating relaying of loads and rappels on the western side, down 400 m to the flat ice and easier travel. The weather had been nearly perfect for their stay so far, but during the last day to Vinson BC, November 25th, it turned for the worse.

To reach the lower Branscomb Glacier, site of Vinson BC, from up on the plateau to the west of the range, one needs to cut through the lower section of Boyce Ridge. While there are two or three gaps that seem possible, only one is really feasible with sleds. On the southern side of Boyce Ridge a steep snow slope reaches down to the Branscomb, but on either side of this the terrain is steeper. On the lower western side of the gap the ridge is actually a serac, overhanging in places, while on the upper eastern side it is higher and rockier. The team approached this area in very poor visibility, with very bad surface contrast and were unsure of their exact location on the map. They were in fact far too high up to the east. They were not roped up but were travelling in pairs, Virelaude and Gryzka close together, about 30 m behind de Choudens and Cayrol around 5 m lower. Suddenly both Virelaude

and Gryzka's sleds slipped and dragged both climbers simultaneously down the slope. Virelaude was not instantly worried, as they were falling quite smoothly, but then they plummeted over a steep drop. Virelaude landed in the soft snow at the bottom and was knocked unconscious. Although his memory of the location of impact and immediate events is hazy, his team mates assured him he was lucky to be alive. But Jean-Marc was not so lucky. He had hit his head on a piece of rock and was killed instantly. The remaining three radioed across to Vinson BC, where their three compatriots had recently arrived on skis from Patriot Hills, and a rescue operation ensued.

Years later Bernard Virelaude would describe this as "my best expedition and my worst expedition". He took part in successful big climbs with a great team in a wonderful location, only to have his euphoria crushed at the final hour by the death of his friend Jean-Marc. In October 2003, Antoine de Choudens was killed when a cornice collapsed during an acclimatisation climb for the south face of Shishapangma.

*Evans Peak was not marked as such on the USGS 'Vinson Massif' map, so the team did not realise that it had already been named for John Evans, who made first ascents on both Vinson and Tyree in 1966-67. Upon making the first ascent of the peak, the French team wanted to name it after their late Commander Alain Esteve. Then, after Gryzka's death and still believing the mountain to be nameless, they formally proposed to the USGS that it be called 'Gryzka Peak', but this did not proceed. They have considered proposing the name 'Gryzka Peak' for the smaller 2950 m peak to the east of Evans, of which they also made the first ascent.

Giovinetto, via its south face. Two days later they set off up the south face of the virgin Peak 4111, the southern summit of Long Gables. Finding terrain similar to the north face of the Matterhorn, they moved unroped for most of the climb but tied in for the last 200 m and reached the summit ridge without problem. However, whilst taking photos on the summit, Destivelle lost her footing on poor snow and fell backwards, somersaulting down the slope before coming tight on the rope. She only fell around 20 m, but landed on hard ice with protruding rocks. She had broken her leg, the open fracture bleeding into her boot, and had also injured her shoulder and elbow but could still use her arm. For a less capable party in this situation, such an injury might have been a death sentence but Decamp managed to lower Destivelle down the 1600-metre face that they had climbed, using only a 50 m rope. The necessary traverses were particularly difficult but fortunately Destivelle could use both arms and was able to rig the many belays. Upon reaching the bottom of the face Decamp rushed back to their camp to retrieve a sled, which he then

‹ **A RAY OF LIGHT HITS CAMILO RADA** high on the southwest face of Mount Epperly during the first ascent of *The Fifth Element*.

˄ **ASCENDING THE FIXED ROPES UP THE BRANSCOMB SHOULDER** on Vinson's normal route.

ANSELME BAUD SKIING THE *ASTURIAS* ROUTE ON VINSON'S WEST FACE, January 1998. In the background are Mount Epperly and Mount Shinn.

THE HIGH PEAKS OF THE NORTHERN SENTINEL RANGE.

used to drag Destivelle back to the tent. They only had a very basic first aid kit with no strong painkillers. She said later that, given their position, she would not have taken any painkillers anyway, so as to remain fully lucid. To make matters worse, poor weather prevented a plane being sent from Patriot Hills, so they had a desperate three-day wait before their eventual evacuation.

Shortly after the French left the Patton Glacier, another team – Conrad Anker, Dave Hahn, Alex Lowe and Gordon Wiltsie – flew in. Anker, Hahn and Lowe quickly repeated the south ridge of Evans Peak then turned to Tyree. On December 16th they climbed the French *Grand Couloir* route, with a variation in the upper section, going right onto mixed ground to avoid bad snow conditions. Hahn turned back in this upper section but Anker and Lowe reached the summit for Tyree's fourth ascent. Anker stayed in the area for the rest of the season, making the first ascent of the right side of the main ice-stream on Vinson's west face, descending by ski the *Asturias* route with Anselme Baud, and setting the current speed record on the normal route of nine hours and eleven minutes return. A week later he skied north and made the second ascent of 'Peak Loretan' by a steep route on the northwest face that he graded 5.8 80° (2100 m) and named *With You In Spirit,* as a dedication to his mentor Mugs Stump.

During this time two Finnish climbers, Patrick Degerman and Veikka Gustafsson, had journeyed north from Vinson BC to the little-known northern Sentinels. They started their campaign with the first ascent of the small 3119 m peak just north of Mount Viets then turned to the bigger unclimbed peaks nearby. Circling around to the west side of the Anderson Massif, they climbed a shallow couloir to the summit of an unnamed central peak approximately 4050 m high that they called 'Sisu Peak'. Coming down from the summit they continued north along the ridge, having an open bivouac, and climbed the south ridge of Mount Bentley (4137 m). Continuing over the summit they descended the north ridge of Bentley and traversed to the lower summit of Mount Davis. The pair descended a line on snow between Davis and Bentley, back down to the flat ice, but still had to cross a lower ridge off Bentley to reach their camp. It had been a 42-hour marathon journey but yielded three significant first ascents of mountains that few had even seen; an extremely fine effort. They even managed the fourth ascent of Mount Gardner on their way home.

The following 1998-99 season proved one of the most difficult in the history of mountaineering on Vinson. Very bad weather prevented a number of flights and only 28 people managed to reach the summit of Vinson, which was less than half the usual number at that time. Conrad Anker was active again, climbing the 1966 route on Gardner with Dave Hahn then soloing the first ascent of the long west ridge of Vinson in an 18 1/2-hour round trip. This obvious feature leads from near Vinson BC up to the minor top of 'Asturias Peak', just west of Silverstein Peak. Anker then attempted the very long and gendarmed west ridge of Mount Epperly (4508 m) with fellow American Jim Donini but they retreated halfway up. Despite the weather some other new climbing was done, and Bob Elias and Rodrigo Mujica were the first people to fly into the Embree Glacier in the northern section of the range. In late November they made the first ascent of two peaks north of Mount Hale. 'Natalie Peak' is around 3400 m and was climbed from the northeast, as was the peak north of it that they named 'Kristen-Julie Peak'. On a rare journey south of Vinson, the New Zealand guide Guy Cotter, who had inherited the late Rob Hall's guiding company, took Terry Gardiner to the summit of the virgin Mount Slaughter (3444 m) by a couloir on the north face.

The good weather returned for the 1999-2000 season but the only new climbing done was on Mount Bentley, where Bob Elias returned, this time with Wally Berg and camped on the Embree Glacier. They climbed up the direct line of the northeast ridge, but were stopped just 60 m from the summit in high winds.

2000 – VINSON CLIMBING EXPLODES & THE OMEGA FOUNDATION

The new millennium started quietly in the Sentinel Range, with the notable exception of the first ascent of Vinson from the east. Conrad Anker and Dave Hahn teamed up again to lead a team of climbers and scientists, landing out near Flower Hills where the Hansen and Dater Glaciers meet the Rutford Ice Stream. From here they ascended the Hansen Glacier, climbing Mount Havener and Mount Mohl along the way, before ascending a 1000 m headwall up onto the Vinson summit plateau, from where they reached the main summit on January 14th 2001.

In November 2002 a strong Chilean team attempted an ambitious project. Landing in the Newcomer Glacier at the far north of the range, they proposed to ski back the 250 km to Patriot Hills, climbing many high peaks along the way. However, travel down the east side of the range requires crossing many ridges and cols, often involving lowering of sleds with ropes and equipment. This proved very time-consuming and the team spent most of their time just making progress south and eventually only made one ascent, the virgin Mount Segers. They also set out for the east side of Mount Giovinetto, only to be turned back by the cold and the scale of the climb. Once out of the Thomas Glacier, however, the team made more rapid progress and proceeded to Patriot Hills without further trouble, thus completing the first and only full traverse of the Ellsworth Mountains. In December 2002, while the Chileans were struggling down the east side, Damien Gildea and Rodrigo Fica spent seven hours camped on the summit of Mount Shinn running a GPS to ascertain a new height. Shinn had never had a published figure for its altitude and had been thought to be around 4800 m. Fica and Gildea, sponsored by the US-based Omega Foundation, had their data processed by the Australian government, which produced the figure of 4660 m. This project heralded the start of a series of expeditions sponsored by the

STEPHEN CHAPLIN DESCENDING THE NORTH RIDGE OF
MOUNT GARDNER, JUST AFTER MIDNIGHT.
The northern Sentinel Range stretches beyond, with Mount Ostenso in
the centre and, in the distance, the rocky pyramid of Mount Anderson.

Omega Foundation that led to significant revisions in the heights, names and knowledge of the Sentinel Range.

During 2003 the company that now owned ANI, having bought it from the previous long-time owners in 2000, decided that the company was not profitable enough and announced they were suspending operations. A group made up of ANI former owners and staff came together to fill the gap, calling itself Antarctic Logistics and Expeditions (ALE). ALE eventually bought ANI, taking over and ultimately improving the facilities at Patriot Hills. In December 2003 Robert Anderson returned to the southwestern side of Vinson and guided several clients up the centre of the southwest face, left of the ridge he had climbed in 1992. Gaining the main summit from here involved crossing the high plateau, an area that was the focus of the Omega Foundation in the 2004-05 season. Gildea and Fica returned, this time with the young Chilean climber Camilo Rada, and spent over a month at or above high camp on Vinson. With the

Gardner and Tyree

1.	**Gardner SW Face**	**3.**	**Tyree West Face**	**5.**	**Peak 4500 / 'Peak of Kindness' SW Face**
	Mugs Stump (1989)		Mugs Stump (1989)		Erhard Loretan (1995)
2.	**Tyree NW Ridge**	**4.**	**Peak 4500 / 'Peak of Kindness' NW Face**		
	Corbet / Evans (1967)		Conrad Anker (1997)		

STEPHEN CHAPLIN ON THE SUMMIT OF MOUNT GARDNER, December 2005. On the left is the upper west face of Mount Tyree, soloed by Mugs Stump in 1989. Right of that is the northwest face of Peak 4500 soloed by Conrad Anker in 1997. Above Chaplin's head is the main summit of Mount Vinson.

entire mountain to themselves initially, they summited Vinson and slept on top in a tent but with no sleeping bags, running the GPS in temperatures of -46°C. This produced a new height for Mount Vinson of 4892 m, within the margin of error of the old USGS height of 4897 m. Over the following weeks the trio made several journeys past Vinson's main summit out onto the plateau where they camped, climbing and measuring the massif's numerous unclimbed sub-peaks. Gildea would later suggested to the USGS that these peaks be named after the 1966 team and this was officially adopted. It was during the 2004-05 season that the number of people attempting Vinson exploded. For most of the previous decade each season had seen 60-70 climbers attempt the summit, with around a 98% success rate. That season saw this figure almost double, with around 130 people on the mountain, and these numbers have gradually increased in the following years.

From high on Vinson the Omega team had a good view of the massif to the south and saw a problem: the summits of the Craddock Massif did not seem to match their representation on the USGS map. In 2005 Gildea and Rada returned, this time with Stephen Chaplin and Manuel Bugueño, and landed low on the Bender Glacier to the south of Craddock. The team eventually climbed a new route on the west face of Craddock, camping halfway up on a site excavated from the rock of the southwest ridge, to make the second ascent of the mountain. After measuring the summit at 4368 m – much lower than the previous official height of 4650 m – Bugueño and Rada made the first ascent of what is now Rada Peak, a small snowy peak north of Craddock's top. From here they could see that, as they suspected, a small summit to the north was actually higher than the peaks they had just climbed. Hence, Mount Craddock was not the highest peak in the Craddock Massif. But the team was scheduled to move on, so they flew north to Mount Gardner. Here they made the sixth ascent of the original route in a nine-hour single push and eventually recorded a new height of 4573 m, only 14 m lower than the old height. A short flight over to the Patton Glacier and they were in position to attempt a repeat ascent of the French

Grand Couloir on Tyree in late December. However, a period of poor weather and high winds meant conditions in the couloir itself were very icy, so they moved onto the unclimbed northeast ridge. Progress was slow and Gildea and Chaplin set a tent around one third of the way up, but decided against climbing any further owing to the icy condition of the couloir higher up and the impending bad weather.

Whilst the team was in the Patton Glacier, they had tasked a satellite to take images of the main part of the range to aid in the production of a new map. This was done successfully and Rada used the images combined with the years of data from the Omega trips to make the map in mid-2006. This gave a new view of the range and consequently the USGS decided to add many new names to features which were now much more obvious than on the previous USGS map. One such change was the designation of the Craddock Massif. Its northern peak – believed to be the highest, but then unproven – was now called Mount Rutford while the southern peak remained Mount Craddock.

The conundrum of the Craddock Massif remained for Damien Gildea, so in 2006-07 he returned, again with Rada and also the American Jed Brown and the Chilean Maria Paz 'Pachi' Ibarra. The team skied a new route from Vinson BC down onto the Nimitz Glacier and up the newly-named Gildea Glacier into a basin beneath the new Craddock Massif and Mount Rutford. They climbed and measured the smaller peaks of Mount Atkinson (3192 m) and Mount Slaughter (3444 m) before Brown soloed the first ascent of the west face of Rutford. The latter, they eventually learnt, was 4477 m, making it certainly higher than Craddock and probably the ninth highest mountain in Antarctica. They returned to Vinson BC where they spent some time with several of the 1966 team who had returned for a 40th anniversary climb. Over a period of three days, Ibarra and Rada climbed a 1600 m new route on the southwest side of Mount Shinn named *Sol de Media Noche* (Midnight sun), Brown soloed a 1500 m new route – *Conjugant Gradients* – on the west face of Vinson in only six hours, and Gildea soloed a minor new route further north on the face. The Omega team then flew north to the Embree Glacier, where they made the first ascent of Mount Press, and the second ascent of Mount Bentley, via the northeast ridge that Berg and Elias had nearly completed in 1999. They then left the area via an untravelled pass north of Mount Hale, to reach the flat ice out to the west, from where they proceeded south.

During the flight north the team had noted a couloir cutting through the rocky west face of Anderson, now the highest unclimbed mountain in the range. They suspected it could prove a key to the ascent, by avoiding the large serac threatening the easier ice slope to the left of the face. On January 8th Brown and Gildea set off, climbing unroped up the lower 800 m face of easy rock and ice, to gain the base of the couloir. This led 400 m up to a notch in the rocky west ridge, and above this the pair used the rope on a couple of rock pitches. There was easier mixed ground from here to the summit with some poor snow just below the summit ridge and some quite exposed climbing on the summit itself. Maria Paz Ibarra and Rada repeated the route the next day, confirming its quality.

The team then moved south, making the first ascent of Mount Giovinetto (4074 m) – the last virgin 4000 m mountain in the Sentinel Range – and the first ascent of the steep Mount Morris (3793 m), which Brown, Ibarra and Rada climbed in extremely bad weather. Reaching Vinson BC in late-January, the team left the area having made nearly a dozen climbs that were either first ascents or new routes, making it the most successful expedition ever to visit the range.

The 2007-08 season was to be the last of the Omega expeditions, with the aim of obtaining GPS heights for the two remaining big mountains they had not measured: Tyree and Epperly. The season provided very poor weather, changing unusually rapidly and one storm caused great havoc all over the range. Climbing on Vinson for acclimatisation, Maria Paz Ibarra, now climbing with Jarmila Tyrril, put a new route up a previously untouched part of the west face. The

JED BROWN CLIMBING THE UPPER SECTION OF THE WEST FACE OF MOUNT ANDERSON during the first ascent.

Maps, Heights & Names in the Sentinel Range

The range was first mapped by United States Antarctic Program (USAP) personnel in the early 1960s, and the first 1:250,000 Vinson Massif topographical map was published in 1965. The range was resurveyed more accurately in the 1979-80 season, and on the revised 1988 USGS map the main summit of Vinson was reduced from 5140m to the more accurate 4897m. The higher figure continued, however, to be erroneously published on many other maps. During the 2004-05 season the Omega Foundation twice measured Vinson at 4892m and that has been accepted as the new official height of Antarctica's highest mountain.

In December 2002 an Omega team occupied the summit of Mount Shinn for seven hours with a Trimble 5700 dual-frequency GPS unit. Mount Shinn had no previously published height and was considered to be around 4800m high. Processing by the Australian Government AUSPOS facility produced the figure of 4660m for Shinn, confirming its position as Antarctica's third highest mountain.

Between the 2004-05 and 2007-08 seasons Omega once again re-measured many high peaks, including all the sub-peaks and some outlying peaks of the Vinson Massif, the Craddock Massif, Mount Epperly, Mount Gardner and its sub-peaks, and other high summits further north in the range. All this new data led to the production, in co-operation with the USGS, of the Omega Foundation *Vinson Massif & The Sentinel Range* 1:50,000 topographical map, first published as a draft in October 2006, with a revised second draft published in 2007. Based on a high-resolution IKONOS satellite image, this map covers the area from Mount Gardner in the north to Mount Craddock in the south. It contains many of the new official names assigned by the USGS ACAN to features in the range, in addition to showing all known climbing routes completed at the time of publication.

1500m mixed route was named the *Chilena-Slovak Route* and was the first new route to be climbed on Vinson by an all-women team. The four-person team returned to their Epperly BC via 'Sam's Col' and on December 27th Gildea and Rada set off up the massive south face of Epperly. They climbed a line on the right of the face, over snow and easy mixed ground into an obvious couloir that narrows at the top and peters out into a rock wall beneath the summit plateau. This was reached after around 15 hours of climbing, mostly on soft snow and bad rock, and the face narrows in to a couloir before ending at a short rock band. The pair stopped to make drinks at the top of the face but were unable to relax in the extreme cold.

Continuing across the wild upper plateau, they ascended the final pyramid over easy mixed ground and reached the summit ridge. Here a rock pinnacle, semi-detached from the bulk of the mountain, loomed a few metres above them. Although obviously difficult and exposed, it was clearly climbable and they could see a piton in the lower section, no doubt left by Loretan in 1995. Nevertheless, the snow across to it was unstable and the two placed the GPS as high as they could on the ice and descended. The conditions were still poor, which meant the descent took as long as the climb: 20 hours up and 20 hours down. Ibarra and Tyrril repeated the climb soon after, retrieving the GPS to give a height of 4508m, not including the few metres of rock pinnacle above. The climb had proven very taxing and at least two of the climbers suffered some degree of hallucinations during the descent. These included the relatively common phenomenon of the imagined presence of an ethereal extra person, which mainly effected Gildea and Rada while climbing the upper couloir. Hence the route was named *The Fifth Element*. Whilst downclimbing the greasy snow of the lower face, after more than 30 hours of continuous climbing, Gildea sensed the continual presence to his left of a woman and two men. The figures were sit-

ELLSWORTH MOUNTAINS

ting at a desk in business attire and observing his climbing, never doing more than whispering a quiet commentary amongst themselves.

After extensive rehydration and rest, Gildea, Rada and Ibarra then skied north to attempt Tyree via the original route over Gardner. They were unsuccessful and turned back twice from high on Gardner due to incoming bad weather. Despite the poor weather reducing success on Vinson early in the season, the mountain saw a record 157 people summit. This brought the total number of people to have climbed Vinson, as of January 2008, to an estimated 1147.

The following season broke records again, with over 190 people attempting the mountain and almost all of them being successful. Damien Gildea returned once more, this time with Austrians Christian Stangl and Walter Laserer, with the aim of climbing Tyree by the northwest ridge route of 1967, over Mount Gardner. The trio acclimatised on Vinson, with Stangl making a solo ascent of Mount Shinn via the south face, above Goodge Col. Soon after they pulled sleds over Boyce Ridge and around to a camp beneath Mount Gardner and quickly set off up the northwest couloir. After camping at a site on the eastern side of Gardner at just over 4000 m, the weather closed in overnight and they retreated to their base camp. A couple of days later they went up once again, and in clear weather the next day reached the summit of Gardner. However, looking across to Tyree they realised the route was too long and involved for just the three of them with no intermediate camp or further resources, so they reluctantly retreated once more. A week later a commercially guided group primarily made up of Australians flew into the Dater Glacier, and made two first ascents of small peaks near their base camp. They then moved up to a new camp on the Crosswell Glacier, from where they climbed a new route to Goodge Col, continuing on to the summit of Vinson. This was only the second ascent of Vinson from the east. During their retreat down to the Dater Glacier a few of the team made the second ascent of Mount Segers, before enduring an extended wait to fly out due to poor weather.

The 2009-10 season saw a reduction in the number of climbers attempting Vinson, with only around 80 making the summit. Austrian alpinist Christian Stangl returned for another attempt on Mount Tyree, this time trying to repeat the 1997 French *Grand Couloir* route on the east face. On November 29th he flew into the Patton Glacier with fellow Austrian Thomas Strausz and Ingrid Schittich of Germany, and they quickly established an advanced base camp beneath the east face. On December 3rd Stangl and Strausz set off up the lower section of the northeast ridge and traversed into the upper couloir. The pair made excellent time, climbing 2000 m in around six and a half hours. Mostly unroped, they did climb a 350 m section on belay due to the extremely hard ice underfoot. At around 4500 m, with the top in sight, Strausz was hit by a single rock, breaking his arm and badly bruising his thigh. He could not continue climbing, so Stangl helped him rappel their route and they arrived at their camp 11 hours later. All three were flown across to Vinson base camp, from where Stangl and Schittich climbed the normal route on Vinson while Strausz was flown back to Patriot Hills and on to Chile for medical care. The other interesting climb from this season was the second ascent of Mount Rutford (4477 m), via the northern flank. Britons David Hamilton and Patrick Bird climbed Mount Shinn first, then Mount Vinson, both mostly on skis, before hauling their sleds south across the high plateau and down on to Hammer Col. From here they skied almost to the summit of Rutford, climbing the last 70 m to top out on January 16th, before retracing their steps to Vinson high camp over the next two days.

DAMIEN GILDEA NEARS THE HIGHEST POINT OF AN UNNAMED PEAK above the Embree Glacier.

Unclimbed Sentinels

Though all the mountains over 4000m in the range have now been climbed, there are still some high 3000ers that remain virgin, in addition to dozens of unclimbed ridges, spurs and faces. All the climbers flying in to Vinson BC fly straight past the unclimbed mountains just south of Mount Craddock such as Mounts Strybing, Allen (3248m), Liptak and Southwick (3087m). The northern end of the range, between the Embree and Newcomer Glaciers, contains some higher and steeper virgin 3000ers, such as Mounts Goldthwait (3813m), Alf, Sharp (3359m) and Dalrymple (3600m), whose top looks particularly

steep. These northernmost Sentinels have not been visited by humans since the scientific parties of the early 1960s, but as they lie only 60km north of Vinson BC they could be reached from there in a few days on skis or via a short airplane flight.

Some truly outstanding lines remain to be done on the higher peaks. The southeast face of Mount Tyree, above the Crosswell Glacier, rises around 2300m to the southern summit and is probably the biggest unclimbed face in the range. The southwestern side of Mount Gardner (4587m) was soloed by Stump in 1989 and the terrain to

‹ LOOKING SOUTH ACROSS THE UNCLIMBED SUMMITS OF MOUNTS STRYBING, ALLEN, SOUTHWICK AND LIPTAK FROM HIGH ON MOUNT CRADDOCK.
The Nimitz Glacier is in the background on the right.

› THE NORTHERN FACES OF MOUNTS ALF, DALRYMPLE AND GOLDTHWAIT IN THE NORTHERN SENTINEL RANGE,
with the Embree Glacier in the foreground.

the right of it is both higher and steeper. In fact, the upper rock headwall on this direct south face of Gardner may be the steepest terrain on any of the highest peaks. There remain a couple of unclimbed ridges on Vinson itself. The most obvious is the long and complicated northeast ridge, now known as the Zinsmeister Ridge, which starts in the Hinkley Glacier and leads to the summit of Schoening Peak. The rarely seen north face of Mount Shinn (4660 m) holds an elegant direct spur up its centre, though the face is not as steep as it appears head-on. On the south face of Mount Anderson (4144 m) is hidden a deep gully con-

taining a stunning – and no doubt very cold – goulotte, though no one has ever been to the base of it.

At only 25 km north of Vinson BC, the south face of Mount Ostenso is somewhat more accessible. The face has never been attempted but contains two soaring buttresses of steep, rocky terrain and two amazingly narrow couloirs, with the right-hand one seeming easier. Even closer to Vinson is the still-unclimbed southwest ridge of Shinn. Rising above 'Sam's Col', the pre-1993 access to the upper Branscomb Glacier, it gives some moderate scrambling to reach the upper

THE HUGE UNCLIMBED SOUTH FACE
OF MOUNT TYREE,
one of the greatest unclimbed objectives on the continent.

southwest shoulder and the normal route. Only slightly north of here, overlooking the old Vinson BC, is the southwestern side of Mount Epperly (4508 m) which has two obvious unclimbed lines. The elegant, soaring buttress on the left of the south face looks to give sustained rock climbing up to the summit plateau. The long, gendarmed west ridge of Epperly seems much more complicated and proved too time-consuming for the strong team of Conrad Anker and Jim Donini on their 1998 attempt.

On the less-accessible eastern side of the main range, the east faces of Craddock, Rutford, Shinn, Epperly, Gardner, Giovinetto and Long Gables have never been touched. This side of Gardner, from the Patton Glacier, also has two extremely large ridges, one of which leads to an unclimbed sub-peak of the Gardner massif. Though teams have landed on the Patton and Dater Glaciers for climbing, surface travel north or south along this eastern side goes against the grain of the land, requiring numerous crossings of ridges and cols

which has proved difficult and time-consuming to the few who have attempted it.

THE STUNNING UNCLIMBED SOUTH FACE OF MOUNT OSTENSO. The 1967 route of first ascent took easy snow slopes on the northwest side.

THE SOUTH SPUR OF MOUNT CRADDOCK soars 2200 metres above the Severinghaus Glacier. Both the spur and the faces either side of it are unclimbed.

40

THE UNCLIMBED NORTH FACE OF MOUNT TYREE, LEFT,
and the unclimbed northeastern side of Mount Gardner, right,
as seen from the summit of Mount Giovinetto.

Heritage Range

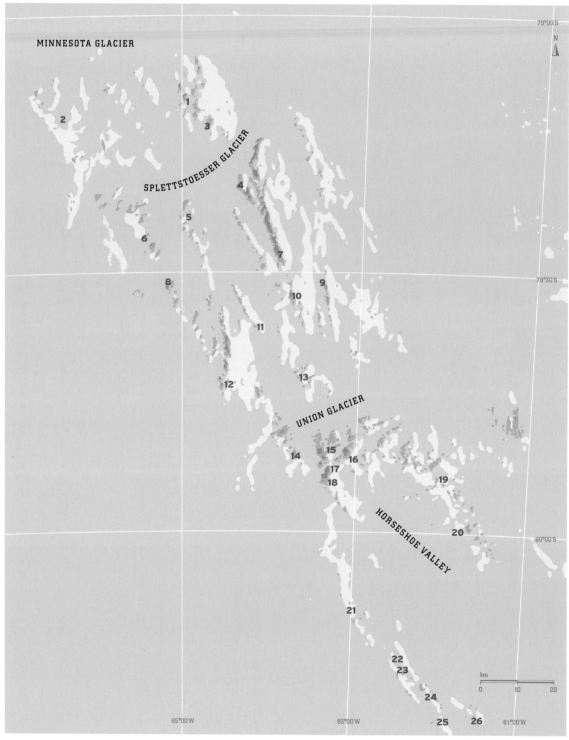

MINNESOTA GLACIER

SPLETTSTOESSER GLACIER

UNION GLACIER

HORSESHOE VALLEY

79°00'S
79°30'S
80°00'S

85°00'W
83°00'W
81°00'W

N

km
0   10   20

42

1. **Anderson Massif** 2190 m
2. **Cunningham Peak** 2170 m
3. **Rullman Peak** 1910 m
4. **Rodgers Peak** 1527 m
5. **Springer Peak** 1460 m
6. **Mount Twiss** 2000 m
7. **Hall Peak** 2169 m
8. **Maagoe Peak** 1850 m
9. **Mount Spörli** 2253 m
10. **Mount Capley** 1830 m
11. **Hessler Peak** 1670 m
12. **Mount Bursik** 2500 m
13. **Mount Rodger** 1410 m
14. **Elvers Peak** 1615 m
15. **Mount Dolence** 1950 m
16. **Hoinkes Peak** 1840 m
17. **Linder Peak** 2010 m
18. **Guarcello Peak** 2050 m
19. **Parrish Peak** 1773 m
20. **Gliozzi Peak** 1477 m
21. **Moulder Peak** 1860 m
22. **Minaret Peak** 1613 m
23. **Beitzel Peak**
24. **Mount Fordell** 1670 m
25. **Mount Simmons** 1590 m
26. **Patriot Hills**

HERITAGE RANGE

The Heritage Range is both lower and wider than the Sentinels, and is a vast scattering of rocky mountains less linear than its higher brothers to the north. In fact the range is made up of several smaller, named mountain groups such as the Soholt Peaks, Pioneer Heights, Enterprise Hills, Liberty Hills, Independence Hills and Patriot Hills. There are large areas of polished blue ice and many smaller glaciers that flow around and between the peaks and rocky escarpments. Though the highest mountain here, Mount Bursik, is only 2500 m high there is a lot of climbing to be done, particularly for those seeking traditional Alpine-style routes with long ridge climbs and traverses. In fact, a lot of climbing has been done here and perhaps half of the major peaks have already had ascents. Some peaks in the southernmost section, near Patriot Hills, have been climbed by people from the ANI/ALE base there, but most of the major climbs have been done by scientific parties from the US and British national programs.

The first visitors to the range came in the summer of 1961-62, led by the legendary Campbell Craddock of the University of Minnesota. He returned the following two seasons, operating out of Camp Gould on the Minnesota Glacier. Using helicopters, the scientific teams explored most of the range, all the way down to Patriot Hills and compiled immense amounts of geological and survey data that was used in the first mapping of the area. Though they did no real mountaineering, the scientists – including a young John Evans and Bernhard Spörli from Switzerland – often landed on mountain ridges to collect samples and travelled around the glaciers of the region.

The most productive period in the range was the early 1990s. New Zealand geologist Paul Fitzgerald arrived in November 1992 and added to his impressive tally of Antarctic first ascents, climbing with fellow Kiwis Charlie Hobbs and Patrick Goldstrand as well as American Tim Redfield. Climbing in the ranges between the Minnesota and Union Glaciers and around the Splettstoesser Glacier, they summited eight peaks, probably only one of which – Landmark Peak (1840 m) – had already been climbed. One of the highest of the rocky Soholt Peaks, around

UNCLIMBED COULOIRS IN THE HERITAGE RANGE, just south of the Minnesota Glacier.

44

2700 m, was also climbed as well as Bingham Peak (1540 m), Mount Twiss (2000 m), Mount Virginia, Welcome Nunatak (1476 m), Pardue Peak (1840 m) and a smaller unnamed peak they called 'Patrick's Peak', after Goldstrand.

British Antarctic Survey (BAS) geologists Mike Curtis and Brian Hull visited the area the following season and made around 13 ascents, including the first ascent of the highest mountain in the Heritage Range, Mount Bursik (2500 m), which they climbed via the northeast ridge. The pair also climbed a 2200 m sub-peak of Bursik and made the first ascents of Springer Peak (1460 m), Eley Peak (2280 m) and one of its sub-peaks, Lester Peak, as well as Elvers Peak (1615 m), Hessler Peak (1670 m), Skelly Peak (1450 m) and Mount Rosenthal (1840 m). In addition to the second ascents of both Bingham Peak and Parrish Peak – the latter first climbed by two New Zealanders in 1979 – they climbed a feature on Mount Spörli (2253 m) known as Mhire Spur, but did not go to the main summit. Hence Mount Spörli remains the highest unclimbed peak in the range. Curtis and Hull's peak-bagging spree of January 1994 was recorded in one of the main British climbing magazines at the time and caused some consternation amongst the BAS authorities, who are loathe to think that their mountain operations might be considered anything other than scientific, particularly by the taxpaying public.

In more recent years there have been several minor excursions into the southern part of the range, north of Patriot Hills. Some small peaks have been climbed here and the Horseshoe Valley is a popular day-trip. British Antarctic specialist Simon Garrod has made a couple of very productive forays into this region. In late 1997 he made around a dozen first ascents, including the first ascent of Gliozzi Peak (1477 m), with the Italian Paolo Gardino, who also made the solo first ascent of Schoek Peak (1810 m). Then in late 2007, Garrod and fellow Briton Peter Clutterbuck undertook a 100 km journey through the area, linking several glaciers and making first ascents of three unnamed peaks.

UNCLIMBED PEAKS AT THE SOUTHWESTERN END OF THE UNION GLACIER. The large rocky pyramid on the right is Mount Dolence (1950 m).

BEITZEL PEAK ON THE LEFT AND MINARET PEAK ON THE RIGHT. Minaret Peak has been climbed only once, but is seen by all the climbers who fly from Patriot Hills to Vinson.

The peak that catches everyone's eye here is Minaret Peak. A small but stunning 1613 m pyramid of marble just north of ALE's blue-ice runway, it was first climbed by Conrad Anker, Alex Lowe and Steve Pinfield in December 1997. Finding they had a spare day shortly after climbing Tyree, Anker and Lowe joined up with Pinfield, the British manager of ANI's Patriot Hills camp at the time, and flew a short hop over to the base of the peak. Lowe led the crux, rated around 5.9, but had to climb it without gloves, finding that although the rock on the peak looks smooth and compact, it actually came away in his hands as he ascended. It has not had a second ascent. The other obvious peaks from Patriot Hills, Mount Fordel (1670 m) and Mount Simmons (1590 m), have also only been climbed once and twice, respectively. Fordel fell to a team led by Pinfield in the mid-1990s and Simmons was first climbed by Jim Donini and Elizabeth Sodergren during a flight delay in the disrupted 1998-99 season. Its west summit was reached in the 2009-10 season by a British pair, Robin Jarvis and Dominic Spicer. They also made the first ascent of Beitzel Peak, next to Minaret Peak, and the second ascent of Gliozzi Peak (1477 m), across the Horseshoe Valley in the Douglas Peaks.

Aside from Mount Spörli, several of the highest peaks in the range remain unclimbed. These include the 2190 m high point of the Anderson Massif, near the Minnesota Glacier, and Cunningham Peak (2170 m) and Zavis Peak (2197 m) at the head of the Splettstoesser Glacier. Further south, Mount Dolence (1950 m), near the Union Glacier, and Guarcello Peak (2050 m) and Linder Peak (2020 m) at the northwestern head of the Horseshoe Valley remain virgin. Many of these peaks have been passed by several expeditions over the years who have approached Vinson on skis from Patriot Hills, but these parties were only focussed on Vinson. To combine first ascents and other technical climbing in the Heritage Range with an ascent of Vinson is surely a worthwhile objective for future expeditions.

ANTARCTIC PENINSULA

This is the most popular and accessible part of Antarctica, and arguably the most beautiful. To many people the Antarctic Peninsula, with its icebergs, penguins, seals, whales, snowy peaks, and glaciers dropping into the sea, *is* Antarctica. No longer unexplored, the Peninsula now draws tourists and other adventurers due to its great natural beauty, a melding of mountains and sea, of rock and ice, of twilight, colour and warmth, far from the vast monochrome inland.

The early years of exploration in the Peninsula region mainly consisted of commercial trips by sealers and whalers, with geographical discovery a secondary aim. The first party to visit the Antarctic for purely geographical exploration was Adrien de Gerlache's 1897-99 *Belgica* expedition. Their ship became trapped in pack ice and they were thus the first people to spend a winter in Antarctica. The expedition not only included a young Roald Amundsen, who would later return south for the Pole and greater glory, but also Frederick Cook who was the ship's doctor. Cook, part of a long and continuing tradition of dishonest polar adventurers, would gain notoriety for making fraudulent claims to have reached both the North Pole first and to have made the first ascent of Alaska's Mount McKinley. Cook would also later spend time in a US prison, where Amundsen was a famous visitor.

Otto Nordenskjöld's Swedish expedition sailed aboard the *Antarctic* in 1901 and wintered on Snow Hill Island in 1902. They explored the east coast of the northern Antarctic Peninsula and contributed greatly to the early understanding of the basic geography of the region. Yet the expedition endured great hardship, spending the winter stranded in three separate groups after their ship was crushed, and were rescued by the Argentines. They did, however, make some of the early ascents in the area and climbed the high points on Snow Hill Island (304 m) and Robertson Island (Christensen Nunatak, 299 m).

In the following decades several expeditions, most notably the Frenchman Jean Baptiste Charcot's two expeditions (1904-07 and 1908-10) and the Australian John Rymill's 1934-37 British Graham Land Expedition (BGLE), discussed later, explored further south down the Peninsula,

SUNSET ON THE WEST FACE OF MOUNT SCOTT, above the waters of Penola Strait.

A TYPICAL PENINSULA SCENE: climbing ice out of the sea.

mainly surveying the coastal areas and travelling short distances inland. However, with a few exceptions, there was generally little mountaineering done in these years. World War II provided an even greater lull in exploration of the region, but this was not to last.

OPERATION TABARIN, FIDS & BAS

After World War II the British presence in the Antarctic Peninsula area was rejuvenated with Operation Tabarin, a somewhat secretive expedition named after a disreputable Paris nightclub and launched in late 1943. The alleged reasons for launching Operation Tabarin are various, ranging from reporting on enemy naval activity, protecting the area from occupation as a Nazi war base, reinforcing the British claim against the competing Argentine and Chilean claims, misinforming potential spies to protect other more critical operations and finally, to dissuade a potentially territorial United States from laying claim to the region. In early 1944 small bases were established on Deception Island in the South Shetlands and further south at Port Lockroy, near Wiencke Island. In both instances the British removed Argentine emblems that they found at these locations, believing the British history of exploration in the region gave their territorial claims supremacy over the Argentine claims.

The following season, in 1945, two more stations were established, on Coronation Island in the South Orkneys and at Hope Bay, on the very tip of the Trinity Peninsula, the northernmost point of the Antarctic mainland. The base on Coronation Island was never really used, as another was built on nearby Laurie Island in 1946. That base itself lasted just one year before a new base was built nearby on Signy Island in 1947, which operated continuously for 49 years. Both the Signy Island and Port Lockroy bases were early centres of mountaineering on the Peninsula, mostly in the name of surveying and exploration and increasingly in scientific fieldwork. In 1945 Operation Tabarin became the Falkland Islands Dependency Survey (FIDS), which was then renamed in 1962 as the British Antarctic Survey (BAS), though for years afterwards many BAS personnel continued to refer to themselves as 'Fids'.

A SHIP RESUPPLIES ROTHERA BASE ON ADELAIDE ISLAND, with Mount Liotard in the background.

AN IMPERFECT HISTORY

Between them FIDS and BAS personnel have been responsible for the vast majority of climbing done on the Antarctic Peninsula, or hundreds of first ascents. The actual number of peaks climbed will never be known, mainly due to the long-standing official attitude that climbing for recreation was frowned upon and that mountaineering should only be employed in the conduct of scientific fieldwork and associated training. The taxpayers of Britain should not be asked to fund the Antarctic holidays of ambitious climbers. Whilst there is fieldwork to justify some of the ascents – particularly those made during the early surveys and some of the geological traverses – countless more FIDS and BAS people have gone climbing on 'jollies', their term for short recreational journeys. Many of these involved repeating moderate ascents done in previous years but, particularly in the earlier years, they sometimes also produced a significant haul of summits. On many other occasions the Field Assistant, or General Assistant (GA), would take time off caring for his scientific colleagues to steal away and tick off a nearby virgin summit. Most of these climbs have not been officially recorded, to avoid the ire of the authorities back in England, and as a result much of this 'history' exists only as rumour and legend. However, most of the major climbs, either of the highest peaks or very difficult routes, were eventually published somewhere – in books, alpine journals and field reports – and thankfully not all of this history has been lost. The notable exception to this is Alexander Island, for which almost no climbing history is known.

Nevertheless, there is a danger of overstating these exploits, as the lack of a verifiable history can lead to stories growing out of proportion to the real events. As a result, previous generations are on occasion generously credited with feats that, upon closer investigation, prove somewhat less dramatic. Areas were explored but no climbing was done. Climbs were attempted but no summits were reached. Summits were reached but not as many as planned. Much tea was drunk. Sometimes history amplifies achievement without adding anything to substantiate it and this is particularly true of histories that are largely oral. This chapter is a very imperfect history, but we should be careful to not make it more so. It should also be noted that although many keen climbers have worked on the Peninsula with the FIDS and BAS, most of them have simply not had the opportunity to climb as much as they would have wished, secretly or otherwise. When in the field the work is the priority, time is nearly always short and the weather in this part of the world rarely agrees with ambitious climbing plans. As many GAs have wistfully recalled in later years, when working for BAS a lot of time in the mountains does not equal a lot of time on summits.

This lack of hard facts is not all bad. It creates a sense of mystery, a beautiful void where adventure is still possible for new travellers going south each year. Some in FIDS and BAS have deliberately maintained a silence for their own private reasons, regardless of the authorities' views. For these people there has been a code of silence amongst colleagues, as a means of preserving good experiences as they remember them, and not having their days of joy cast out into a world to be collected, bested and belittled by the latest record-breaker. Though modern professional media 'extremists' may wish it otherwise, adventure is relative; it is in the eye of the beholder. If you're not claiming to be first yourself, then does it really matter who was?

It is impossible to list all the summits ever reached by FIDS/BAS personnel over the decades and this becomes increasingly difficult as generations pass. The fact that an area or mountain is not listed in this book does not mean that no one has been there, although interesting objectives known to be unclimbed are included here whenever possible. But if it lies between 60° S and 75° S and 75° W and 60° W there is a good chance that a FIDS team travelled past it and, if it was not too hard or dangerous and time and weather allowed, maybe they even climbed it. If you need to claim to be first on some piece of Antarctica, you should go elsewhere.

49

Antarctic Peninsula

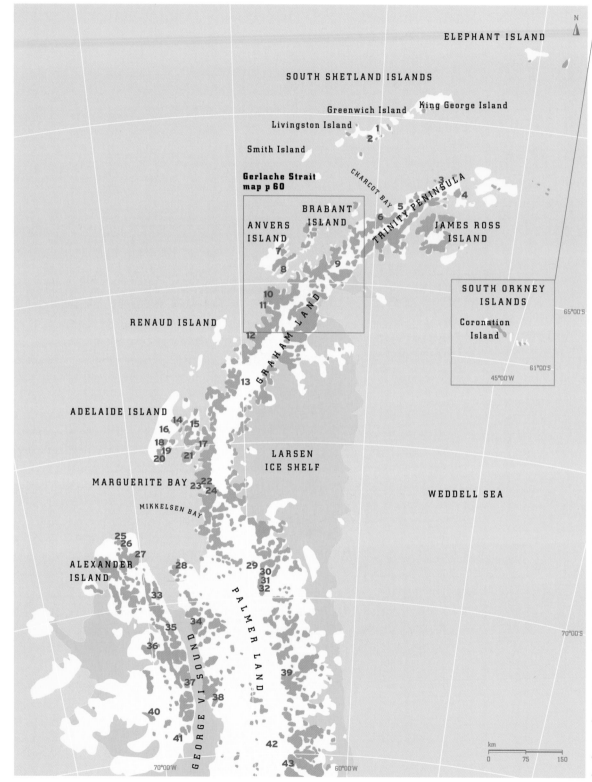

ELEPHANT ISLAND

SOUTH SHETLAND ISLANDS

Greenwich Island

King George Island

Livingston Island

Smith Island

Gerlache Strait map p 60

BRABANT ISLAND

ANVERS ISLAND

CHARCOT BAY

TRINITY PENINSULA

JAMES ROSS ISLAND

SOUTH ORKNEY ISLANDS

Coronation Island

65°00'S

RENAUD ISLAND

GRAHAM LAND

61°00'S

45°00'W

ADELAIDE ISLAND

LARSEN ICE SHELF

WEDDELL SEA

MARGUERITE BAY

MIKKELSEN BAY

ALEXANDER ISLAND

GEORGE VI SOUND

PALMER LAND

70°00'S

70°00'W

60°00'W

km
0   75   150

1. **Mount Bowles** 822m
2. **Mount Friesland** 1700m
3. **O'Higgins Base**
4. **Hope Bay**
5. **Crown Peak** 1184m
6. **Mount Bris** 1673m
7. **Mount Français** 2822m
8. **Port Lockroy Base**
9. **Mount Johnston** 2139m
10. **Mount Scott** 880m
11. **Vernadsky Base**
12. **Mount Bigo**
13. **Slessor Peak** 2370m
14. **Mount Reeves** 2210m
15. **Arrowsmith Peninsula**
16. **Mount Mangin** 1955m
17. **Blaicklock Island**
18. **Mount Gaudry** 2565m
19. **Rothera Base**
20. **Mount Liotard** 2225m
21. **Pourqoi Pas Island**
22. **San Martín Base**
23. **Stonington Island**
24. **Neny Fjord**
25. **Les Dents / The Needles**
26. **Mount Paris** 2800m
27. **Mount Calais** 2345m
28. **Mount Edgell** 1675m
29. **Davies Top** 2361m
30. **Mount Faith** 2650m
31. **Mount Hope** 2862m
32. **Mount Charity** 2680m
33. **Mount Stephenson** 2895m
34. **Mount Courtauld** 2105m
35. **Mount Edred** 2195m
36. **Colbert Mountains**
37. **Fossil Bluff Base**
38. **Mount Bagshawe** 2200m
39. **Mount Jackson** 3184m
40. **Staccato Peaks**
41. **Stephenson Nunatak**
42. **Sky-Hi Nunataks** 1753m
43. **Sweeney Mountains**

The main mountain regions of the Antarctic Peninsula will be described here from north to south, detailing where possible the significant peaks of those areas and the climbing that has been done there, focusing on first ascents, significant events and remaining unclimbed objectives. For the purposes of this book the term Antarctic Peninsula refers to both the Peninsula mainland itself as well as the outlying islands. The South Orkney Islands and South Shetland Islands, whilst not geographically part of the Antarctic Peninsula, are included here owing to historical connection and for logistical efficiency.

SOUTH ORKNEY ISLANDS

The South Orkneys are a small group of mostly ice-covered islands in the Southern Ocean, around 1500 km southeast of Ushuaia and 750 km northeast of the tip of the Antarctic Peninsula. The main islands are Coronation Island, Laurie Island, Signy Island and Powell Island, though there are numerous smaller islands close by. Coronation Island, discovered by the American sealer Nathaniel Palmer in 1821, is the largest, most mountainous and heavily glaciated of the group, rising to 1265 m on Mount Nivea. For such remote and tiny islands, much climbing has been done here over the years, mainly by FIDS and BAS personnel stationed at Signy. The Signy Island base was built by FIDS in March 1947 and was continuously occupied until 1996, when it became a summer-only base. The first facility on the island was a meteorological station built by the Scottish explorer William Speirs Bruce, who arrived aboard the *Scotia* in early 1903. After wintering and surveying the island he departed in 1904, having sold the station to Argentina. They have operated the facility ever since, renaming it Orcadas in 1951.

The first recorded summit reached in the South Orkneys was the highest of the John Peaks (415 m) climbed by personnel aboard *Discovery II* in 1933, who also climbed some of the other minor points on the other islands. However, climbing did not really start on the main peaks on Coronation Island until the 1950s. The first ascent of Wave Peak (997 m) was made by Frank Johnson on September 13th 1952. This was climbed several times over the next two decades, after the second ascent by Lance Tickell in August 1956. The west face is particularly impressive when viewed from Signy, while from the east it is an easy climb that is often done on skis. Devil's Peak (744 m) is more accessible from Signy and was ascended via the south ridge by Allan Grant and Lance Tickell on February 14th 1956. Later that year the island's highest peak was climbed for the first time. On September 11th 1956, Allan Grant and Lance Tickell made the first ascent of Mount Nivea (1265 m), up the northwest ridge after approaching from the north. Though conditions in winter were generally considered to be good for climbing, they noted considerable avalanche activity. The second ascent in November 1966 was via a new route up the much steeper west face, by Burgin, Lindsay and Thornley.

In early September 1969 John Edwards, Martin Pinder, Dave Rinning and Eliot Wright hauled sleds for seven days across the Laws Glacier to the west of Coronation Island and climbed all of the Sandefjord Peaks, the highest being 635 m. Difficult ice over rock had turned back a previous party in March 1966 on these shapely snow and ice cones. Mount Napier (1070 m) had its first ascent in winter, Adrian Gilmore and Jerry Light climbing it in early July 1970 from the Sunshine Glacier. The next month Gilmore and Light, joined by Bob Cook and Peter Hardy, reached the eastern end of the island by snowmobile across the sea-ice and made first ascents of the Divide Peaks (640 m), the rocky Breccia Crags (305 m) up their north face, and the prominent Pulpit Mountain (945 m) via the south face. This eastern end of the island was considered to hold the best climbing on the island, though other areas also proved acceptable for shorter climbs, such as the Cragsman Peaks and Beaufoy Ridge. It must be noted here that meticulous records and reports kept by Lance Tickell, John Edwards and others have made Coronation Island the best-chronicled mountaineering area in all the British Antarctic Territory.

LIVINGSTON ISLAND FROM THE EAST.
The highest peak, Mount Friesland, is visible at right.
The high mountain on the left is Falsa Aguja, the island's
second highest peak.

SOUTH SHETLAND ISLANDS

The South Shetlands are an extensive group of small islands approximately 100 km northwest of the coast of the Antarctic Peninsula. The group stretches over 500 km and contains many small islands. From a climbing perspective the main ones are King George Island, Livingston Island, Smith Island and the northern outliers Elephant Island and Clarence Island. Sealing and whaling dominated the early history of the region and relics from these activities can still be found, most notably on Deception Island and Livingston Island.

ELEPHANT ISLAND & CLARENCE ISLAND

Small, remote and well north of the main South Shetland Islands, Elephant and Clarence islands nonetheless have some interesting climbing on them, if one can brave the wet and windy maritime climate. The 1976-77 British Joint Services Expedition (BJSE) made several successful ascents on Elephant Island, including the first ascent of the highest peak, Mount Pendragon (974 m), by Furse, Simkins and Wimpenny on March 11th 1977. Chris Furse would become a regular visitor to the far south, most notably leading the 1984-85 Joint Services Expedition to Brabant Island.

Clarence Island serves as a visual introduction for climbs further south, as it is essentially a small mountain sitting in the ocean. It rises steeply from the ocean to a rather improbable height of 1924 m on the summit of Mount Irving, first climbed by Highton, Monteith and Wimpenny of the BJSE on January 9th 1977. Elephant Island is also famous as the starting point for Ernest Shackleton's famous boat voyage to South Georgia.

KING GEORGE ISLAND

King George Island has often been described as the 'capital of Antarctica' due to the presence of stations for nine national Antarctic programs, making it the second most densely populated part of Antarctica after the US base McMurdo, across the continent on Ross Island. On the Fildes Peninsula at the southwestern tip of the island there is a gravel runway, operated by the Chilean Air Force (FACH). It is close to the Chilean station Eduardo Frei, and is used by planes of various sizes, including C-130 transport planes from Chile and Uruguay. The commercial airline Aerovías DAP also flies to the island from Punta Arenas and in recent years their service has been used by private expeditions of various kinds to access the area, sometimes utilising additional shipping or other transport options.

King George Island is dominated by a large icecap comprising several icefields and numerous smaller glaciers, and ski tours have been done around many of them. Although there are no high mountain peaks here, the icecap is very crevassed and suffers the typical bad weather of the region, making adventures a serious undertaking. King George Island is no longer a climbing destination and is more of a base for adventures further a field, but some climbing was done here in the early days of FIDS, when they operated a base at Admiralty Bay. Many minor points were climbed for the first time around 1948-49 amid journeys across the island, including traverses of the Keller Peninsula, first done in full by J. Ewer and Ken Pawson in February 1948. Geoff Hattersley-Smith and friends did some more technical climbing in the winter of 1949, which most notably included ascents of Ternyck Needle (365 m) with Ken Pawson, and The Tower (345 m) with Pawson, Jardine and Jefford. Ternyck Needle is a prominent nunatak, or rocky feature, on a peninsula halfway along the southern coast of the island and was probably the highlight of their climbing here. Hattersley-Smith and Pawson later joined forces again to climb Melville Peak, the 500 m high summit of Cape Melville, from the northeast in September. They also climbed another summit they named 'Pyramid Peak', which was the highest of a group of peaks at George's Bay.

AN AERIAL VIEW EAST ACROSS THE UNCLIMBED SUMMIT OF HELMET PEAK, Livingston Island, with Greenwich Island in the distance.

Southwest of King George Island, Greenwich Island has no real climbing history, although it has been visited in modern times by non-government vessels. The island's highest mountain, Mount Plymouth (520 m), is in the northern part of the island, although there are some rockier 275 m summits in the Crutch Peaks to the west of it. There are also some coastal crags up to 425 m high on the southern tip of the island and a good yacht anchorage in the distinctly shaped Yankee Harbour. If the weather is good this is a relatively accessible venue for short ski tours and moderate climbs.

LIVINGSTON ISLAND

At around 70 km long, Livingston Island, together with King George Island, is the largest of the South Shetlands. Much of the western half of the island is quite flat and regularly visited by scientific field parties from the United States and other nations. Visitors to Deception Island looking north can often see the southern side of Livingston Island, and it appears as a high range of snowy mountains rising steeply from the sea.

The southeastern section of Livingston is dominated by the Tangra Range. The main part of the range is a high ridge, which has just four genuine peaks up high and a couple of minor summits lower to the southwest, and forms a peninsula between False Bay and Brunow Bay. A yacht-based Italian team did the first recorded non-government climbing on the island in 1976. But the highest peak, Mount Friesland (1700 m), was not climbed until December 1991, by Jorge Enrique and Francesc Sàbat from the Spanish Juan Carlos station at South Bay, west of the mountains. In 1993 another Spanish team did a south-to-north ski traverse from Elephant Point to Cape Shirreff and back, but there was no climbing done on the high peaks during the rest of the 1990s.

In December 2003 the Omega Foundation sent a team to measure the altitude of Mount Friesland, as there was some ambiguity about this. Australians Damien Gildea and John Bath were joined by Chileans Rodrigo Fica Perez and Osvaldo Usaj and all flew to King George Island with DAP in early December. Using three flights in a BO-105 helicopter specially chartered from DAP for the expedition, they established a base camp in beautiful weather on the Perunika Glacier, a high plateau north of Mount Friesland. During the next 26 days only three days were totally clear, with most of the time spent stuck in light storms, wind and snow. The team made the second ascent of Mount Bowles, a straightforward snow peak situated on the northern side of the plateau that they re-measured and gave 822 m. They also skied to various other points around the area, such as Orpheus Pass.

With time running out Bath, Fica and Gildea set off on December 19th in a brief clearing of good weather for the east ridge of Mount Friesland. This was gained by climbing south up a gentle glacier toward a col, named the Catalunyan Saddle, but the glacier was very crevassed and route-finding was slow in the deteriorating weather and twilight. After a short, cold bivouac the three continued up the easy ridge, to reach the broad summit, which was split in two by a narrow crevasse. Here they ran the GPS unit for nearly three hours, as the weather closed in again, then descended in a blizzard to their base camp. The team flew out on December 22nd in perfectly clear blue skies, back to King George Island and returned to Punta Arenas with DAP. Later in 2004 the Omega Foundation produced a new map of the island, based on 1991 satellite imagery generously provided by the University of Barcelona, Spain. The new map incorporated the recent Omega GPS results, which found that Mount Friesland was exactly 1700 m high, or 16 m higher than the old official figure and up to 90 m below other figures in circulation. The map also included many new feature names that the Scientific Committee of Antarctic Research (SCAR) had accepted in the intervening period since BAS had published the first map of the island. In keeping with its stated aims, the Omega Foundation distributed the map worldwide for free, to all interested parties.

A BASE CAMP ON THE PERUNIKA GLACIER, LIVINGSTON ISLAND.
The north face of Mount Friesland is visible in the background, with the east ridge route forming the left skyline.

DAMIEN GILDEA AND RODRIGO FICA climbing through the night on the east ridge of Mount Friesland in December 2003.

JOHN BATH AND OSVALDO USAJ
approaching the summit of Mount Bowles
on Livingston Island. In the background
to the south is the Tangra Range,
with Lyaskovets Peak on the right and
the unclimbed Levski Peak on the far left.

In December 2004 a Bulgarian team climbed in the region, camping on the Perunika Glacier, after skiing from their occasionally occupied Klement-Ohridski base 13 km to the west, on the shores of South Bay. Lyubomir Ivanov and Doychin Vasilev followed the existing route up the glacier to the Catalunyan Saddle, before turning left for a short distance to make the first ascent of Lyaskovets Peak (1473 m). Ivanov continued along the ridge to another minor summit they named Zograf Peak (1011 m) before descending. The Bulgarian pair then completed a ski journey in the northeastern sector of the island, climbing several minor tops along the way.

There are a number of high, unclimbed peaks in the Tangra Range, notably Levski Peak, which is just east of Lyaskovets Peak, and Falsa Aguja, which is probably only slightly lower than Mount Friesland and has never been attempted. The attractive and unclimbed Helmet Peak is further east again, forming the westernmost top of an attractive line of smaller summits running down to the sea at Renier Point. As the western and northern sections of the island are relatively flat, the topography of Livingston Island lends itself to ski traverses, with a lot of gentle terrain north of the high mountains. This may also be a better way to see the island than trying to climb the highest peaks in the occasional spells of fine weather. In 2008 a team of eight Spaniards skied from Lister Cove south to Juan Carlos base over four days and no doubt the island will see similar trips in the near future. To traverse the entire 30 km of the Tangra Range

‹ CLIMBERS ON 'RICK'S RIDGE'
during the first ascent of Mount Foster in January 1996.

^ LOOKING ACROSS TO THE WEST FACE
OF THE UNCLIMBED FALSA AGUJA,
the second highest mountain on Livingston Island.

in either direction, over all the main summits, would be a significant climbing achievement, but feasible only by moving fast in rare windows of good weather.

It is important for all potential visitors to this area to realise that these islands contain important and environmentally sensitive Specially Protected Areas (SPA), as designated under the Antarctic Treaty. Such areas should be totally circumvented to avoid disruption to wildlife and areas of valuable scientific fieldwork.

The horseshoe-shaped Deception Island is actually the remains of a volcano, with part of the crater wall blown out, and there is still thermal activity in the region. There is no real climbing on the island, but it is one of the most popular destinations for cruise ships, as vessels can venture inside the crater and disembark passengers to enjoy thermal pools and visit the rusted remains of an old whaling station. The highest peak on Deception Island is Mount Pond (542 m), the first recorded climb of which was by the prolific Richard Brooke and Ken Pawson in April 1950, yet it was almost certainly climbed much earlier by sealers.

SMITH ISLAND

Smith Island is the steepest island in the South Shetlands and epitomises the mountain-in-the-sea nature of the climbing here. It is the highest island and, being the most westward, bears the worst of the incoming weather. Few people ever see Smith Island in its entirety, as it is often invisible thanks to fog or is raked by storm clouds. The edges of the island are not beaches but crumbling ice cliffs, occasionally interspersed with small rock promontories that may grant access to the terrain above. The highest peak on Smith Island is Mount Foster (2105 m), which until its first ascent in January 1996 had been attempted at least twice and was one of the greatest unclimbed prizes in Antarctic mountaineering.

Legendary mountain explorer Harold William 'Bill' Tilman took to sailing voyages in his later

A RARE VIEW OF SMITH ISLAND FROM THE WEST
with the highest point of Mount Foster (2105 m)
visible in the centre.

years and first planned to reach Smith Island in the southern summer of 1959-60. In the midst, and mist, of a typically shambolic voyage on board his Pilot Cutter *Mischief*, Tilman did lay eyes on Smith Island, but not more, and sailed to Kerguelen and the Crozet Islands. In 1977 Tilman, at 79 years old, set off for Smith Island once again, this time invited to crew aboard *En Avant*, a converted tug. The boat was skippered by Simon Richardson, a young Briton who had sailed with Tilman to Greenland. The expedition reached Rio de Janeiro as planned, then headed for the Falkland Islands as a last stop before Antarctica. They never reached the Falklands and no trace was ever found of the ship or its crew. In 1991 and 1994 Mount Foster was the objective of British military expeditions led by John Kimbrey that attempted the mountain from the south, using a helicopter from ship to shore. The 1994 expedition was beaten back from the main summit, but reached a subsidiary top of around 1700 m that they named 'Mount Catherine James'. Thus by the mid-1990s the mountain that had eluded the great Bill Tilman and defeated two heavyweight military expeditions had gained a considerable cachet.

Enter *Northanger*. This steel-hulled yacht was especially built for high latitudes by two ex-BAS men Rick Thomas and Mike Sharp. Rick Thomas used it to climb Mount Saint Elias from the sea and sail the Northwest Passage, but was killed in 1989 by a falling cornice on Mount Waddington, in Canada's Coast Range. A Canadian, Keri Pashuk, and a New Zealander, Greg Landreth, who had both crewed on *Northanger*, eventually rescued the yacht from rusting away in a Canadian port and began sailing adventures, with a view to realising Rick Thomas's dream of climbing Mount Foster. Mike Sharp moved on, spending many years managing the ANI base at Patriot Hills, guiding on Vinson and eventually running ALE, when it took over from ANI.

In January 1996, Pashuk and Landreth sailed out of Ushuaia with Bruce Dowrick, Anna Kemp, Dan and Veronica Mannix, Jo Stratford and Roger Thomson on board, bound for Smith Island. Upon arrival five days later the weather was typically poor, so they waited it out in the Melchior Islands, before returning to drop Dowrick, Landreth, Mannix and Thomson at a small landing on the southeast side of the island. As with so many other places in the region, getting up onto the shore from the water was steep and difficult. In the process of climbing and hauling their six weeks worth of supplies up crumbling vertical ice, they dropped the main radio into the sea, leaving them with just a small VHF unit. They were now only able to call Northanger at close range, where it could not safely stay. Travel to other points on the island from here would have been impossible given the surrounding terrain, so it was either up or off.

After an initial attempt ended due to poor visibility, they launched up the central ridge on the southeast face in what would certainly be only a short spell of good weather. Hard ice climbing took them through a rock band, above which they climbed 11 pitches along a knife-edge ridge, through cornices and up onto easier ground. Using the VHF radio here they were able to contact *Northanger* to begin the retrieval journey. Mount Foster has three summits, with the south being the highest. They reached this after one more hard section, through the upper ice cliffs. After years of obsession and toil, only minutes were spent on top, suspended in the Antarctic alpenglow. Descent was back down the way they had come, now in deteriorating weather, and they reached their base camp 27 hours after starting. Nearly 30 years after Tilman had first gone for it, Mount Foster was done, and by the route named *Rick's Ridge*.

In January and February of 2010 a trio of French alpinists visited the Antarctic Peninsula aboard Isabelle Autissier's yacht *Ada II*. Mathieu Cortial, Lionel Daudet and Patrick Wagnon enjoyed great success this summer, the first of which on Mount Foster. The French decided to try a new route on what they referred to as the western spur of the northeast summit. The first 1000 m were uneventful, but the terrain got harder as they climbed higher and both Cortial and Daudet took falls on the rope, the latter while climbing an overhanging serac which plunged 1000 m toward the sea. After tunnelling through steep mushrooms of rime, they eventually reached the summit at around 2 am on January 12th, after 15 hours of climbing. They then began the 15-hour descent. They named their new 1600 m new route *Le Vol du Sérac* (The Flight of the Serac).

There is a lot of unclimbed mountain terrain on Smith Island, but given the long, high nature of the landmass, an obvious objective for the future is a full skyline traverse, up to 30 km long. Beginning at the southwestern tip may be too difficult, but at least starting up Mount Foster from the southeast and continuing northeast would take climbers over several other high tops, including the unclimbed Mount Pisgah (1860 m), six kilometres northeast of Mount Foster, and Mount Christi (1280 m), five kilometres further again northeast of Mount Pisgah. Suffice to say, a successful party will need some luck with the weather.

GRAHAM LAND

TRINITY PENINSULA

The section of the Antarctic Peninsula north of 66° S is named Graham Land, and the northernmost part of Graham Land is the Trinity Peninsula. Most of the mountains here are quite low, but FIDS were very active along here in the 1950s, exploring south from their base at Hope Bay and regularly climbing summits during surveying work. Often though, as elsewhere in Antarctica, the summits used for erecting the theodolite were not the highest in the area. Sometimes men could take a break and climb from their survey point to the highest point nearby, yet this was often not possible due to the traditional Antarctic factors of time, weather and risk. Hence, while not offering spectacularly difficult climbing, various high points in the region may still be untouched. Worthwhile areas to visit may be the ranges around the northern end of the Detroit Plateau, south of Sirius Knoll

∧ JULIE STYLES CLIMBING AN UNNAMED PEAK
with 'Wiltsie's Peak' in the background.

› AN UNNAMED PEAK NEAR PILCHER PEAK
east of Brialmont Cove.

(1012 m), possibly moving inland from Bone Bay. Additional factors here are difficulties in getting ashore due to ice cliffs, and the need to travel inland up to 20 km to reach the higher summits.

Probably the most significant journey through this region was the 1957 dogsled traverse from Hope Bay base to Charlotte Bay, led by Wally Herbert (see profile in Transantarctics chapter). The team battled the foul weather so typical of the northern Peninsula region, with difficult navigation made worse by having a relatively narrow strip of terrain along which to travel. They traversed high along the Detroit Plateau south to the Foster Plateau. These two were linked by a smaller area now known as the Herbert Plateau, which is only joined to the other plateaux by high, narrow sections: The Catwalk in the north and The Waist in the south. Descent was west from the Foster Plateau, down the Reclus Peninsula to the coast at Charlotte Bay, a route pioneered in advance by FIDS men Bayly and Evans, for just this purpose. This route along the Peninsula from Hope Bay was also used, with some variations, by the 1989-90 International Transantarctic Expedition, which drove dogs from Hope Bay the whole way across Antarctica to Mirny station on the opposite side. Plans have often been touted for various manhauling traverses along the length of the Antarctic Peninsula, as it is such an obvious geographical feature for such a trip, but no full journeys have been completed.

As one moves south along the Detroit Plateau the Trinity Peninsula region comes to an end and one finds oneself in Graham Land. The inland terrain becomes higher and more mountainous the further south one goes, but the edges of the peninsula and the outlying islands also become steeper and more dramatic. Once again FIDS explored much of this region, although there are few records of any climbing here. One notable exception was a private expedition from Australia in January 1999 that sailed aboard the yacht *Tiama* to the mountains east of Brialmont Cove. Robyn Cleland, Stefan Eberhard, Chris Holly, Kieran Lawton, Geoff Moore and Julie Styles were inspired by a photograph taken years before by Gordon Wiltsie. It showed a skier beneath a sharp snow spire above the Calley Glacier that Wiltsie had captioned 'Pilcher Peak', and there was no record of Pilcher Peak having been climbed. However, upon arriving in the area and hauling sleds inland, the Australians realised that Pilcher Peak was actually a larger, but less im-

Gerlache Strait

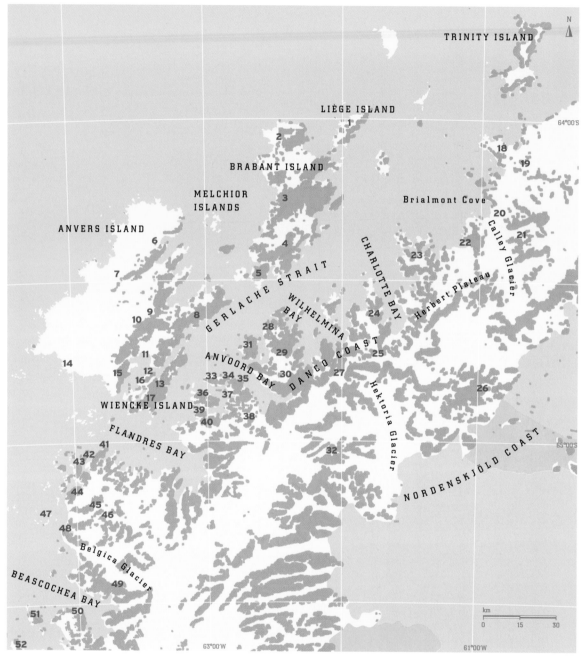

TRINITY ISLAND

LIÈGE ISLAND

BRABANT ISLAND

MELCHIOR ISLANDS

Brialmont Cove

ANVERS ISLAND

Calley Glacier

GERLACHE STRAIT

WILHELMINA BAY

CHARLOTTE BAY

Herbert Plateau

DANCO COAST

ANVOORD BAY

Hektoria Glacier

WIENCKE ISLAND

FLANDRES BAY

NORDENSKJÖLD COAST

Belgica Glacier

BEASCOCHEA BAY

64°00'S

65°00'S

63°00'W

61°00'W

km
0   15   30

60

1.	**Pavlov Peak** 852 m	**7.**	**Mount Helen** 1370 m	**13.**	**Wall Range**
2.	**Mount Hunter** 1410 m	**8.**	**Osterrieth Range**	**14.**	**Palmer Station**
3.	**Mount Parry** 2520 m	**9.**	**Mount Français** 2822 m	**15.**	**Mount William** 1515 m
4.	**Galen Peak** 1540 m	**10.**	**Mount Agamemnon** 2570 m	**16.**	**Port Lockroy Base**
5.	**Mount Bulcke** 1032 m	**11.**	**Borgen Bay**	**17.**	**Savoia Peak** 1415 m
6.	**Mount Nestor**	**12.**	**Jabet Peak** 550 m	**18.**	**Penaud Peak**

19.	**Mount Cornu** 1530 m	**25.**	**Mount Johnston** 2139 m
20.	**Pilcher Peak**	**26.**	**Andersson Peak** 1600 m
21.	**Baldwin Peak** 2100 m	**27.**	**Mount Walker** 2350 m
22.	**Mount Morton** 1400 m	**28.**	**Zeiss Needle** 696 m
23.	**Mount Zeppelin**	**29.**	**Arctowski Peninsula**
24.	**Harris Peak** 1002 m	**30.**	**The Downfall**
		31.	**Rongé Island**
		32.	**Mount Bistre** 1295 m
		33.	**Lemaire Island**
		34.	**Gonzalez Videla Base**
		35.	**Mount Hoegh** 890 m
		36.	**Bryde Island**
		37.	**Paradise Harbour**
		38.	**Mount Inverleith**
		39.	**Mount Bancke**
		40.	**Kershaw Peaks**
		41.	**Cape Renard**
		42.	**Booth Island**
		43.	**Wandel Peak** 980 m
		44.	**Mount Scott** 880 m
		45.	**Mount Shackleton** 1300 m
		46.	**Mount Peary** 1800 m
		47.	**Vernadsky Base**
		48.	**Mount Demaria**
		49.	**Valiente Peak**
		50.	**McCollum Peak** 735 m
		51.	**Lahille Island**
		52.	**Magnier Peaks**

pressive mountain, and that the snowy spire captured by Wiltsie was merely an attractive peak on a ridge leading up to the plateau. So they attempted both, and referred to the attractive sharp peak as 'Wiltsie's Peak'. Pilcher Peak was climbed from the south and the whole team summited on January 16th. Lawton and Styles attempted 'Wiltsie's Peak', spending four days climbing the south ridge, only to be turned back just 50 m from the summit by horrendous snow conditions. The team skied back to Brialmont Cove and made three other minor ascents in the area before reboarding *Tiama*. They then sailed south to Booth Island, where Eberhard, Lawton and Styles climbed an ice couloir on the southwest face of the southernmost peak on Booth Island.

GERLACHE STRAIT REGION

Mount Johnston (2139 m) on the Detroit Plateau is the only big plateau peak to have seen private expeditions. It was first climbed in January 1957 by FIDS men Maurice Bayly, Evans, Leslie Harris and Arthur Shewry, as part of an effort to find a way from Portal Point up the Reclus Peninsula to the plateau. They needed to find a route that Wally Herbert's traverse party could descend after their journey from Hope Bay. This route up and down the Reclus Peninsula to Mount Johnston has now been followed at least twice by private teams in recent years, often on skis, taking in an ascent of Harris Peak (1002 m) along the way.

To the south of Johnston is another high plateau peak of around 2000 m, Mount Walker. It was the objective of an international team aboard the yacht *Gambo* in January 2001, which followed a route first done in 1956 by a FIDS team from the old Danco base (UK). From the Errera Channel they went up onto the Orel Ice Fringe and climbed a 1500 m peak, incongruously named The Downfall, because that is as far as they got. Its extremely steep east face stopped the FIDS team from continuing over it up to the plateau, and it was on The Downfall that the *Gambo* team also stopped in December 2001, this time due to poor weather.

LOOKING INTO THE ERRERA CHANNEL FROM THE GERLACHE STRAIT.
The small rock peak is Cuverville Island.
This photo was taken in 1897 during the first exploration of the area by Adrien de Gerlache.

The *Gambo* team had previously been climbing in one of the most popular areas for all private expeditions to the Peninsula, the region around Rongé Island, the Errera Channel and Andvord Bay. On Rongé Island they made an ascent of Mount Britannia (1160 m) by two different routes, the east ridge and the southeast ridge, and the latter mostly on skis. The other main peak on Rongé Island, Mount Tennant (688 m), had been climbed by another international team – Ronald Naar of The Netherlands with the Spanish pair Vicente Castros Sotos and Javier Selva Serrano – who were based aboard the cruise ship *Grigory Mikheev* in March 2001. Tennant presents a steep rock face to the west, overlooking the Gerlache Strait, but the ascent from the north up to the east ridge was straightforward. Opposite Rongé, on the mainland of the Arctowski Peninsula, the *Gambo* team made an ascent of Stolze Peak (1580 m) on skis and also the westernmost peak of the Laussedat Heights. The Arctowski Peninsula was also the scene of some extreme skiing and snowboarding in February 2000. An American team did short day-trips in the area, based aboard the cruise ship *Akademik Shuleykin.* Several ascents and descents were completed, the highlight being a ski descent of the impressive Zeiss Needle (696 m), where the top section was less than two metres wide, but pitched at 60°. In February 2006 a commercially organised trip aboard the yacht *Evohe* visited the area, after climbing a few peaks further south around Wiencke Island and Prospect Point. Three guides on the boat Luis Benitez, Guy Cotter and Mark Sedon made a possible first ascent of a relatively high peak above the Errera Channel, noting that problematic ice cliffs marked on their nautical chart had fallen away, making access ashore easier than expected. Initially climbing on showshoes, the trio then climbed seven pitches to gain a ridge, which they followed over moderate ground and up one steeper slope to arrive on a rounded dome of a summit around 1300 m high. They referred to the peak as 'Hiddleston Peak', in honour of David Hiddleston, a guiding colleague who had recently died. One of the benefits of this region is the good anchorage available at Cuverville Island. In January 2010 Ludovic Challéat's French team aboard *Podorange* visited the area, making the probable first ascent of Scheimpflug Nunatak (1150 m) on the southern side of the Laussedat Heights and climbing to 650 m on the higher Pulfrich Peak, a high peak in the northern half of the Arctowski Peninsula.

62

with the enormous northwest ridge dropping from the summit down diagonally left to the sea.

Across from the Laussedat Heights above the waters of Andvord Bay lies Mount Hoegh (890 m). The peak may well have been climbed in previous years, but it certainly received an ascent by a New Zealand team in January 2000. They came ashore near the Chilean station Presidente Gonzalez Videla and approached the mountain from the south, climbing to a high col. In addition to climbing Mount Hoegh from this col they also ascended an 805 m peak and a 730 m peak, both to the southeast. In December 2001 the *Gambo* team made a joint ascent of Mount Hoegh with a small British military team in the area sailing aboard the yacht *John Laing*. A long ridge runs down to the west of Mount Hoegh and finishes at Waterboat Point, near the Chilean station Presidente Gonzalez Videla, which provides easy access to this area. Two small peaks near Gonzalez Videla were climbed by a Spanish team in December 2000, one 318 m and another 581 m, both of which the team believed to be first ascents. Mount Hoegh was climbed again, via the west face in 2006, by Darrel Day, Grant Dixon and Jytte Christensen, who were

**CLIMBERS LOW ON THE WEST FACE
OF JABET PEAK.**
Across the waters of the Neumayer Channel is Anvers
Island, with the southern end of Mount Français at
the extreme right.

climbing in the area and based onboard *Spirit of Sydney*. This area has been a successful venue
for one unique commercial operator. The Australian company Aurora Expeditions, founded by
climber Greg Mortimer, has been the only operator of passenger cruises that regularly puts
guided parties ashore specifically for climbing. Over the last decade they have made a number
of minor one-day ascents, some of them probably firsts, on Rongé, Lemaire and Twin Hummock
islands and adjacent mainland points.

Lemaire Island separates the Gerlache Strait from the northern side of Paradise Harbour. It is
a particularly attractive mountain mass with two summits around 780 m high linked by a long
ridge, that would provide a potentially aesthetic coast-to-coast traverse for the right party. The
suitably named Paradise Harbour, often erroneously called 'Paradise Bay', is a very popular venue
for cruise ships, due to its accessibility, landing sites and sheer beauty. Surrounding the harbour
are numerous peaks, some of which have been climbed by yacht-based parties, particularly those
peaks around Neko Harbour and Andvord Bay. These small peaks near the coast offer good day
climbs, as preparation for bigger climbs or as enjoyable half-day trips in their own right.

BRABANT ISLAND

Brabant is a mountainous and heavily glaciated island, lying around 25 km across the Gerlache
Strait from the Danco Coast of the mainland and barely 10 km north of Anvers Island. The island itself is around 53 km long north-to-south and 25 km across, with the terrain rising toward
the centre of the island and culminating in Mount Parry (2520 m). Though the eastern side of
the main range is relatively easy-angled, the western side of this central area drops to the sea in
a very steep escarpment, with several big ridges. The northwestern ridge of Mount Parry, for
example, drops over 2500 m from the summit to the sea in an unbroken sweep, one of the biggest
such climbs in the world.

Mount Parry was first climbed by the 1984-85 British Joint Services Expedition (BJSE) led
by Chris Furse, who had been on a similar previous expedition to Elephant Island in 1976-77.

The second ascent was by a Chilean team in 1993, with support from the Chilean navy in the form of the ship *Piloto Pardo*. The Chileans initially thought they were the first to summit Parry but, finding the hut left behind by the 1984-85 British expedition and making some enquiries, realised they were the second. Both ascents were from the easier eastern side. The 1984-85 BJSE climbed most of the main peaks on the island, so any more significant first ascents here are unlikely, but it still remains an interesting mountaineering venue. In early 2008 a Belgian team made what was probably the second ascent of the 1375 m Celsus Peak, as part of an expedition celebrating the 110th anniversary of Adrian de Gerlache's 1897-99 journeys in the area. For Parry's third ascent, French guide Ludovic Challéat led Alwin Arnold, Arnauld de Fouchier, Thierry Garnier, Ulrich Goerlach, Vincent Logerot and Philippe Poncin, climbing from the south and east, on skis. After one camp on the route, they had a spectacularly clear, but extremely cold and windy, summit day on January 13th and quickly returned to their yacht, *Podorange*, crewed by Caroline and Hervé Olagne, Julien Hélène and Brice Monégier du Sorbier.

Only days later and having just spent time moored safely at the Melchior Islands, the *Ada II* arrived and delivered Mathieu Cortial, Lionel Daudet and Patrick Wagnon to the prime objective of their expedition. Dropped near the base of the northwest ridge, the three climbed over 1000 m up soft snow before deciding to bivouac due to the poor weather. Some 39 hours later they set off again, enjoying another 1000 m of climbing up an elegant arete, hampered only by some crevasses. The last 500 m of the route are decidedly steeper and here the climbers encountered the hardest

THE YACHT *PELAGIC*, SAILING PAST WIENCKE ISLAND.
At left are the rocky summits of Noble Peak, with the smaller Jabet Peak to the right. In the right background is the southern end of the Wall Range.

ADRIEN DE GERLACHE'S *BELGICA*
off Anvers Island in 1897.

climbing on the route, on soft wet snow. Wagnon and then Daudet took four hours to climb the last 100 m, but all three arrived on top around 6 pm on January 23rd. It took them 19 hours to descend, but their pickup was delayed by rough seas. This did not appear to be a problem, as they had brought sufficient food and equipment for just such a delay. Unfortunately, a giant wave hit their site and washed away most of their food and gear and they shivered away the night until the *Ada II* was able to retrieve them the next day. Over the years there have been several incidents of large and unexpected waves hitting climbers and camps close to shore, sometimes causing injury and loss of equipment. Prospective Antarctic climbers would do well to take this into account when operating in such areas, no matter how briefly. The French named their ridge route *Nouvelle Vague*, meaning 'New Wave'. After their climb on Mount Foster, it was their second grand route in less than two weeks. A New Zealand team was also in the area, with Parry's northwest ridge as their main objective, but after the French success they did not attempt the route and climbed elsewhere.

MOUNT FRANÇAIS AND ANVERS ISLAND

At 2822 m Mount Français is the highest peak on Anvers Island. It is also one of the highest mountains in the Antarctic Peninsula area, a local landmark and one of the most photographed mountains in Antarctica. It was named after Charcot's 1903-05 expedition ship, but its first reported sighting was by de Gerlache, who sailed around the southeast corner of Anvers Island on the *Belgica* in 1898.

The first ascent of Français was by the FIDS team of Hindson, Rennie and Shewry, who climbed a route at the western end of the mountain, from the William Glacier, on November 28th 1955. The trio also made the first ascent of nearby Molar Peak (1065 m) and three smaller peaks above the William Glacier. Rennie, Shewry and Hindson now have three peaks named

MOUNT FRANÇAIS AS SEEN FROM JABET PEAK with the main summit at right. The most common route of ascent is the Bull Ridge, seen here dropping from the summit before curving down left into the small rocky peaks right of centre.

after them, running along a ridge in the southern part of the island, near Mount William. Hindson had already made an attempt on Français the previous September, with Canty and Hooper, but they retreated, having already made the first ascent of the nearby Mount Helen (1370 m) a few days before. In 1982 a large Chilean survey team visited the area and made what is thought to be the third ascent of Français, another British team having climbed the mountain in the intervening years since 1955. The Chilean leader was Jorge Quinteros, a celebrated Chilean climber and scientist. He had sailed with Bill Tilman years before and on one occasion narrowly avoided disaster after their boat was swept out into the Drake Passage, their rudder having been damaged navigating a Chilean fjord. Also on the team was a young Gino Casassa, who was one of the first Chileans to climb on the big peaks of the Himalaya and who would go on to become a significant figure in Patagonian and Antarctic glaciology.

The first ski descent of Mount Français was made by New Zealander Greg Landreth, after accomplishing the fourth ascent of the mountain, in January 1987. This ascent, from the *Northanger* still under the hand of Rick Thomas, was the first time that the giant peak had been climbed by a private, yacht-based expedition. It was to be more than a decade until climbers stood atop Mount Français again. In 1999 the cruise ship *Professor Molchanov* dropped Australian climbers David Adams and Duncan Thomas on Wiencke Island for a three month stay in the area, during which time they made the fifth ascent of Français, by the Bull Ridge. This ridge is an obvious 'fish-hook' shaped feature on the south face of the mountain that is visible to all who sail past down the Neumayer Channel. The two climbed steep ice out of the water to get ashore, before ascending the ridge in a long single-push, undoubtedly energised by the sight of an avalanche obliterating their tracks to the base of the ridge. Adams and Thomas summited in calm, midnight twilight with a marvellous view far south down the coast of the Peninsula. Returning to the edge of the seracs above the water, they found ice movements had drawn their inflatable boat metres up out of the water, leaving it dangling by a solitary ice screw.

Mount Français was the objective of a strong group of Australian and New Zealand climbers who arrived aboard *Spirit of Sydney* in early 2003. One of the team, Rob Rymill was a descendant of John Rymill, leader of the 1934-37 British Graham Land Expedition that explored so much of the surrounding area. By the time the 2003 team arrived on Anvers they had already climbed Mount Johnston via Harris Peak, been up the Reclus Peninsula, made a ski descent of Mount Demaria above Waddington Bay, and climbed around Mount Scott. Getting ashore at Anvers Island, Theo Kossart, Jon Morgan, Stuart Morris and Chuck Olbery crossed between Billie Peak (725 m) and Copper Peak (1125 m) to gain the western side of the Bull Ridge. They climbed this to the summit, completing the sixth ascent of Mount Français, before making the second ski descent of the mountain. An obvious challenge on Français is a traverse from end to end, possibly on skis, and although this has been talked about, it has yet to be attempted.

Mount William (1515 m), on the southern end of Anvers Island, about 20 km from Mount Français, is one of the most beautiful mountains in the entire Peninsula area and provides an elegant companion to the long, rounded bulk of Français. It has had four ascents and several more attempts, proving a big climb with some serious objective danger from its numerous seracs and cornices. The first ascent was achieved by FIDS personnel John Bull and John Thompson in November 1956 (the Bull Ridge on nearby Mount Français is named after the former). In 1982 a Chilean team, mentioned above, made the second ascent of the mountain, via the north ridge, then Jorge Quinteros and Gino Casassa climbed a new route up the southwest ridge. The fourth ascent of the mountain was in January 1994, by an international team – Matt Dickinson, Denis Ducroz, Doron Erel, Julian Freeman-Atwood, Chantal Mauduit and Frank McDermott – sailing aboard Skip Novak's *Pelagic*. They climbed a bold and threatened line up the northeast face, under the seracs of the east ridge, to finish up the north ridge. *Pelagic* returned in early 2003 to

THE WESTERN SIDE OF THE SOUTHERNMOST
PEAK OF THE WALL RANGE,
ON WIENCKE ISLAND.
The prominent central buttress is the line of the 1997
route *Whoz Una?*, probably the hardest route
yet climbed on the island.

deposit Doug Stoup and Andrew McLean on Anvers, where they made an ascent of The Minaret (1065 m), a sharp peak on the ridge northeast of Mount William. The two Americans skied down from a point just 100 m below the rocky summit.

THE EAST FACE OF THE BEAUTIFUL
MOUNT WILLIAM AT THE SOUTHERN END
OF ANVERS ISLAND.
The 1994 route gains the ice directly in front of the camera, before traversing right to ascend under the seracs of the northeast face, right of the visible rock, and reaching the north ridge down to the right from the summit.

WIENCKE ISLAND

The most popular destination for yacht-based climbers on the peninsula has been Wiencke Island. This is largely due to the protected harbour at Port Lockroy, but also because of the attractive peaks around the area and the good access between them. Wiencke Island is around 25 km long from northeast to southwest and relatively narrow for most of that length, but for a bulge in the central section of around 10 km from west to east. A narrow mountain range runs up the middle of the island for its entire length, broken into three sections. The northernmost section of the range lies north of the Channel Glacier and holds the two smaller summits Nipple Peak (675 m) and Nemo Peak (865 m). South of the Channel Glacier is the central section, the Wall Range, an impressive barrier as the name would suggest, with snowy summits above steep rock walls.

The first known ascent of the 1097 m high-point of the Wall Range was in 1976 by a team of Italians from the famous 'Lecco Spiders' club. The team used siege tactics to reach a nearby top, then traversed to the highest point. In early 2000 the Welsh bad-weather specialist Crag Jones visited the area with Julian Freeman-Atwood, aboard *Pelagic*, after their aborted attempt on Cape Renard Tower. Jones soloed a straightforward couloir on the west face of the Wall Range that took him to the north ridge of the main peak, which he then followed to the top in poor weather. This route was repeated by climbers from *Gambo* in December 2001. There are plenty of other hard climbing options available on the Wall Range, too hard for the early FIDS people who worked here. The hardest climb done here so far was by the two Canadian climbers Jia Condon and Rich Prohaska, with New Zealander Greg Landreth, who arrived at the island in January 1997 aboard *Northanger*. Point 1050 m is at the southern end of the Wall Range above the Thunder Glacier. Its steep buttress gave 18 pitches of mostly granite climbing up to 5.9, the top five pitches having some added mixed terrain, leading to a difficult summit cornice. Caught by a storm on the summit the trio could not see an easier way off the top and so were forced to rappel their route. They named it *Whoz Una?* in reference to the popular name for Cape Renard, further south. Reaching the Thunder Glacier below in terrible conditions, they skied back to Port Lockroy to end a 40-hour round-trip. At this southern end of the Wall Range the Thunder Glacier cuts through from west to east. On the south side of the Thunder Glacier is Savoia Peak (1415 m), the highest mountain on the island.

69

Savoia Peak was first climbed by Charcot's men, Pierre Dayné and Jacques Jabet, on February 7th 1905. With the extent of Dayné's climbing on Wandel Peak unverified, it can be said that Savoia Peak was the first big peak to be climbed on the Antarctic Peninsula. It is an aestheti-

SAVOIA PEAK
with the peaks of the Sierra du Fief stretching south.

cally impressive mountain, particularly seen from the west, and has had numerous ascents since then, with a moderate route to the summit via the northeast ridge on snow and ice up to 50°. Pierre Dayné was actually Italian and the first professional mountain guide to be employed in Antarctica, and has a pyramidal 730 m peak at the southern end of Wiencke Island named after him. The name of Savoia Peak derives from the great Italian mountaineer and explorer Luigi di Savoia, the Duke of Abruzzi, and originated with Charcot. Hence this peak has often been called variations of the Duke's name, most commonly 'Luigi Peak'. In February 1988 Hamish Laird and Skip Novak made what was almost certainly the first non-government ascent of Savoia Peak. It was *Pelagic's* first journey to the Peninsula and, as with ascents of Savoia Peak, there were many more to come. In December 2001 it received its first snowboard descent, by members of a team aboard *Gambo* that had been climbing in the region, as noted above. There is potential for some steep technical routes on Savoia Peak, but it has often been noted that there is also significant avalanche danger from the upper sections of the mountain. Nonetheless, this did not deter the marauding French trio aboard *Ada II* in January 2010. They spied the narrow ribbon of ice on the left of the west face that had had climbers talking for years. Cortial, Daudet and Wagnon approached Savoia on skis, pulling sleds, but were turned back by poor weather on their first attempt on January 28th. Two days later they tried again. The route gave 800 m of steep ice climbing in the gully, followed by another 300 m up the ridge to the summit, reached after 13 hours of climbing. They named their route *Bon Anniversaire Tristan* (Happy Birthday Tristan) and graded it ED+. The trio descended the south ridge, thus making a traverse of the peak, and rappelled the gully separating Savoia from the first peak on the serrated ridge running south.

This ridge is the Sierra du Fief, to give it its official name, though the peaks are often called the 'Fief Mountains' or even the 'Seven Sisters of Fief' due to the seven obvious peaks. In December 2001 members of the *Gambo* expedition climbed the Fief summit nearest to Savoia Peak, the 'First Sister', via the steep and loose northwest ridge. This route had been attempted by Roger Haworth and Luke Milner in February 2000, who were unsuccessful due to poor snow conditions. The Sierra du Fief is a clear target for a traverse of all the summits but this has yet to be done. On the southeast side of the Sierra du Fief lies Janssen Peak (1085 m), which was climbed by a yacht-based group on January 17th 2000. Four New Zealanders – guides Mike Roberts and Anton Woperis with Steve and Lizzie Craddock – climbed 13 pitches of 45°-50° snow on the east face.

THE TWIN TOWERS OF CAPE RENARD AT EXTREME LEFT. The lower summit of the twins is unclimbed. In the centre is False Cape Renard, on which only the left summit of the three has been climbed.

The island is at its widest in the centre and is around 10 km from west to east. On the west side of the Wall Range the Harbour Glacier parallels the mountains, running northeast to southwest. West again of the Harbour Glacier is a short parallel range formed by two peaks – Jabet Peak (550 m) and Noble Peak (720 m) – and on the west of them is the Neumayer Channel. On May 9th 1948, when Ken Pawson and W. Richards made the first ascent of Jabet Peak, they could never have dreamed that within their lifetimes it would become the most popular peak ascent on the entire Antarctic Peninsula. Other than Mount Vinson and Mount Erebus, Jabet Peak is probably the only significant Antarctic mountain to have received over 100 ascents. From Port Lockroy it is a steep snow climb. It is even easier from the west, as you traverse up the west face to reach the southern end of the summit ridge, which can be soft and narrow. Noble Peak also fell to Blyth and Pawson, on November 6th 1948. Between climbing Jabet and Noble, Blyth, Pawson and Richards travelled to the north of the island to make the first ascent of Nemo Peak (865 m) on October 13th, in addition to climbing high during an unsuccessful attempt on the nearby Nipple Peak. Just over a week after their first ascent of Noble Peak, they took their climbing one step further and traversed the entire ridge between Noble Peak and Jabet Peak, a considerable feat that may not have been repeated. As noted above, Pawson moved north up to King George Island and made numerous first ascents with Geoff Hattersley-Smith in 1949. He returned to Port Lockroy in March 1950, for the third ascent of Jabet Peak with Richard Brooke. Like many FIDS personnel, Pawson moved around the world in later years, following geological work where it took him, and eventually settled in Canada, where he continued to ski and enjoy the mountains into the 21st century.

Various points on the ridge between Noble Peak and Jabet Peak have been reached over the years. In 1976 an Italian team reached a point on the ridge via a face route, and in March 2000 Richard and Roger Haworth reached the highest point on the ridge via a route from the west. In late February 2003, the German climber Ed Birnbacher and Briton Niel Fox approached from the eastern side and climbed one of the ice runnels giving 400 m of 50°-60°. They reached the top of the ridge at around 700 m and turned across loose rock to a small point on the ridge, from where they rappelled off pitons and slings.

The British base Port Lockroy was established in February 1944 during Operation Tabarin. It operated intermittently over the years, but through all seasons during the 1950s and up to 1962.

In early 1996 the main building, Bransfield House, was restored and designated an official Historic Site. Since late 1996 it has been open every summer, receiving tourists from ships and yachts, selling souvenirs and educating visitors about the geography and history of the region. The station is actually on the tiny Goudier Island, barely separated from the larger mass of Wiencke Island.

To the southwest of Wiencke Island is Doumer Island, a low-lying dome of snow and ice. It rises to a height of 515 m near its centre, called Doumer Hill, which provides no real climbing challenge but can be an enjoyable ski journey. This summit was first climbed on June 12th 1948 by Blyth, Pawson and Richards on a day trip from Port Lockroy and has been visited many times since.

CAPE RENARD

There is one mountain that has become almost synonymous with the Antarctic Peninsula: Cape Renard. The striking 747 m high spire of rock and ice is often referred to as 'Cape Renard Tower', though it is more accurately two steep towers that share a common base. This unique symmetry lent itself to the other popular, but more prosaic, name for the mountain: 'Una's Tits'. The famous woman to which this referred was the wife of a Governor of the Falkland Islands, the last stopping place for FIDS people on their way south. Cape Renard looks steepest when viewed from the west, in the northern section of the Lemaire Channel and from this aspect the lower tower is also visible, thus giving rise to the anatomically derived knickname. From the north, however, the lower tower is not seen and the main tower looks much wider; a steep rock face capped by snow and cut by two obvious couloirs.

Less than three kilometres southwest of Cape Renard is a second group of three very steep peaks named False Cape Renard. When the *Belgica* expedition first sighted the area, the two massifs were referred to collectively as 'The Needles'. But with up to five sharp peaks visible in the region at once, such a name was considered too ambiguous, and too inaccurate for navigational purposes. The need to distinguish the two, quite separate, massifs led Charcot, on his second expedition in 1908-10, to rename the southern massif False Cape Renard and the northern twin towers Cape Renard. In addition, 'The Needles' is an old name on some maps for Les Dents, the impressive unclimbed spires on the northern tip of Alexander Island, much further south. Cape Renard is also significant as it marks the divide between the Danco Coast to the North and the Graham Coast to the South.

The first known attempt to climb Cape Renard was in February 1996, by Crag Jones and Julian Freeman-Atwood, both of whom by this time were veterans of tough climbing in the southern regions. *Pelagic* delivered them to the base of the cape and they set up camp on top of the seracs, 25 m above the sea. Their initial attempt up the obvious central couloir on the north face found good rock but bad avalanche danger. They then traversed east across ledges to gain the base of another gully that slants up from left to right, initially on rock before it reaches a hanging couloir of snow and ice. The couloir provided 12 pitches of Scottish III terrain, with a few harder sections. However, upon reaching the base of the upper rock headwall, bad weather set in and stayed, forcing them down. Another attempt days later, with a slight variation over new rock pitches, ended in Jones pulling off a flake and taking a minor fall, his injuries forcing them to descend once again.

In February 1997 *Northanger* landed the Canadians Jia Condon and Rich Prohaska at Cape Renard, fresh from their climbing in the Wall Range on Wiencke Island. The duo was aiming for the first ascent of the main tower, by the east buttress, a line well left of the 1996 British attempt. The pair fixed ropes up the first half of the route, then pushed up beyond. On February 4th they came to the top of the buttress on a subsidiary top, but the cornice from there to the main summit was dangerously unstable, so they rappelled from that point. Their route

THE NORTH FACE OF CAPE RENARD, SHOWING THE ROUTES ATTEMPTED:
Purple – 1996, Freeman-Atwood/Jones, first attempt
Yellow – 1996, Jones/Novak, second attempt
Green – 1997, Condon/Prohaska, *Una's What?* (5.9, A2)
Red – 2000, Freeman-Atwood/Jones, attempt

FALSE CAPE RENARD
showing the 2007 route *Azken Paradizua* (600 m, 7a, M6).

LOOKING ACROSS THE LEMAIRE CHANNEL
to the unclimbed summits of the Humphries Heights
on the right, with the Cape Renard towers visible on the left,
from the northern end of Booth Island.

– *Una's What?* – is primarily rock climbing with some easier mixed ground, and received the classic Canadian Rockies grade of 5.9 A2. After leaving the cape, Condon and Prohaska, with Greg Landreth and Keri Pashuk off *Northanger*, moved across to the north ridge of Wandel Peak where they became the first of several teams in recent years to turn back up high due to poor snow and ice conditions.

The first ascent of Cape Renard finally happened in 1999, when renowned German climber Stefan Glowacz arrived with Kurt Albert, Hoger Hoeber, Hans Martin Götz, Gerhard Hiedorn and Jürgen Knappe, aboard the yacht *Santa Maria*. They climbed the dark rock wall of the west face via a 17-pitch, 900 m high route, with free-climbing up to 5.12. The team bolted the belays, eventually calling the route *Against The Wind*. Though the ascent was not widely reported, it is almost certainly the most technically difficult route yet climbed on the Antarctic Peninsula.

Julian Freeman-Atwood and Crag Jones returned to Cape Renard in February 2000, once again attempting the left couloir on the north face. *Pelagic*, under owner Skip Novak, put them ashore further east than in 1996 and the team fixed a line over an ice cliff to gain the flatter ground above, where a camp was set and loads hauled up from below. From this camp their route traversed west across the ice to reach the ledges that give access to the base of the couloir, thus rejoining the start of their 1996 line. The duo took two days to overcome the difficult rock pitches at the bottom, before entering the hanging couloir itself. Fixed ropes were used initially, but then abandoned for a single-push attempt from their high point. Freeman-Atwood descended at this time and Jones was joined by Novak for the summit push. This pair climbed a dozen pitches in the couloir then went up and across a snow ramp, on which they bivouacked without sleeping bags. The next day started with very difficult climbing on the headwall and it soon became even harder. Around 150 m below the summit, only two pitches from easier ground, but low on fuel and faced with loose, wet, overhanging rock, Jones and Novak decided to retreat. Eighteen rappels took them to the traverse ledges, and base camp on the glacier was reached soon after.

In December 2007 *Northanger* made yet another pilgrimage to the cape, this time carrying a Spanish team looking to climb a steep new route. The renowned rock climbers Eneko and Iker Pou were joined by a film crew and eventually decided to attempt the westernmost summit of the three tops of False Cape Renard, which they referred to as 'Zerua Peak' ('Sky Peak'). The brothers and their two-man film crew were put ashore on December 20th, but were forced to endure four days of bad weather in camp. The weather cleared unexpectedly during their Christmas Eve party, so they stopped drinking and set off for a single-push up the mixed northwest buttress. Though the lower section is easy terrain, it soon gave way to difficult rock climbing, often with a covering of verglas, all done in freezing conditions. They had only taken one set of ice tools, so the M6 mixed pitches took longer than normal and much of the steep rock was shattered, somewhat intensifying the F6b+ pitches climbed up high. After reaching the summit, eight hours of rappelling got them down and they reached their friends in base camp 24 hours after leaving. They named their route *Azken Paradizua*, and with 600 m of F7a and M6 it is one of the hardest routes on the Antarctic Peninsula.

Just right of the Pou brothers' line is an unusually straight and narrow goulotte of ice that had attracted the eye of passing climbers but had not been touched. Fresh from their new route on Savoia Peak, the *Ada II* climbers Cortial, Daudet and Wagnon climbed 550 m of ice up the line. They named it *42 Balais et Toujours pas Calmé* (42 Years Old and Still Thriving) as a tribute to the fact that it was Daudet's 42nd birthday and that he has clearly lost none of his burning energy to climb such adventurous routes.

There has been no known attempt on the lower, southern Cape Renard tower and it remains unclimbed. Though overshadowed by its nearby twin that is steeper and rockier, it is one of the major unclimbed objectives on the peninsula. The remaining two virgin summits of False Cape Renard are also attractive. Access from the southwest, above the waters of the northern Lemaire Channel, seems relatively straightforward, although this can change and the climbing above is clearly much harder. As one moves into the northern end of the Lemaire Channel the terrain south of False Cape Renard appears as a chain of summits dropping steeply to the water. This is the Humphries Heights area, and no climbing has been recorded here.

BOOTH ISLAND AND THE LEMAIRE CHANNEL

The Lemaire Channel is a contender for the most photographed area in Antarctica, which has led to the popular name 'Kodak Gap', and as one moves south, the coast of the mainland is on the left and Booth Island lies on the right. The northernmost point of Booth Island rears up to the steep and rocky sides of Mount Lacroix, whose 640 m high point is Cléry Peak. Mount

Lacroix is connected to the rest of the island by a very low isthmus, south of which the terrain rises into the north ridge of Wandel Peak (980 m), the highest point on Booth Island. Charcot visited Booth Island in 1905 and one of his geologists, Ernest Gourdon, climbed at least one peak with the guide Pierre Dayné. From Charcot's writings it seems that they may have climbed to Wandel Peak, the highest point of the island. If true, this is quite remarkable, as several teams have failed to climb Wandel in modern times, often being stopped by bergschrunds and other difficult ground high on the north ridge. In February 2006 a very strong Spanish team led by Jose Carlos Tamayo climbed almost to the top of Wandel Peak, stopping around 15 m short of the summit due to an unstable snow mushroom. The east face of Wandel Peak presents a fantastic couloir dropping down directly from the summit to the waters of the Lemaire Channel. This straight shot to the summit is steep and somewhat threatened from above by seracs and severely overhanging cornices. In early February 2010 the French trio from *Ada II* climbed the couloir, reaching the summit ridge just north of the summit and negotiated the sinuous crest and some wild cornicing. They could look over 900 m straight down into the Lemaire Channel, where they could see cruise ships unwittingly pass by. Near the summit was a large crevasse that Cortial fell into on the descent. The trio found that the top of Wandel Peak consists of two summits separated by a short and narrow ridge. Visting both, they found the smaller and steeper second summit to the south to be a few metres higher than the first. The French named their direct route *La Mystique des Corniches...ons* (The Mystical Cornices), a lighthearted play on the French word 'cornichons' that also gives The Mystical Idiots! There is more mountain terrain on Booth Island besides Wandel itself, and some climbing has been done in couloirs on peaks at the southern end of the island. There are also some attractive unclimbed rock walls that form the western aspect of Wandel Peak and the lower summits to the south.

BOB LEWIS NEAR THE SUMMIT OF MOUNT SCOTT
during the first ascent in November 1962.

THE LONG AND SERIOUS NORTH RIDGE OF MOUNT SCOTT
climbed by Chris Jewell and Lucas Trihey in January 2000.

SCOTT, SHACKLETON AND VERNADSKY

As you emerge from the southern end of the Lemaire Channel you are greeted by a steep rocky peak up to your left: Mount Scott. Though they did not climb high, the first people to set foot beneath the mountain were members of Charcot's second expedition, in 1909, looking for a route from the coast up to the spine of the mainland. The 880 m Mount Scott has become one of the most popular and most photographed peaks on the Peninsula and the normal east ridge route, accessed from the south, is much easier than the steep western side would indicate. The first ascent used this east ridge, but it was approached from the Leay Glacier to the north. It was climbed on November 20th 1962 by three FIDS members – Edward Grimshaw, Peter Kimber and Bob Lewis – in a long day trip from Faraday base, much of it on skis. There are three other established routes on Scott: the west ridge, southwest face and north ridge.

Italians Gian Luigi Quarti and Fulvio Mariani made the first non-government ascent of Scott in 1985, based aboard the yacht *Basile*. Their mixed route up the prominent west buttress required one bivouac. The southwest face was climbed by Skip Novak and Alex Lowe in January 1996, in a rapid nine hour journey from shore to shore, based aboard the yacht *Pelagic*. This route, graded Alpine TD by Lowe and Novak takes the obvious couloir up the face and climbs mostly 60° ice leading to the crux, a near vertical exit on to the summit snowfield. In January 2000 Australian climbers Lucas Trihey and Chris Jewell climbed the north ridge, finishing on a northern peak of Scott. This long ridge rises out of the water and the pair climbed around 35 pitches, at least 10 of them on poor rock up to 5.7, with the rest of the climb being ice and mixed, often along a razor-thin ridge. The ascent required at least one rappel off a gendarme and in all Trihey and Jewell took 29 hours to reach the summit. This serious route is one of the harder climbs accomplished on the Antarctic Peninsula.

˅ **MOUNT SCOTT FROM THE WEST.**
The 1996 Lowe-Novak route takes the steep ice couloir dropping down from the summit, just right of centre.

› **CHRIS JEWELL CLIMBING ONE OF THE MANY ROCK PITCHES** on the north ridge of Mount Scott.

Mount Scott is really the northwestern end of a wide horseshoe-shaped massif, opening to the southwest onto the Penola Strait, with a small line of rocky peaks forming the southeastern end of the horseshoe. Several of these peaks were climbed, skied and snowboarded by private teams in early 2000 and again in March 2001. The massif rises to a broad snowy summit around 980 m high at the back of the horseshoe, and gives an easy ascent and superb views north along the Lemaire Channel, past Booth Island. This point was first climbed by Grimshaw, Kimber and Lewis on November 20th 1962, after their first ascent of Mount Scott. Most of the climb was done on skis, ensuring a relatively fast descent.

Faraday base was established in the Argentine Islands in 1947; first on Winter Island, before being moved to Galindez Island in 1954. The station was occupied by FIDS, then BAS, until February 1996 when it was transferred to the fledgling Ukrainian Antarctic program for a token amount, whereupon it was named Vernadsky. In January 1997, the very next summer after they took possession of the base, Ukrainian personnel made ascents of Scott, Shackleton and Peary, having already climbed Mount Demaria and Mount Mill in March 1996. The base is now the longest continually operating scientific station in Antarctica and is a popular stopover for cruise ships and yachts. Passengers can view the buildings and enjoy the hospitality of the personnel working there, often partaking of their home-made vodka around the pool table.

Southeast of the Scott horseshoe lies Mount Shackleton, a steep massif running east-west, between the Leay Glacier to the north and the Wiggins Glacier to the south. Shackleton, like Mount Scott, has an east ridge easier than its other aspects and this was the route of first ascent by Bob Lewis, Edward Grimshaw and Brian Porter on 17th October 1962. Operating from a camp at the junction of the Leay and Wiggins, they were the first to explore this area since Charcot and, like his expedition, were searching for a way to get up onto the plateau from the coastal area

LOOKING ACROSS LEROUX BAY TO MOUNT RIO BRANCO ON THE PEREZ PENINSULA from high on Chavez Island. In the centre foreground is Edwards Island and behind that a low unnamed peninsula. Mount Rio Branco is around 35km away.

accessible from Faraday. Shackleton has been climbed a few times in recent years, but there has only been one additional route. Shortly before their climb on Wandel Peak, mentioned above, the Spanish team of Sebastian Alvaro, Esther Sabadell, Carlos Tamayo and Alex Txikón climbed Shackleton by the south face. This face looks over the normal route up the Wiggins Glacier and has been the scene of some large avalanches. It is an attractive target though, and more direct than the east ridge route, which also has a broken icefall. On February 1st 2006 the four set up camp on the Wiggins, under the face, and the next day climbed around 600 m of 55°-60° snow and ice to reach the west ridge, which they followed for a further 200 m to the summit. They started descending the normal east ridge route but after 300 m could no longer find the way in the thick mist that had developed. They waited until dawn on February 3rd but the situation did not improve so they re-ascended to the summit and rappelled their route on the face. Shortly after the Spanish ascent, Australian climber Grant Dixon and Dane Jytte Christensen left *Spirit of Sydney*, skied up the Wiggins and repeated the east ridge to make the third non-government ascent of Mount Shackleton.

Appearing more like a dark rock peak as the climber approaches from the coast, Blanchard Ridge (520 m) is a steep outlier of Shackleton. Blanchard was first climbed on August 14th 1965 by BAS men Bushell and Stacey. This marked the end of a productive week for the BAS group. On August 6th Bushell, Hope, Stacey and Tallis had made the first ascent of the massive Mount Peary (1900 m), a great rounded dome on the edge of the mainland plateau. On August 10th they made the first ascent of Lumière Peak (1065 m) via the west face, after a failed attempt on August 8th. Lumière had also been attempted in late November 1962 by Peter Kimber and Bob Lewis, climbing from the Bussey Glacier, but they turned back less than 200 m from the summit confronted by loose rock and deep snow. Lewis reported the terrain to be very difficult for travel with dogsleds, with numerous large crevasses and icefalls on the Bussey Glacier, particularly around Mount Peary. Lumière Peak

LOOKING EAST INTO THE WIGGINS GLACIER. On the left is Mount Shackleton, with the dark rock spire of Blanchard Point visible in front of it. South across the Wiggins Glacier the terrain rises to the distant cloud-topped summit of Mount Peary. In front, much closer, is the angular rock summit of the popular Mount Mill.

lies on the southern side of the peninsula formed by Demaria and Cape Tuxen, and has not been climbed by non-government parties. On a small rock island, Rasmussen Island, just west of the Wiggins' terminus and the northern extremity of Waddington Bay, there is a small cove that allows good access up onto the Wiggins itself. On the seaward side of this island – formerly thought to be joined to the mainland – there is a cross erected to Hargreaves, Walker and Whitfield, three BAS men who died in a storm high on Mount Peary in 1976. The three climbers are thought to have made the third ascent and to have reached the summit on September 6th 1976, shortly after which bad weather enveloped the mountain. Signs of their equipment were reportedly found around 300 m below the summit, but no trace of their bodies was ever found and there is no evidence that they did reach the top. In August 1975, Walker and Whitfield had made the fourth ascent of Mount Shackleton, an ascent of Mount Mill and also attempted Chaigneau Peak (760 m) and Mount Balch (1105 m), and were quite experienced at climbing in the area. They are part of the surprisingly small number of climbers who have ever died whilst actually mountaineering in Antarctica.

Winter climbing, impractical in other Antarctic ranges, has been quite popular on the Peninsula. Not only are conditions slightly warmer here, but in earlier years BAS personnel could travel efficiently by dogsled over the frozen sea and access some areas more easily than in summer. It gave them a break from being cooped up inside base during the dark months. Moreover, during this time most of them had less scientific fieldwork than during the summer months. Indeed it provided good preparation for that work.

On January 23rd 2010 the French team aboard *Podorange*, led by Ludo Challéat, made an ascent of Mount Peary, climbing on skis all the way and encountering numerous crevasses. They started from a base camp on the Wiggins Glacier, as they had made an ascent of Mount Shackleton the previous day. The upper reaches of Peary were almost flat and they skied across nearly horizontal terrain for almost an hour before reaching the summit, which their GPS showed as being 2080 m, significantly higher than the official height.

VIEUGE ISLAND FROM HIGH ON CHAVEZ ISLAND with the yacht *Evohe* sailing the waters of the Grandidier Channel below. The low flat ice on the right horizon is the distant coast of Renaud Island.

80

Just south of where the Wiggins empties into the Penola Strait lies the small inlet of Waddington Bay. The shore of the bay is home to a cluster of small peaks: Mount Demaria, Mount Mill and Mount Balch. Mount Demaria is thought to have been first climbed by Joe Farman and others in the 1950s after the establishment of Faraday base. But members of Charcot's 1904 expedition climbed high on Cape Tuxen, the feature running down from Demaria to the water, so they may well have reached the summit. Bob Lewis and others climbed Demaria shortly before their first ascent of Mount Scott in November 1962, and it has become very popular in recent years as it offers good access and a straightforward climb up an obvious snowy arete to a distinct summit with great views. Mount Balch was first climbed on September 3rd 1963 by Peter Blackley, Peter Kimber and Bob Lewis, with some support from Terry Tallis, using dogs. The trio started from a base camp behind Mount Mill and actually took three attempts to get up the complex ridge. From that camp they also made the first exploration of the Bussey Glacier, with three attempts to find a route up Mount Peary and hence onto the main plateau. In recent years Mount Mill and Mount Balch have also seen more ascents from climbers on yachts, helped somewhat by the good anchorage available at nearby Petermann Island, where several lines can be secured, and the relative civilisation of the Vernadsky base.

BEYOND THE TOURISTS

**LOOKING EAST FROM HIGH
ON CHAVEZ ISLAND.**
The large massif on the right contains
the high peaks of Mount Perchot (left) and
Mount Bigo (right). In front of them are the
sharp rocky features of the Magnier Peaks.
The waters of Leroux Bay are on the left.

Most cruise ships and yachts go no further south than the Mount Scott-Vernadsky base area, for various reasons. The peaks to the north, around Paradise Bay, and Wiencke Island are so beautiful and accessible that most cannot bear to sail past them without stopping off to climb or ski. Those areas also have the advantages of known anchorages for yachts, and well-known peaks, such as Jabet Peak, Mount Français and Mount Scott, for climbing. The impressive mountains of Adelaide Island (let alone Alexander Island) are still a long way off, while getting ashore here is

not easy and there are fewer proven safe anchorages along this stretch further south. Time is the other factor, as in all Antarctic expeditions. Most yacht charters are around 30 days and by the time the Drake Passage is crossed twice, Ushuaia and Puerto Williams are departed and returned to, and the less mountainous northern Peninsula is passed, teams usually have barely two weeks remaining and the notorious maritime weather of the Peninsula means good climbing days are a rare blessing. Hence there is not usually enough time left to push further south and many interesting mountain areas remain just out of reach for most modern Antarctic Peninsula climbers.

However, for those willing to face these challenges, this area can be rewarding. The coastal region around Collins Bay and Beascochea Bay, with the promontory of Cape Perez in between, is home to many fine peaks. East of Cape Perez toward the Belgica Glacier there is a multitude of summits never visited by private expeditions and the terrain eventually rises to Valiente Peak, the southern side of which overlooks the northern arm of Beascochea Bay. This area was visited by de Gerlache and Charcot but not charted until Rymill visited in 1934-37. The official USGS altitude of Valiente Peak is 2165 m, but other sources show nothing this high anywhere in the vicinity. Such a high altitude is possibly a mistranslation between feet and metres, as a height of 650-750 m would be more in keeping with the surrounding terrain. Hubert Wilkins flew over Beascochea Bay in December 1929 and in following years all visitors noted the large ice cliffs around the shore, still presenting a serious obstacle for any potential climbing teams. However BAS teams have climbed here since the 1960s. In October 1965, for example, they climbed the high point of King Island and two unnamed peaks either side of McCollum Peak (735 m).

LOOKING SOUTHEAST TO UNCLIMBED PEAKS in from Cape Perez.

In February 2006 a group, primarily made up of New Zealand climbers, visited the area further south around Leroux Bay, climbing to the summit of Edwards Island and climbing high on Chavez Island. From Chavez the mainland peaks of Mount Perchot and Mount Bigo are clearly visible to the east, but there is no record of ascents of these peaks, nor of the nearby Magnier Peaks. The altitudes of Mount Perchot and Mount Bigot are recorded as being over 2000 m, but may be considerably lower. Similarly there is no record of climbers on Mount Rio Branco, a high summit with a steep south face, on the ridge running down to Perez Point. Of course, these lower peaks may well have been visited much earlier by FIDS and BAS personnel from the old Faraday base.

Going south from here, Renaud Island and Lavoisier Island are relatively low and flat compared to most of the other islands and are of little interest to climbers. Between Renaud and the mainland lies Larrouy Island, which had a visit from the *Pelagic* in February 1991 when Skip Novak, Jacapo Merrizi and Marco Preti climbed the highest summit, Pilot Peak (745 m). Novak returned to this region in 2004 for a slightly unusual expedition. A team of Palestinian and Israeli climbers wanted to climb a virgin Antarctic peak in the name of peace. Using both *Pelagic* and Novak's new *Pelagic Australis*, the team arrived at Prospect Point, southeast of Larrouy Island. Guided by Denis Ducroz and Doron Erel (who had made the fourth ascent of Mount William in 1994) the team of seven novices climbed a summit that they estimated to be 882 m high, via an easy ascent to the head of the glacier above Prospect Point. They referred to their peak as the 'Mountain of Israeli-Palestinian Friendship'. The Prospect Point area was visited again in early 2006 by a mainly Australian team aboard the *Spirit of Sydney* skippered by Ben Wallis. Grant Dixon and Danish climber Jytte Christensen climbed the southern summit of the Miller Heights, a high ridge running inland from Sharp Peak (475 m). Another commercially organised trip of New Zealanders aboard *Evohe* also visited around the same time, unsuccessfully attempting Sharp Peak, but climbing a smaller peak to its west, and a larger peak slightly further inland. Aside from these minor forays around Prospect Point, no non-government climbers to anyone's knowledge have ever visited the region's larger coastal and inland peaks.

The highest peak here is Mount Dewey (1830 m) and the mountainous coast around it may provide a worthwhile new area for private expeditions to explore, if they can afford the time and find a way ashore. Though Mount Dewey may be lower than 1830 m, it appears steep and broken from the south and east, so an attempt from the northwest would be a long and serious journey. Further south again, but high up on the inland plateau, Slessor Peak (2370 m) is one of the highest peaks on the Peninsula. Though not as far south as some of the other high mainland peaks, it has not had an ascent in recent years due to the usual difficulties of getting up high onto the spine of the plateau. Slessor rises only a few hundred metres out of the ice of the Bruce Plateau, but it has a short, steep north face of exposed rock. The summit was first climbed by BAS personnel from Stonington base, David Matthews and J. Steen, on January 8th 1966, though a sled party had passed by the area in the 1940s. Matthews and Steen sledded up from sea level, taking the dogs up a route via the Forel and Finsterwalder Glaciers. Further south again is Castle Peak (2380 m), rising just over 600 m out of the Avery Plateau. It was ascended from the northeast by FIDS personnel in November 1957 but had been known about since the 1940s.

ARROWSMITH PENINSULA

Although only tenuously joined to the mainland, the Arrowsmith Peninsula is large and mountainous, its peaks running approximately north to south and rising to 1465 m in the southern section of the Tyndall Mountains. BAS teams have explored and surveyed here over the years but there are few records of any peak ascents and only one private expedition of climbers has ever visited these mountains. Unfortunately, it ended in tragedy.

ANTARCTIC PENINSULA

A group of experienced, mostly American, adventurers arrived in the area aboard a yacht in early 1990, for filming and other activities. They included climber and filmmaker Mike Hoover, Mike Graber and renowned Yosemite climber Beverley Johnson, the first woman to climb The Nose on El Capitan. Also on board were the Chilean Antarctic veteran Alejo Contreras and the Briton Giles Kershaw. Kershaw was the most famous and respected polar pilot of his time. Renowned for his skill and bravery, he had flown around the world via both Poles and won a medal for a daring Antarctic rescue. In more recent years he had formed ANI, which revolutionised Antarctic travel by opening up the Vinson Massif and South Pole to private adventurers. The team was filming a variety of climbing and skiing action, flying ultralight aircraft and Kershaw was experimenting with his new gyrocopter. As Contreras would recount later, during a flight on March 6th Kershaw disappeared over a ridge, after which a loud noise was heard and then the high-pitched whine of a racing engine. When the rest of the team arrived at the site they found the aircraft had crashed and Kershaw was dead.

Beverley Johnson gave one of the eulogies at Kershaw's memorial service at the Royal Geographical Society in London in April 1990. She recited a poem that Kershaw had written, where he expressed a desire to be buried near Alexander Island. Kershaw is buried on a ridge above Jones Sound, on the northern side of Blaiklock Island. In April 1994 Beverly Johnson was killed in a helicopter crash in the mountains of Nevada, which Mike Hoover survived. Also killed in the Nevada crash was American businessman Frank Wells who, with Dick Bass, had funded the first private expedition to the Vinson Massif in 1983. Organised and flown by Kershaw, that trip had started the whole Seven Summits phenomenon and gave birth to ANI. In 2007 the remains of Kershaw's gyrocopter were discovered in a warehouse in Punta Arenas.

The highpoint of Blaiklock Island is a 1200 m summit that was first climbed on May 15th 1971 by the BAS men Collister, Davies and McArthur. Collister had already been involved in some other significant climbing in the area when, with Shaun Norman and four others, he attempted to make the first ascent of Mount Wilcox, a sharp 1981 m peak looming above the southeast corner of Square Bay, just south of Blaiklock Island. The team attempted the southwest side of the peak, turning back just 100 m from the summit and this was almost certainly the first time fixed ropes were used on a climb on the Antarctic Peninsula (fixed ropes were used during the ascents of Mount Gardner and Mount Tyree in the Ellsworth Mountains in January 1967).

POURQUOI PAS ISLAND

Pourquoi Pas is a small but mountainous island at the northern end of Marguerite Bay, east of Adelaide Island and south of the Arrowsmith Peninsula. It was named by Rymill's 1934-37 British Graham Land Expedition, after the ship used by Charcot on his second expedition in 1908-10. There are several peaks on the island but it rises in the southern part to the highest peak, Mount Verne (1630 m). Though the peaks of Pourquoi Pas look impressive, the rock is reportedly quite unstable and not the best for climbing. Verne was first climbed on November 3rd 1965 by David Matthews and J. Steen, based at Stonington. They approached by dogsled from the north, made camp then climbed six and a half hours up the north side of the mountain to the summit. There had been at least one previous attempt on the peak, in the 1950s, via the south ridge. Matthews and Steen attempted several other peaks, but reached no summits, and Matthews had a small peak – Matthews Peak (1100 m) – in the northwestern part of the island named after him.

Pourquoi Pas and Mount Verne are particularly notable in this area because they have seen at least four visits by private, non-government climbing parties. In 1983 a French expedition visited the area aboard Philippe Cardis's boat *Graham* and made several ascents on Pourquoi Pas Island. Philippe Cardis and Luc Fréjacques attempted Mount Arronax (1585 m), stopping just short of the summit in

85

a storm. Another member, Christian de Marliave, made an attempt on Mount Verne (1632 m) with Jérôme Poncet, the French skipper of the yacht *Damien II*, which purely by chance was visiting the island at the same time. Poncet was sailing with his family aboard the *Damien II* and soon after the steel-hulled yacht froze into the waters of Marguerite Bay and spent the winter there. Both Arronax and Verne were skied down. Michel Franco made many reconnaissance flights around Marguerite Bay in an ultralight aircraft. Jérôme Poncet would become one of the senior figures in Antarctic sailing, launching many expeditions to the Peninsula over the following years from his base in the Falkland Islands. Christian de Marliave would later spend a lot of time in the Arctic, but not before achieving one of the most impressive Antarctic climbs ever: a solo, single-push ascent of the massive Nordenskjöld Peak on South Georgia, starting from the deck of the *Damien II.*

In February 1991, the other big name in Antarctic yachting, Skip Novak, arrived at Pourquoi Pas aboard his *Pelagic*, with the Italians Jacapo Merrizi and Marco Preti. In addition to some other climbing, the trio made the first ascent of the south face of Verne on February 23rd. They started from the shore, climbed through the night and reached the summit after 33 pitches of 50°-55° ice and snow, naming the climb the *Nautilus Wall*. In February 2010 the *Ada II* arrived with Cortial, Daudet and Wagnon eager to add to their tally of routes for the summer. They made the probable first ascent of Mount Statham, at the southern end of Perplex Ridge on Pourquoi Pas Island, involving some very hard climbing up the west-northwest face. Perplex Ridge runs northeast to southwest in the northwestern section of Pourquoi Pas Island and has two named high points, Statham Peak and Matthews Peak. Approaching Statham Peak on February 18th, the French climbed up a couloir to tackle a goulotte of extremely steep and overhanging ice, probably the steepest technical ice climbing ever done in Antarctica. However, part of the way up Wagnon backed off, and they traversed on to easier ground to reach the summit after 12 hours of climbing, naming their route *Bohemios y Locos* (Gypsies and Mad Men). The team originally referred to their peak as 'Peak Ada 2', not realising at the time that they were on Mount Statham.

‹ **APPROACHING THE SOUTH COL OF MOUNT GAUDRY** from the west, in October 1997.

⌄ **THE EASTERN SIDE OF MOUNT GAUDRY,** the highest mountain on Adelaide Island.

MOON OVER MOUNT LIOTARD
from near Rothera.

SIMON ABRAHAMS AT THE SOUTH COL
OF MOUNT GAUDRY with the south ridge
rising up behind him.

ADELAIDE ISLAND

Discovered by John Biscoe in February 1832 and seen by Charcot in 1904, Adelaide Island was not recognised as an island until the 1934-37 BGLE. The island is around 125 km long and 30 km wide and, with Pourquoi Pas Island, forms the northern boundary of Marguerite Bay. It has also been one of the main centres of Antarctic mountaineering for nearly 50 years, both as a base from which to launch longer journeys, and as a climbing venue in its own right.

The mountains of Adelaide Island are on the eastern side of the island in two groups: the Bouvier-Reeves group in the north and the larger Gaudry-Mangin-Liotard group in the south. To the west of the mountains lies the Fuchs Ice Piedmont, a broad expanse of ice stretching over 100 km from northeast to southwest. Jutting out from the lower east coast of the island is the Wright Peninsula. Its southern tip is Rothera Point, the location of the BAS station Rothera, which has been in operation since 1975. Before the establishment of Rothera all FIDS/BAS activity on the island was based out of another station on the southern tip of the island, Base T, which had been operating since 1961. Rothera now houses up to 130 people in summer and is also fully operational every winter. It receives direct Dash-7 flights from the Falkland Islands and Punta Arenas, which land on the reliable gravel airstrip. Twin Otters fly further south from here, to Fossil Bluff on Alexander Island and onward to Sky Blu near the Sky-Hi Nunataks, from where field operations are conducted in various regions, including the northeastern Ellsworth Mountains.

The highest peak on Adelaide Island is Mount Gaudry (2565 m), which has been climbed at least twice, though attempted several times more. It is a longer and more serious trip from Rothera than Mount Liotard or Mount Ditte and is quite formidable from the east, so has not seen

nearly as many climbers as those smaller peaks. The first ascent of Mount Gaudry was made during the 1962-63 season, by Royal Marines from *HMS Protector*. T.J Wills, T. McAuliffe and J.R Green reached the summit in reportedly appalling weather conditions. They had unsuccessfully attempted the northwest ridge the previous February, before moving on to Mount Liotard. On October 1st 1997, climbing in winter conditions, Simon Abrahams and Mike Austin approached from around the western side of Gaudry. They reached a col to the south then ascended the southeast ridge, moving on to the south face before reaching the top. It is not known how many, if any, ascents were made in addition to these two. In June 1970 an attempt was halted at 1550 m by an avalanche, while another attempt in April 1986 via the northwest ridge also failed.

Just to the south, Mount Liotard (2225 m) is another of the major peaks on the island and one climbed numerous times by BAS personnel, as it sits in full view of Rothera station, across the waters of Ryder Bay. However, BAS missed out on the first ascent. *HMS Protector* was in the Marguerite Bay area in February 1962 and some of the men onboard decided to attempt the unclimbed Mount Liotard. Upon being informed of the crew's plans to climb the mountain, a BAS team from Base T immediately set out to do the climb but failed after enduring two weeks of poor weather. Subsequently, a detachment of Royal Marines from *Protector* landed to try the ascent, using dogs and sleds lent to them by the BAS. Malcolm Burley, Gordon McCallum and Terry Speake eventually made the first ascent, via the south ridge. The terrain down low was very crevassed but up high, around 200 m below the summit, the route ascended a steep wall of blue ice threatened by seracs. As they had forgotten the ice pitons, the trio were forced to cut steps and belay off their ice axes, but reached the summit soon after. Liotard received its third ascent, and first winter ascent, on June 2nd 1970 by Chambers and Pashley. They also attempted Mount Gaudry but were forced to turn round by an avalanche at 1550 m, as mentioned above.

NENY MATTERHORN, LITTLE THUMB AND THE SPIRE FORM THE BLACKWALL RANGE on the southern shore of Neny Fjord, Marguerite Bay. These peaks were the scene of the first technical climbing done in Antarctica.

GRAEME NOTT, BELAYED BY ROB JARVIS, on the first winter ascent of *James' Chimney* (Scottish V) on Reptile Ridge, Adelaide Island, August 2004.

South of Liotard and across the Sloman Glacier is a smaller peak, Mount Ditte (1400 m), that was first climbed in July 1963 by Cousins and Lambert. The area soon became a popular climbing destination for BAS people in the area, often in winter and sometimes in combination with an attempt on Liotard from the south or west. Numerous smaller features in the nearby area were also climbed by various routes over the years, such as Window Buttress, via the south face and southwest ridge. The latter was first done by McKeith and Willey in September 1968.

During October and November 1968 McKeith, Dave Rinning and Willey did a lot of climbing on and around Mount Bouvier (2230 m), the second highest peak on the island lying around 40 km north of Rothera. McKeith soloed around half a dozen minor summits, and he and the other two made the first ascent of the west face of Bouvier on November 6th, via a line they named the *Snake Ridge*. Their attempt on October 27th had failed lower down. The other high peak here, Mount Reeves (2210 m) has also been climbed. Its north face received an ascent in four hours in September 1998 by Mark Smith and Phil Wickens, though it is thought to have been climbed before that. It was certainly visited in February 1981 by Geof Somers and A. Moyes, who ascended to the col between Reeves and Bouvier but did not go to either summit.

Bugs McKeith was a Scottish climber who, after leaving Antarctica, emigrated to Canada and played a pivotal role in the development of climbing the frozen waterfalls for which the Rockies have now become famous. The skills that were refined on lower crags around Base T, and further south around Stonington, were put to use on routes that had taunted generations of Canadian climbers. McKeith's pioneering first ascents of the *Weeping Wall* in 1973, *Takakkaw Falls* in 1974 and the multi-day, epic group ascent of *Polar Circus* in 1975 were seminal breakthroughs in ice climbing, establishing routes that would become internationally famous classics of their kind.

Moving back south across the Shambles Glacier towards the Mount Gaudry group we find Mount Mangin (1955 m) and Mount Barré (2140 m). The first ascent of Mount Mangin has not been recorded, but it was unsuccessfully attempted a number of times. One team turned back just 30 m from the summit in September 1970, after ascending from the col between Mangin and Barré. Conversely, Mount Barré was the first big peak on the island to be climbed. Not surprisingly it was the legendary Scottish climber John Cunningham who wasted no time and bagged the summit with J. Green in 1961, soon after Base T had been established.

Rising up to the northwest above Rothera station is the 3 km long Reptile Ridge. This has proved to be both a playground and training arena for generations of Rothera locals. Numerous climbs have been done on the flanks and gullies of the ridge, some to quite a high technical standard, and there is even a guidebook maintained for the use of incoming personnel.

MARGUERITE BAY

Before the existence of Rothera, the centre of west Antarctic mountaineering was Stonington. This British station sits on a tiny rock island, close against the northern coast of Neny Fjord, a large inlet on the eastern side of Marguerite Bay. Charcot, sailing aboard a damaged *Pourquoi Pas?*, discovered this large and picturesque bay in January 1909 and named the area after his wife. Rymill's BGLE spent the winter of 1936 here, at a base in the Debenham Islands, north of Neny Fjord, from where they sledged far south into and along George VI Sound past Alexander Island. They could not reach the mainland plateau from near their base, but did so further south, eventually reaching the Wakefield Highland. The first major station in the Marguerite Bay area was East Base, established in 1939 by Admiral Richard Byrd's United States Antarctic Service (USAS) expedition. From here Finn Ronne and Carl Eklund followed in the steps of Rymill's expedition, exploring and surveying the region down to Alexander Island, where they made a couple of minor ascents near the coast in January 1940. The base was evacuated in 1941 due to the escalation of World War II.

Amid latent post-war tensions between Britain and the US regarding their presence in the Antarctic, the British built a new base here in 1946, just a few hundred metres away from the existing American East Base. This British base became known as Stonington Island, or Station E, or sometimes Marguerite Bay. It was unoccupied through most of the 1950s, but from 1960 it was continuously occupied until 1975, when Rothera became the main BAS station in the area. In 1951 Argentina erected San Martín station at the site of the BGLE base, in the Debenham Islands, around 8 km northwest of Stonington.

The eastern shore of Marguerite Bay is generally mountainous, so over the years it became relatively easy for FIDS teams to go climbing in close proximity to Stonington. South of the base, at the northwest corner of Neny Fjord, is Neny Island, a 676 m high rocky mountain in the sea. Over the years it would become a popular climb for FIDS personnel. The first ascent, however, was made on March 14th 1940 by James Wiles, an American from the USAS expedition at East Base. Vivian Fuchs found a note that Wiles left in a glass jar on the summit, when he and John Huckle made an ascent on January 24th 1950. To the northwest of Stonington Island is the much larger and 969 m high Millerand Island, another FIDS target. However, of particular note is a later ascent when a mainly French team, based aboard Jérôme Poncet's *Damien* and Philippe Cardis's *Graham*, made a ski ascent of the island's 786 m subsidiary peak. Some of the group, including Christian de Marliave, skied on Millerand while others rockclimbed on Red Rock Ridge, a feature on the southern side of Neny Fjord that had been climbed many times by FIDS. The group from these yachts had earlier made some ascents on Pourquoi Pas Island, and not since the days of Rymill's BGLE had a private expedition climbed this far south on the Antarctic Peninsula.

Inland to the east from Stonington, the more difficult Mount Nemesis (788 m) overlooks the north side of Neny Fjord. It was unsuccessfully attempted during the winter of 1947 by FIDS men Arthur Butson and Kevin Walton, together with the Americans Bob Dodson and William Latady, all of them finding the climbing technically quite difficult. Months later the two nations were to team up again. On the southern side of Neny Fjord lies the Blackwall Range, a short line of steep rock peaks admired by all who visit the Marguerite Bay area. The highest is Neny Matterhorn (1500 m), but Little Thumb (825 m) and the smaller pinnacle of The Spire (330 m) are also impressive. In January 1948 both the American and British expeditions were working in the area and Neny Fjord became the venue for an impromptu climber's meet between personnel from each program. The group that had attempted Mount Nemesis was joined by Frank Elliott, an experienced British alpinist, who had just arrived from further north via a 900 km dogsled journey. As Kevin Walton was later to write in the 1949 *Climbers' Club Journal*, it was certainly

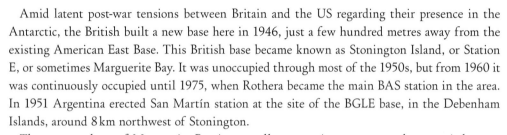

‹ **BOB METCALF HIGH ON NENY ISLAND**, looking north across the Northeast Glacier, with Butson Ridge behind and the McClary glacier beyond. The prominent peak beyond the McClary Glacier is Mount Wilcox. The peak to the right of Metcalf is Blow-Me-Down Bluff.

^ **ON THE SUMMIT OF NENY ISLAND**. In the background is the Centurion Glacier and Mount Nemesis with Mt Rhamnus behind.

not an official gathering, but it just happened that everyone there was a member of either the Climbers' Club or the Harvard Mountaineering Club. In fact, Latady was President of the HMC and had made the second ascent of Alaska's Mount Saint Elias (5489 m) just two years earlier.

The international team's first target was The Spire, which at the time they referred to as 'Sanctuary Pinnacle'. The climbing was steep, with a lot of loose rock but good belays between short pitches. Elliot led the hardest pitches using rubber sneakers, and led to the summit that consisted in two razor-like flakes on which only three of them could sit à cheval at any one time. It was the first truly technical climbing done anywhere in Antarctica. Descent was via downclimbing, and one rappel from a piton. Two days later they moved on to attempt Little Thumb, but their initial attempt up a rib on the shadowy south side ended just over 100 m up on very bad volcanic rock that even Elliott in his sneakers was not willing to force. After a few days rest they left at midnight on January 10th to attempt Neny Matterhorn. The team skied to 500 m then cramponed up a steepening snow ridge that soon turned to hard ice. A 20 m deep bergschrund only 30 m below the summit stopped their progress, as they carried insufficient technical ice gear. After admiring the view of the USAS ship still frozen into the ice off Stonington Island, they descended and reached base 12 hours after having left it.

By this time the British had found a way to reach the upper plateau from Stonington Island, via a route north of Neny Fjord. Such a route had eluded Rymill a decade earlier and similar difficulties still plague expeditions that venture all along the Peninsula trying to get up high on the mainland. After their attempt on Neny Matterhorn, Dodson, Latady and Walton decided to find a new, more direct climbing route to the plateau. This they did without any trouble, cramponing up to break through the cornice at 1520 m, emerging on flat ground that Walton likened to climbing up onto a table. In the following days they climbed another rock route on The Spire, a cold chimney of rotten rock. They also made a final attempt on The Thumb, via the north side, but stopped 300 m from the top on steepening ground, as the sun disappeared from their route.

Around this time, one of the scientists, Harries-Clichy 'Pete' Petersen, was out on a glacier. He was travelling unroped for speed in deteriorating conditions and fell 30 m into a crevasse. Dodson, who was with him at the time, marked the location of the fall and skied the remaining 15 km back to camp in three hours. Members of both the USAS and British expeditions returned to the crevasse with little hope of finding Petersen alive. Upon arrival they rigged a system to lower Arthur Butson into the depths, where he found Petersen alive. Butson assumed Petersen would soon die, owing to his position. Six men hauling from the surface almost failed to displace Petersen, but when they finally freed him he shot up out of the crevasse and flew two metres into the air with the force of his release. Despite 11 hours in the crevasse, he was not seriously injured and the rescuers concluded that the calm, close depths had kept him relatively warm – warmer in fact than his rescuers on the surface who had endured bitterly cold conditions. Butson was awarded the Albert Medal for his part in this rescue.

The following decade saw little activity, with Stonington largely unoccupied during the 1950s. The base reopened in 1960 and a new surge of activity started in the area, particularly from 1963 to 1966. This was primarily due to the presence of various members of the Creagh Dhu Mountaineering Club. Its members originated from the rough working class areas of Glasgow, particularly the shipyards, and had a reputation for drinking and fighting as hard as they climbed. The leading light of the club was John Cunningham, who had spent time on South Georgia in the mid-1950s with Duncan Carse, and was Base Commander at Stonington in the early 1960s. In 1962 Cunningham, Ben Hodges, Ian McMorrin, Bob Metcalf and Ivor Morgan travelled using dog teams among the mountains and glaciers north of Stonington. These men all did various climbs around the area, but Cunningham in particular was not backward in snaring first ascents. He had already snatched Mount Barré soon after Base T opened on Adelaide Island in 1961, and would later steal the grand prize of the peninsula, Mount Jackson, with fellow Creagh Dhu men in 1964 (described later).

In addition to first peak ascents, Creagh Dhu climbers and others often practiced climbing on short ice cliffs and gullies during winter, honing techniques that later influenced ice climbing in Scotland and North America. An example of their hard local climbing was the *Pinnacle Buttress* on Roman Four Promontory, an attractive wall of rock up to 830 m high and riven with ice gullies, three of which form the Roman numerals 'IV'. Roman Four Promontory is southeast of Stonington, west of Mount Nemesis, and runs down to the sea, forming a northern boundary to Neny Ford. The Creagh Dhu route climbed the left side of a steep rock pillar, clearly visible from base. Richard Brooke, writing years later in the 1973 *Alpine Journal*, described it as 'probably the first rock climb of alpine length and standard to be done in the Antarctic'[4]. It took Mike Cousins, Jimmy Gardner, John Noble and Davie Todd five hours, climbing over rock at UIAA grade IV. The route was repeated in later years and more routes of similar difficulty were put up on the promontory by later generations. Avalanches were not unknown, and Ian McMorrin and Ivor Morgan had a close call during a 1962 winter ascent of Neny Island, when a slab released

[4] Brooke, Richard, *Alpine Journal*, #78, 1973, p. 219.

The Uemura plan

The Argentine station of San Martín was to be the base for one of the best expeditions that never happened. The legendary Japanese explorer and mountaineer Naomi Uemura planned to over-winter at the base, then dogsled from there to Vinson, climb it and return the same way. Uemura was uniquely qualified for such a trip, particularly in those times. He had become famous in Japan for summiting on the first Japanese ascent of Everest in 1970, shortly after which he made the first solo ascent of Mount McKinley (6194 m) in Alaska. Given that he had

also climbed Kilimanjaro, Uemura was one of the earliest front-runners, with Messner, in the quest to be first up the Seven Summits. In 1978 he became famous around the world for being the first person to reach the North Pole solo, which he did by dogsled. Uemura later dogsledded from Greenland to Alaska, as part of his preparation for his Antarctic project, and the final part of this training was to be McKinley solo in winter. Naomi Uemura died in February 1984 on Mount McKinley, after making the first solo winter ascent of the mountain; his flag was

found on the summit but multiple rescue teams never found Uemura himself. There has yet to be an overland ascent of Vinson from the sea to the summit*.

* In 2006 an Australian expedition flew from Patriot Hills to a point near sea-level at the inside edge of the Ronne Ice Shelf – around 700 km from the sea – and from there skied to Vinson before climbing to the summit.

near Stonington base in the early 1960s
with Neny Island rising behind.

› JOHN CUNNINGHAM AND BEN HODGES
on the north side of Butson Ridge overlooking the
McClary glacier, north of Stonington in the early 1960s.

beneath Morgan, almost taking him with it. Climbing this far south, on unclimbed mountains and untravelled glaciers, with no field radios or satellite phones, no means of rescue and no GPS in whiteouts, was extremely serious, making the sheer amount of hard climbing done in the area all the more remarkable.

Peaks further afield were also climbed, but only when time, weather and safety allowed; the work was still the priority. Around 1962, Ivor Morgan made the first ascent of the highest peak (1306 m) on the Butson Ridge, northeast of Stonington between the McClary and Northeast glaciers. With Ian McMorrin, and later with Dave Nash, he ventured much further south to the Batterbee Mountains where they claimed the elegant ice pyramid of Mount Cadbury. Climbs in the Eternity Range during the 1960s were also based from Stonington and they are covered later in this chapter. Closer to base, the 500 m high Pavie Ridge, south of Rymill Bay, was climbed in November 1968 by Shaun Norman, D. Postlethwaite and Ian Sykes. Norman and Lawrence Willey climbed Walton Peak (826 m) via a snow gully in 1968, and in September 1969 a party climbed Deschanel Peak (750 m) and the Triune Peaks, overlooking the north side of the Wordie Ice Shelf at the southern end of Marguerite Bay.

ALEXANDER ISLAND

Around 380 km long, 80 km wide in the north and 240 km wide in the south, Alexander is by far the largest of the islands off the Peninsula, from which it is separated by the frozen sea of George VI Sound. It was first sighted in 1821 by the Bellingshausen expedition, but it was not until the 1947-49 Ronne Antarctic Research Expedition that it was flown over, photographed, and subsequently proven to be an island and not part of the mainland. Though areas of the northern and eastern coast were initially surveyed in the late 1940s, a complete map of the island was not produced until 1960, by FIDS surveyor Derek Searle.

Journeys into the high mountains of the north did not really begin until 1970, but there had been some visits to the central part of the island prior to this, and some smaller peaks had been climbed. Though much of the island is quite low, the northernmost quarter and most of the eastern coast is very mountainous, with several peaks well over 2000 m. The Douglas Range is the highest group, running north to south down the eastern side of the island, with massive drops down both the east and west sides. Mount Stephenson is 2985 m but there is also Mount Spivey (2135 m), Mount Huckle (2500 m), Mount Ethelwulf (2590 m), Mount Ethelred (2470 m) and at the southern end, Mount Edred (2195 m). The Rouen Mountains, in the far north, are not as steep but still have Mount Paris (2800 m), Mount Cupola (2500 m) and the conspicuous Mount Calais (2345 m), first seen and named by Charcot in 1909. Calais protrudes eastwards from the island as if on a neck, and rises high before dropping nearly 2000 m to the sea-ice of Schokalsky Bay.

Alexander Island has never really been visited by private mountaineers. Being so far south, the island is beset by pack ice often until late December, thus it is usually impossible to approach by ship early in the summer. In what remains of the summer, it is too far south to reach and climb on as most modern, private climbing expeditions are based on yachts or ships. Flights have been made to the island by ALE, operating from their Patriot Hills base in the southern Ellsworth Mountains, but this has been to pre-position Search And Rescue teams for private South Pole flights by small aircraft. So far no private climbers have used this method to explore the island. ALE deposited an SAR team of Di Gilbert and Heather Morning in the centre of the island to ensure the safety of a private helicopter flight that passed over the Peninsula on its way to Patriot Hills and the South Pole. Over 10 days in December 2003 the two Scotswomen climbed four minor peaks in the region north of Scarlatti Peak, around 30 km east of the Walton Mountains.

However, as elsewhere on the Peninsula, BAS personnel have worked around the island, often accessing the region from the summer-only facility at Fossil Bluff, around two-thirds of the way down the east coast. This is around 90 minutes in a Twin Otter from Rothera base, while the perpetually frozen George VI Sound also provides an avenue for surface travel up and down the coast of both Alexander Island and the adjacent coast of Palmer Land. There are no recorded ascents of high peaks such as Mount Stephenson (2985 m), Mount Huckle (2500 m) and Mount Calais (2345 m), but based on anecdotal history it is possible that at least some of them have been climbed at least once by FIDS or BAS personnel.

The first recorded climbing on Alexander Island was actually just off the southern coast, in George VI Sound, when Americans Carl Eklund and Finn Ronne ascended the highest of the Eklund Islands on December 14th 1940. At this time the other smaller islands were covered in ice, so only the 410 m highest one was prominent. They had visited the area during a sledging trip of over 1600 km, surveying south from their base at Stonington Island in Marguerite Bay. Nine years later the FIDS team of Ray Adie and Vivian Fuchs again climbed this highest Eklund Islands summit and found a cairn on top with a white cloth bag inside. In the bag, labelled 'Finders Keepers', was a note from Eklund and Ronne. The British pair took the note and replaced it with one of their own, mentioning the first ascent and noting the date of their own climb, November 20th 1949. The other summit climbed and surveyed by FIDS in this area during these years was Swine Hill (550 m), a rocky crag northwest of the much higher Mount Bagshawe that was climbed in 1948. Fuchs later became one of the major figures in British Antarctic history, leading the 1955-58 Commonwealth Trans-Antarctic Expedition, authoring several books and becoming Director of the BAS.

On November 23rd 1969, almost 20 years to the day after its second ascent, Eklund Island received its third ascent, this time by Mike Burns and Shaun Norman, who had climbed the lower eastern island the day before. They then moved on to climb Stephenson Nunatak (640 m) in the south of the island on December 5th. Shaun Norman was to become a veteran of Antarctica's mountains and one of the few climbers to make multiple ascents in multiple Antarctic ranges. These were early ascents around the Peninsula, many seasons in the Transantarctics and later in the Ellsworth Mountains, and he worked on Vinson nearly 40 years after Stephenson Nunatak. Norman and colleagues also attempted the second ascent of Mount Jackson, in January 1970, but were forced back from close to the summit in poor weather. Some smaller peaks on Alexander

PYRAMID TENTS WITH THE WEST FACE OF MOUNT JACKSON IN THE BACKGROUND.
The northwest ridge forms the left skyline.

Island were climbed during the final years of the 1960s, by the same strong and enthusiastic group of climbers based at Stonington that attempted Mount Wilcox and climbed in the Eternity Range, taking whatever opportunities their work afforded them to reach any summits.

BAS people were in the mountains of Alexander again in 1976, climbing peaks around the Bartok Glacier in November, including an unnamed 1515 m ridge top they judged to be the highest in the area. Around the same time Bernard Care made ascents of Mirny Peak (750 m) and Enigma Peak (1000 m) in the Desko Mountains of Rothschild Island, off the northwest coast of Alexander, and also travelled in the Havre Mountains and Staccato Peaks around this time. The Rouen Mountains, Debussy Heights, LeMay Range, Colbert Mountains and the western side of the Douglas Range were certainly visited by BAS personnel in the 1980s.

As an example of BAS activity, from November 19th 1992 to January 22nd 1993, one team climbed around two dozen peaks, in this instance based aboard *HMS Endurance*. Mount King, Nonplus Crag, Olreg Ridge, Stephenson Nunatak and Zebra Ridge were all climbed, often in fast time. One of the climbers, Brian Hull, also climbed Mimas Peak (1000 m) with Paul Doubleday. Some of this group continued to make minor ascents. Mount Ariel (1250 m) via the east ridge has always been a popular trip, Coal Nunatak and Citadel Bastion were also climbed, athough they suspected the latter two may have been ascended by Vivian Fuch's team in 1949. One of the climbers in this 1994 team, Nick Lewis, later became one of the owners of ALE, running operations on Mount Vinson and other similar activities.

PALMER LAND

THE ETERNITY RANGE

The Eternity Range is a short but high group of mountains comprising three major peaks, which are, running from north to south, Mount Faith (2650 m), Mount Hope (2862 m) and Mount Charity (2680 m). The range was first sighted from the air in November 1935 by Lincoln Ellsworth as he flew from Dundee Island at the tip of the Peninsula, across Marie Byrd Land toward the old Little America base on the Ross Ice Shelf. Hours later he would also see a small part of what would become known as the Sentinel Range. The first to approach the range by land were members of a sledding party from John Rymill's 1934-37 BGLE. They saw Mount Hope but originally named it 'Mount Wakefield', a name later given to the Wakefield Highland, a high plateau to the north of the Eternity Range. Rymill's expedition only climbed a minor summit in the area, but this is the furthest south that any private, non-government expedition has ever climbed on the Antarctic Peninsula. Rymill's expedition carried out a great deal of exploration and discovery, a highlight of which was proving that the Antarctic Peninsula did indeed join the mainland of the continent, and that there were no large straits in this area separating the two landmasses. Earlier flights by Hubert Wilkins, in 1928, had reported seeing such a strait, as well as other channels, and he even named it 'Stefansson Strait'. The existence of 'Stefansson Strait' had even been 'confirmed' by Ellsworth.

Mount Hope was first climbed on December 23rd 1964 by BAS members Mike Cousins and Keith Holmes, from a camp to the north of the mountain. Mount Faith was not climbed until six years later when BAS personnel Donaldson, Skinner and Sykes summited on January 24th 1970. Their colleagues Hill, Skinner and Wormald made the second ascent of Mount Hope shortly after, and Hill and Wormald subsequently made the second ascent of Mount Faith. Sykes and Donaldson finished with the third ascent of Mount Hope, finding the west ridge quite chal-

95

AN AERIAL VIEW OF THE SUMMIT OF MOUNT JACKSON, the highest mountain on the Antarctic Peninsula. The northwest ridge is the left skyline.

lenging. The third peak in the trilogy, Mount Charity, was climbed around this time, by Burns, Bushell and Pashley, who also climbed Mount Courtauld (2105 m) and some other lower peaks closer to the coast. These mountains have rarely been visited since, though there have been scientific parties working up around the Wakefield Highland. Davies Top (2361 m), a high summit on the eastern side of the Wakefield Highland and about 30 km northwest of Mount Faith, is possibly unclimbed, as is the 2070 m Mount Sullivan, around 20 km east of Mount Faith. It may be possible to access the peaks here by a long sled journey, over 100 km inland, starting from where the Clarke Glacier empties into Marguerite Bay, but it will require an experienced and organised team that will need luck with both the weather up high and the sea-ice down low.

Mount Jackson is the highest mountain on the Antarctic Peninsula. It is officially given as 3184 m, but is often quoted at various figures from 3050 m up to more than 4000 m, with the latter certainly wrong. The mountain has some long ridges on the south side with exposed rock areas, while the west side has much less relief and rises mildly out of a high plateau. The first ascent of the Peninsula's highest peak fell to a team led by John Cunningham, on his 37th birthday, November 23rd 1964. It comprised his Creagh Dhu cohorts Jimmy Gardner and Davie Todd, while John Noble and B. Smith, also in the team, remained at base camp. Showing the boldness for which the club members were known, Cunningham and friends 'borrowed' an aircraft to fly to the mountain from Stonington, much to the displeasure of expedition leader Sir Vivian Fuchs. By this time, Todd and Gardner had already made the first ascent of Mount Bagshawe (2200 m) in the Batterbee Mountains, as far south as Jackson, but on the coast opposite Alexander Island.

In Cunningham's biography *Creagh Dhu Climber*[5], their route on Mount Jackson is described as the northeast ridge, the book shows an aerial photo of a ridge, and an extract from Cunningham's diary notes that they climbed the northeast ridge. However, with the benefit of more informa-

[5]   Connor, Jeff, *Creagh Dhu Climber*, Ernest Press, London, 1999.

tion from the second ascent in 1997, conducted in much clearer weather than the thick cloud that plagued the Creagh Dhu team, it now seems that in 1964 they actually climbed the northwest ridge. Todd later described the climbing on their ridge: absorbing cramponing over hard ice, cornices and mushrooms up an impressive narrow arete of snow and ice. This exactly matches the terrain on the northwest ridge, whereas the northeast ridge clearly has significant sections of rock and mixed terrain with a large gendarme – obvious characteristics not mentioned by Todd.

Jackson was attempted again in January 1970 by Shaun Norman, Mike Burns and Mike Pashley but they were forced back just 60 m from the summit by bad weather. Another attempt in the 1970s by Dave Birkitt and partners also turned back, but this time high on the south ridge due to a difficult gendarme. In January 1997 the BAS team of Adrian Fox and Simon Garrod made the second ascent of the peak, from a camp on the plateau to the west. They skied up into the bowl beneath the west face then traversed left over onto the northwest ridge. Finding the climbing spectacular and the north face to their left quite daunting, they soon reached the summit pyramid. As in 1964 this was steep, hoary ice that was so unconsolidated as to be almost impossible to climb. Cunningham had led a final pitch like this in 1964, using one long axe and an old ice piton, finding a way up through an improbable narrow chute that cut through the mushroom. Garrod had noticed a similar feature on an aerial reconnaissance, but only reached it after traversing around onto the south face, not having found one on either the north or the west face. Garrod led the pitch, finding it a similarly narrow chute (though not an enclosed tunnel) leading to the summit. Fox and Garrod conducted a GPS survey then descended the same way they had come.

Creagh Dhu Climber also includes a photo of two of the 1964 team on the ridge, overlooking a large drop. The terrain in one of Garrod's photos from his 1997 ascent of the northwest ridge matches this 1964 shot exactly, more evidence that the Creagh Dhu team was on the northwest, and not the northeast, ridge. Given the poor weather the 1964 team had and considering they were the first people ever to visit this uncharted area, it is understandable that they got disoriented. The large face they describe overlooking was actually the steep north face and not the east face, which is even bigger. The top section of Jackson is relatively symmetrical and the upper sections of the ridges are all quite alike. They were certainly neither the first nor the last Antarctic mountaineers to make such a mistake.

A non-government ascent of Mount Jackson, probably preceded by a long sledding journey from either Marguerite Bay or George VI Sound, is one of the greatest – but still realistic – challenges remaining in Antarctic mountaineering. There are other high tops around the Mount Jackson area that remain unclimbed, including a conspicuous massif to the northwest of Jackson. If the access and timing difficulties can be overcome, and the journey routed so as to take in the Eternity Range and surrounding unclimbed high peaks, then it is surely the expedition of a lifetime for a team with the right resources, ability and experience.

South of Mount Jackson the Antarctic Peninsula broadens, and this area contains some lower mountain ranges but there are no major mountains until the Ellsworth Mountains around 78° South. On the eastern side of the peninsula there are a number of smaller ranges and there has been much activity here by US and British scientific teams. Many ascents have been made in the Sweeney Mountains, Hauberg Mountains and Behrendt Mountains, though rarely of any significant technical difficulty. Given their generally mild nature and extreme remoteness, they are unlikely to attract visits from non-government climbers any time soon.

QUEEN MAUD LAND

If there is one part of Antarctica that has fired the imaginations of climbers around the world in recent years it is Dronning Maud Land, now more popularly known by the English translation of Queen Maud Land. While many consider Antarctica a flat land of snow and ice, Queen Maud Land offers steep rock spires jutting out of the horizontal ice, all sharp summits, blank faces and ridges at crazy angles. They are not as high as the Sentinel Range, nor as deeply hidden as the central Transantarctics, but they are real climbing – narrow, steep, technical and cold.

The Orvinfjella is the most famous and popular area, consisting of the smaller ranges of Fenriskjeften ('wolf's jaw') Massif, the Holtedahlfjella and Conradfjella. East of here is the Wohlthat Massif where less climbing has been done. Much further east are the Sør Rondane and Queen Fabiola Mountains (also called the Yamato Mountains), which are high and steep, but not to the same degree as the spires of the Orvinfjella.

West of the Orvinfjella are the Mühlig-Hofmann mountains, home to the region's highest mountain, the 3148 m Jøkulkyrkja (whose highest point is Kyrkjeskipet Peak) as well as some smaller steeper massifs to its east, such as Gessnertind. There has been no climbing in the Mühlig-Hofmann Mountains west of Jøkulkyrkja. Around 400 km further west again is the Borg Massif, a group of steep rocky peaks rising to over 2700 m. No climbing has been done here and no private expeditions have even seen it, so it is probably the most adventurous and exciting climbing destination remaining in Queen Maud Land. Finally, in the far west of the region lies the much less dramatic Heimefrontfjella, where some non-technical ascents have been made by BAS scientists in one of its sub-ranges, the Tottanfjella.

EARLY EXPLORATION

The coast of Queen Maud Land was initially explored and mapped by Norwegian expeditions, beginning in 1928. During the next decade the wealthy whaler Lars Christensen sponsored nine expeditions to East Antarctica, which established the basis for the Norwegian claim to part of the region. Several of these expeditions employed airplanes to explore and photograph the nearby coastal area and some closer inland areas. The eastern edge of the Norwegian claim

ASCENDING FIXED LINES ON RAKEKNIVEN.
In the far distance Ulvetanna rises above the other peaks of the Fenriskjeften massif.

HOLTANNA FROM THE SOUTH.

The main peak is on the left, with the west face in profile.
The dark pyramid in the centre is Kinntanna and left of it is
the steep summit of Holstinnd, the northern summit
of Holtanna.

bordered what was then British territory at 45° 00' E and was agreed upon in 1930 during a
meeting on the ice between Hjalmar Riiser-Larsen and Douglas Mawson. The western edge of
the Norwegian territory was originally considered 37°00' W, but later the entire claim was ex-
panded to include all the land between 20°00' W and 45°00' E. Aside from gaining more land,
the expansion also meant that the Norwegians had inadvertently claimed the most spectacular
peaks in Antarctica.

The inland rock peaks of the Orvinfjella, however, were not seen until 1939. In late 1938 the
German government – Adolf Hitler's Third Reich – sent an expedition to the area. Though it was
not a military expedition, its primary aim was to claim Antarctic territory for Germany, a nation
that had been active in the Antarctic since the original International Geophysical Year (IGY)
in 1882-83 and later through the expeditions of Drygalski and Filchner. Clearly this plan chal-
lenged the Norwegian claim in the region, and in retrospect this was hardly surprising for the
Germany of the late 1930s. In response, on January 14th 1939 King Haakon of Norway formally
proclaimed his country's rights to the territory between 20° E and 50° E. The Germans ignored
this declaration, believing that sovereignty should be established by actual occupation, or at least
by physically marking out the desired territory in some way, rather than claiming unseen land
within a partially explored 'sector'.

It should be noted that at exactly the same time, American millionaire aviator Lincoln Ellsworth
was not far away, doing exactly the same thing. Having spent previous seasons attempting to fly
across Antarctica – discovering the Ellsworth Mountains in the process – Ellsworth now decided

to ignore the Australian territorial claim and brazenly claim Wilkes Land for the United States. On January 11th 1939 Ellsworth and his pilot J.H Lymburner started from their ship the *Wyatt Earp*, off the coast of Princess Elizabeth Land and well west of Wilkes Land, and flew to 70° S. On the way they dropped a canister of documents claiming the territory, now known as the American Highland, for the United States. Ellsworth then left Antarctica and never returned.

The 1938 German expedition sailed aboard the *Schwabenland*. Owned by the German company Lufthansa and under Captain Alfred Ritscher, it left Hamburg on December 17th 1938 and reached Antarctica via Gough Island and Bouvetøya, in an attempt to outflank any pack ice lying out from the Queen Maud Land coast. The ship eventually stopped around 69°14' S 04°30' W and using the two Dornier-Wal seaplanes (*Boreas* and *Passat*) carried on board, it began flying operations, with the planes launched off the ship by catapult and retrieved with a crane. Though ostensibly mapping the terrain they were claiming, they did no ground control to complement the aerial photogrammetric survey (a common flaw in early Antarctic aerial exploration) as they were rushing to cover as much ground as quickly as possible. Their main aim was to claim territory and they planned to return in following seasons to do survey work on the ground. The result of other German territorial adventures, mainly in Europe, from 1939 onwards meant that this never happened.

The German expedition, possibly influenced by the earlier Christensen expeditions, considered the airplanes more suitable than dogs and sleds, neither of which was used. They also planned to drop 1.5 m long metal arrows (with a swastika stamped on one of the three stabilising fins) every 20-30 km along the flight paths, to mark the territory they claimed. Tests in the European Alps had shown that the arrows penetrated approximately 30 cm into the ice, when dropped

THE SOUTH SIDE OF FENRIS SEEN RIGHT OF CENTRE

with the minor peaks of the Fenriskjeften to the left ('the lower jaw of the wolf').

from an altitude of about 500 m. However, there is no real evidence that any of the arrows were ever dropped – no conclusive photos survive, nor have any arrows ever been found – and there is some minor anecdotal evidence that many of them were dumped overboard by the ship's crew, long before they reached Queen Maud Land.

The first flight, made by *Boreas* on January 21st, flew 600 km south over the inland ice to 74° South. But it turned around as the crew felt they could not fly high enough – their maximum height was 4150 m – to clear the higher land further south, which at the time they believed rose to 4000 m. In fact, although the highest mountain in Queen Maud Land is only 3148 m, the inland ice rises in places to over 3800 m. The second plane, *Passat*, flew slightly further the next day and a shorter flight operated the day after that. Neither plane ever landed on the inland ice, only on the water at the edge of the ice-shelf. According to the translated version of the original expedition report, the arrows *were* dropped, with those at the corners of the claimed areas also bearing the German flag. Several more flights took place and some of them landed in bays in the pack ice, enabling access up on to the ice shelves for scientific work, whilst others carried out more photography inland. In increasingly cold weather, the ship left the area on February 6th. Again travelling via Bouvetøya, the ship reached Cape Town on March 3rd and finally Hamburg, on April 11th 1939. Much of the trip had been conducted in secret, its achievements only announced publicly in March 1939. Upon its return the expedition was immediately congratulated by Hitler and the new German territory named 'Neuschwabenland'. For many years afterward, speculation and rumour abounded as to the existence of secret Nazi bases supplied by mysterious submarines, UFO flights, nuclear explosions and other sensational events, but later research proved all such accounts to be groundless; nothing more than entertaining fantasy at best, and at worst, neo-Nazi propaganda.

The planes took a total of 11,600 photographs, covering an area of 350,000 square kilometres. They observed from a distance an estimated additional 250,000 square kilometres and thus produced a map covering 600,000 square kilometres, which they felt delineated 'Neuschwabenland'. Unfortunately, nearly all the photographs and maps, including a 1:50,000 map of the Wohlthat Massif, were destroyed by fire during the 1943 bombing of Hamburg. Looking at the few photo maps that survived, it is interesting that the massifs now visited by climbers were given German names, most of them since changed to Norwegian. One crew member, having spent hours flying over flat ice, was quoted as saying, "Then, suddenly, like needles sticking out of it, mountains

1957 AERIAL VIEWS of the Sør Rondane (left) and the Belgica Mountains (right).

FENRISKJEFTEN PEAKS FROM THE NORTHEAST.
From left to right: Holtanna, Kinntanna, Hel and Ulvetanna.
The 2008 German route on the northwest buttress of
Ulvetanna is seen in profile on the right. Just behind and to
the right of Ulvetanna is Midgard.

and peaks become visible, shining in a strange, rust-brown colour,"[6]. The Germans also noted the presence of large areas of flat ice, some over 6 km long, which they thought were frozen lakes that would make suitable airstrips for future operations. It is these blue-ice areas that are now used to land aircraft transporting scientists, climbers and other adventurers to the mountains of Queen Maud Land.

Spurred somewhat by the 1938 German expedition, an effort was made after World War II to organise an international expedition to work in Queen Maud Land with more scientific, and less political, ambitions. Thus, the 1949-52 Norwegian-British-Swedish Antarctic Expedition (NBSAE) was formed. The leader was an experienced Norwegian polar researcher, John Giaever, and he was initially accompanied by 13 other men. Among them was a 22 year old Charles Swith-inbank, who would go on to become Antarctica's pre-eminent glaciologist and the initiator of the private aircraft landings on the blue-ice runways of Patriot Hills and Blue-1 that have enabled so much modern adventure. The team built their own base, Maudheim, and spent more than two full years working there, a considerable period of time even in that era. Three men were killed when they drove a tractor over the edge of the ice front into the sea and one man had his eye surgically removed by the team after another accident, but in general the expedition was very successful. Intermittent scientific work was also done in the summers by the Norwegian ship *Norsel*, which had transported the team there, and the Air Forces of Britain, Norway and Sweden.

[6] *Antarctica*, Reader's Digest, 1985, p. 264.

The NBSAE used the surviving photography-based maps from the German expedition and completed ground surveys to correct many of them, as German estimates of the mountains' locations had put some of them up to 50 km away from their true positions. In doing this, the NBSAE were the first people to visit the mountains of Queen Maud Land, though they only made very minor ascents during their work. More significantly, it was the first genuinely international Antarctic scientific expedition, the success of which provided an inspirational model for future international cooperation in Antarctica on a larger scale, most obviously in the 1957-58 International Geophysical Year (IGY).

The IGY started a period of occupation of the area by scientists from Norway, Belgium, Japan, South Africa, Russia, Germany and eventually Sweden, Denmark and India. Over the following decades work was done in a number of the mountain areas of Queen Maud Land but little significant climbing was undertaken. Belgian teams first explored the Sør Rondane Mountains in the 1957-58 season, as did a Soviet team some years later, but mountain activity here did not really increase until the 1980s. A Norwegian team first visited the Orvinfjella in the 1958-59 season. During the 1960s the Japanese personnel based at Syowa station explored most of the Yamato Mountains, where many meteorites were found. The highest peak in the Yamato Mountains is Mount Fukushima (2494 m), which was climbed by a team of Japanese scientists in November 1960. The Japanese Antarctic Research Expedition (JARE) established a winter station 40 km north of the Sør Rondane Mountains in 1985 and occupied it for several winter seasons. During the 1980s Japanese scientists climbed some higher peaks in the Sør Rondane, such as a 1743 m peak in the Brattnipane ('steep peaks') massif in January 1985, Mount Tekubi (2355 m, one of the highest points of the Brattnipane massif) in January 1987, and two unnamed peaks (2790 m and 2730 m), the latter in the Lunckeryggen Massif, in the Widerøefjellet area. The nearby flat-topped Vikinghögda (2751 m) was climbed in September 1990. It seems that the highest point of the Sør Rondane Mountains, a 2996 m peak in the Widerøefjellet, remains unclimbed.

Thus, at the beginning of the final decade of the 20th century the great rock peaks of Queen Maud Land were known to only a handful of people in the world, all of them scientists, and almost no photographs had ever been published, just a few in obscure scientific journals and far from the eyes of ambitious climbers. All this changed in 1993.

A CLIMBER'S PARADISE

Ivar Tollefsen was a successful young Norwegian businessman who had turned his talents to mountaineering projects. In the course of researching one such endeavour he was at the Norsk Polarinstitutt and was shown old, largely forgotten, aerial photographs of spectacular mountains in Norway's Antarctic territory. This was the genesis of an expedition that was to open up a part of Antarctica in a way not seen since the Seven Summits revolutionised activity in the Ellsworth Mountains. The hook for the sponsors and media was Jøkulkyrkja, at 3148 m the highest mountain in Queen Maud Land, which had never been climbed (though a helicopter did visit the summit in the 1992-93 season). Thus the expedition aimed to achieve 'the first ascent of Norway's highest mountain'.

At the time there was no established air access to the region, so great machinations were put in place to enable transport by ship, the Russian icebreaker *Akademik Federov*. The *Federov* sailed from Cape Town, South Africa, on Christmas Eve 1993 and anchored off the ice shelf near the Russian base Novolazarevskaya. Helicopters on board the *Federov* transported the team and their 2000 kg of supplies ashore to a base camp on the north side of Ulvetanna and another camp near Jøkulkyrkja. A somewhat disorganised ascent was made of Jøkulkyrkja via its long but easy

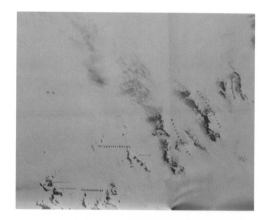

THE PRE-WORLD WAR II GERMAN MAP OF THE ORVINFJELLA showing Ulvetanna named as the Matterhorn.

EARLY EXPLORATION OF THE SØR RONDANE during the late 1950s.

BELGICA MOUNTAINS IN 1957. An exhausted member of a Belgian plane crew resting on the snow while attempting to walk back to safety after their small plane crashed while exploring the range.

Orvinfjella

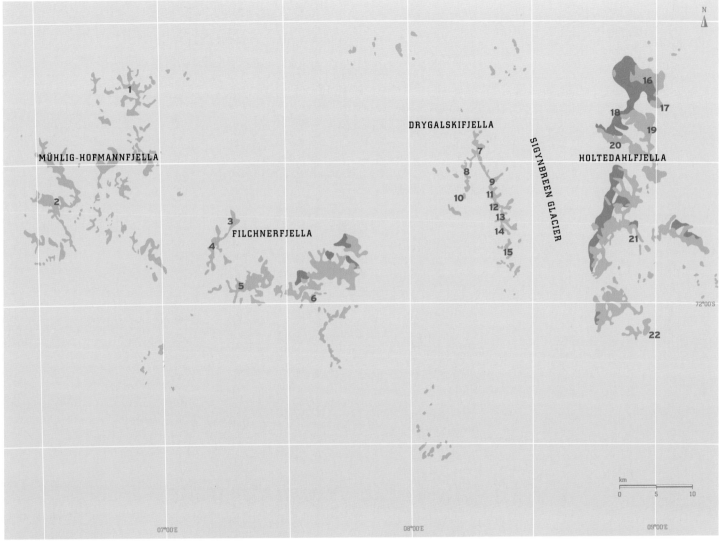

MÜHLIG-HOFMANNFJELLA

DRYGALSKIFJELLA

HOLTEDAHLFJELLA

FILCHNERFJELLA

SIGYNBREEN GLACIER

07°00'E   08°00'E   09°00'E

72°00'S

km
0   5   10

1. Gessnertind 3020 m	**7.** Tungespissen 2277 m	**13.** Holstinnd 2577 m	**19.** Vinten-Johansen Ridge
2. Jøkulkyrkja 3148 m	**8.** Fenris 2480 m	**14.** Holtanna 2650 m	**20.** Steinskaregga 1960 m
3. Rakekniven 2365 m	**9.** Ulvetanna 2931 m	**15.** Mundlauga 2455 m	**21.** Svartnupen 2745 m
4. Trollslottet 2740 m	**10.** Midgard 2345 m	**16.** Gruvletindane	**22.** Halisstonga 2790 m
5. Kubus Mountain 2985 m	**11.** Stetind 2558 m	**17.** Andersnuten 2136 m	
6. Klevetind 2910 m	**12.** Kinntanna 2724 m	**18.** Kubbestolen 2070 m	

106

ROBERT CASPERSEN LEADING OUT A TRAVERSE
ON THE NORTH FACE OF ULVETANNA IN 2006.
The Gruvletindane massif is behind on the left, with Kubbestolen and
Steinskaregga to the right. The isolated massif far beyond is Sandeshatten,
with the small spire of Sandnesstaven to the left.

QUEEN MAUD LAND

QUEEN MAUD LAND

southern slopes, with all team members on top by 9 pm on January 10th 1994. The official expedition objective had been achieved. Now the real climbing could begin.

The ski team of Odd Eliassen, Bård Stokken and Jo Toftdahl immediately set off on their grand tour, which would eventually take them along the southern edge of the Mühlig-Hofmann Mountains, east beneath the Orvinfjella and into the unexplored Wohlthat Massif, before exiting north to Novolazarevskaya. On the way they summited 13 peaks including the highest peak in the Conradfjella – Sandeggtind (3053 m) – and a 2906 m high peak nearby they called 'Stokkantoppen'.

Gessnertind (3020 m) was the first 'real' climbing done by the team, with Robert Caspersen, Jan Åge Gundersen and Sjur Nesheim summiting on January 14th via the northern ice slopes. Now the main target was surely Ulvetanna (the 'wolf's tooth'), probably the most impressive single mountain in Antarctica. The mountain is daunting from all angles and clearly not easy to climb from any side. But from the north it is incredible: a storybook rocket ship thrusting out of the ice, wide smooth fins tapering steeply to a high point. So, in the ultimate climbing destination, why not try the ultimate climb? On January 18th, Tom Cosgriff and Sjur Nesheim launched up the wall, with Robert Caspersen, Trond Hilde and Ivar Tollefsen waiting below to follow. Yet on the first day they only climbed 15 m and progress was slow on the poor rock that

108

IVAR TOLLEFSEN

ROBERT CASPERSEN
leading on the north face of Ulvetanna.

HOLTANNA FROM THE SOUTH
with the summit of Holstinnd just visible at right.
Holtanna's south ridge runs down toward the camera
and was climbed by an international team in 2000.

the leaders were to encounter over the following days. So the team split amicably, with Cosgriff and Hilde persisting on the north wall, and Caspersen, Nesheim and Tollefsen moving onto the seemingly easier mixed terrain of the northwest face. The latter three soon placed a tent on the northwest shoulder, having gained 700 vertical metres in good time over easy ground. Progress above was slower, but for the two over on the north wall it was much worse, as they were still 600 vertical metres from the summit and moving slowly. Their attempt soon ended after Cosgriff, desperate for upward movement but 15 m out from his last protection and facing a loose flake, lunged sideways with a Spectre ice hook in each hand, sticking the landing on a better flake but finding more blank terrain above. The north face attempt was finished.

Tom Cosgriff had done a lot of hard aid climbing – and hard living – in the United States before moving to Norway, where he quickly established himself as one of the bolder and more proficient climbers on their big walls. Considered a brash and forthright character, he had been schooled in the Yosemite dirtbag style of climbing and it was difficult for him to see his ambitious project for the north face end in failure, no doubt exacerbated by the ski team claiming so many less-technical summits. There was friction and arguments, as on most expeditions of this kind, but eventually things were settled. Tollefsen was not the best climber in the team, but then Amundsen was not the best skier in his team, nor Shackleton the best navigator in his boat. Cosgriff and the others were there solely because of Tollefsen and what he had been able to create, so any compromises they had to make to be part of his expedition were minor compared to the incredible opportunity and privilege he offered to be the first climbers in this new wonderland.

So it was probably fitting that Tollefsen would get the great prize of Ulvetanna, summiting on February 2nd with Caspersen and Nesheim, after much convoluted climbing through the upper section of the northwest face. Demoralised from pushing to failure on the rotten rock of Ulvetanna and now running out of time, Cosgriff, Jan Åge Gundersen and Trond Hilde decided to go for the buttress up the centre of the 600 m north face of Kinntanna. They spent a few days fixing their ropes 400 m up the line, a mix of free and aid climbing done only in the more sunny hours, and retreated down to camp each 'night'. On the last day of the expedition the three rushed for the top, which turned out to be less than a metre wide, before rappelling the 11 pitches they had climbed.

At the southern end of Fenriskjeften, Holtanna ('hollow tooth') is shaped like a giant molar with an oval wall, rising higher at each end, and space inside. But one wall of the tooth, on the southeastern side, is broken away. On the western side, toward the south, a beautiful smooth wall rises up to 800 m high. This southern aspect of Holtanna changes as the viewer moves around it from west to east. When viewed in profile from the west, the southern face appears as an incredibly sheer wall, which it is. But as one moves around to the south it appears less narrow and eventually reveals itself to be quite wide and flat across the southwestern side, presenting a huge canvas of smooth brown rock when viewed straight on. Continuing around to the south the wall ends abruptly, forming a sweeping pillar.

The northern end of the molar is much narrower, but appears from due north as a soaring steep tower and one of the most spectacular pieces of mountain on the continent. Moving around to the east a section of wall angles down before the terrain eases considerably. Here the open southeast side of the tooth is filled in by a large snow slope which forms the much more moderate southern face of the northern summit. This face was used by the Norwegians to make the first ascent of the tower, which they named 'Holstinnd', with Caspersen, Nesheim and Tollefsen going to the summit on February 6th 1994. In later years the other sides of this beautiful broken tooth would attract much more attention. In 1999, only months before his death in Tibet, Alex Lowe pointed to a photo of Holtanna's southwestern face in profile and declared it 'the next big thing to do in Antarctica'.

The Norwegians summited 23 peaks in all, many of them quite minor, and including the ski team's exploits the expedition achieved 35 summits, which by numbers alone is one of the most successful Antarctic expeditions in history. After the expedition Tollefsen produced a stunning book titled simply *Queen Maud Land*.[7] Incredibly detailed, often embarrassingly funny, it not only tells the story of the expedition with anecdotes, facts and lots of dialogue, but includes dozens of superb photos and also unique watercolour paintings, by expedition artist Vebjørn Sand. Probably not since the books of Shackleton and Scott has one publication had such a direct influence on motivating adventurers to throw themselves at Antarctica.

In the 1996-97 season American climber and photographer Gordon Wiltsie was one of the first to capitalise on the inspiration that Tollefsen's book was creating. Wiltsie was a veteran of previous seasons on the ice with ANI and now the company was looking to operate in Queen Maud Land, where they hoped to find a suitable blue ice runway inland from the Novolazarevskaya area. Such a location was found and named Blue-1. Wiltsie had scouted the Queen Maud Land mountains in the 1995-96 season and returned the following season with an extremely strong and well-sponsored team. Conrad Anker and Alex Lowe were the lead climbers, with Mike Graber and Rick Ridgeway filming the event, Wiltsie taking photos and Jon Krakauer writing it all up

MIKE LIBECKI'S VIEW SOUTH FROM THE TOP OF FENRIS. At right are the lower peaks of the western wall ('lower jaw') of the Fenriskjeften. Far left is the southwest side of Ulvetanna, with the tops of Hel, Kinntanna, Holstinnd and Holtanna stretching to the right.

7   Tollefsen, Ivar, *Dronning Mauds Land Antarktis*, Oslo, 1994.

for *National Geographic* magazine. Their main objective was a stunning pillar named Rakekniven ('the razor'). Though the western side of Rakekniven is a ridge of snow and rock, the sheer east face overhangs gently as it rises above the ice for more than 600 m, and this was their route.

Arriving at Blue-1 in late December, the team quickly got on the face but found terrible loose granite that came off in the leaders' hands. After 10 days they had only pushed the route up 500 m, delayed by the poor rock, the demands of filming, and a half-day holiday at Christmas. After using a portaledge camp at the top of the tenth pitch, the end of the 14th pitch led them to the narrow, flat summit on January 3rd 1997. Here they found the tiny tracks of a snow petrel and named the route *Snow Petrel Wall*, grading it VI 5.10 A3+. Though not as big as some of the other routes climbed on these walls, it involved probably the steepest and most sustained technical difficulty of any route done in Antarctica up to that time.

Following the Rakekniven climb the team did a few easier climbs. Anker, Krakauer and Lowe made the first ascent of the 2740 m Trollslottet ('troll castle') by a V 5.11 A0 route they named *The Three Sons*. The climb ascended several pitches of huecos up a buttress and face to a snowy summit, all of it watched from the summit of an adjoining peak – 'Media Peak' – that Graber, Ridgeway and Wiltsie had climbed via a moderate snow arete. Anker, Krakauer and Wiltsie also climbed, and skied, the nearby Kubus Mountain (2985 m) to the southeast, while Graber, Lowe and Ridgeway made the second ascent of Jøkulkyrkja, Lowe descending on skis.

As the Americans were battling the razor, Ivar Tollefsen had returned to the ice, also using ANI and Blue-1, but this time to the Sør Rondane Mountains, almost 500 km further east. Here, in the Birger Bergersen Mountains, lay another spectacular virgin spire – Rondespiret ('round spire') – and more untouched rock walls. Venturing into this region was a very bold move, but perhaps a suitable one for the man who started it all here anyway. The Sør Rondane are more isolated than the Orvinfjella, blasted by the katabatic winds rushing down off the higher plateau to the south, and lack the familiar facilities of Blue-1 or Novolazarevskaya nearby. To pioneer technically hard first ascents here was one step beyond a point already considered by most people to be about as extreme as it gets.

The climbing team was again Tollefsen and Caspersen, but joined only by Aslak Aastorp and Håkon Staver. There was also a two-person media team to send video back to Norway, plus Tina Jorgensen, who became the first woman to climb in Queen Maud Land, and Vebjørn Sand was back with his paints. The 2427 m Rondespiret was eventually climbed in 21 pitches up its 800 m northeast face, mostly on surprisingly good rock, but in almost constant strong winds. A few days after summiting Rondespiret, Jorgensen, who had made small solo climbs on four smaller peaks whilst the team were on the wall, joined the climbers to summit a 1639 m feature of dark marbled rock named Bautaen (similar to a headstone) via a four-pitch climb up its west face. Aastorp, Caspersen and Tollefsen finished off with three pitches up the southeast face of a squat 1782 m tower they referred to as 'Cap Gemini'. When planning the trip back in Norway, the team had originally set themselves another objective, to be attempted after Rondespiret. Named Tårnet ('the tower'), they considered it second only to Rondespiret in terms of the best of the Sør Rondane peaks. Lying out to the west of Rondespiret, rising steeply for 600 m above the ice, it remains something for the future.

In the summer of 1999-2000 the experienced Swiss pair of Cestmir Lukes and Irene Oehninger arrived in the area, openly acknowledging the inspiration they drew from Tollefsen's *Queen Maud Land*. Their first climb, on New Year's Day no less, was the west face of Mundlauga, ascended on moderate snow and ice, after which they attempted a rock rib on Midgard. They then spent three days travelling across the Sigynbreen Glacier to the Kurze Mountains at the northern tip of the Holtedahlfjella, where they made six first ascents and the first climbs done in this massif. On January 9th they climbed a 1780 m peak in the north of the Steinskaregga peaks, via its west face and west ridge on moderate snow and broken rock, and named it 'Byrd Peak'. The next day they climbed a 55° ice route up the right side of the northwest face of another summit in the massif that they named 'Elvia Peak'. Back on the south side of the massif, the duo reached the southern 1960 m summit of Steinskaregga, climbing from the southwest and the south over broken rock. The funnel-shaped west face of the 2080 m Kubbestolen ('log chair') was next on the list, and was climbed on January 12th from an approach via the glacier between it and the Steinskaregga massif. They felt this 650 m ice-line with two steep bulges was the most difficult of their routes. Over the next three days the duo used the same approach to climb two more peaks, which they named 'Carasole Peak' climbed by the east ridge and 'Soglio Peak' (2325 m) climbed by the icy northwest face. This very bold and successful smaller expedition showed that there are many interesting climbs to be done in these mountains that need not be aid ascents of the big walls.

In the 2000-01 summer Holtanna was the objective of two strong expeditions that arrived with ANI, now using a Hercules transport plane from Cape Town. An international team of Alain Hubert (Belgium), Ralf Dujmovits (Germany), André Georges (Switzerland), Daniel Mercier and René Robert (France), and Fabrizio Zangrilli (USA) skied 70 km to the mountain from the Blue-1 strip. They first tried a route on the 2577 m northern tower, named 'Holstinnd' by Tollefsen's team, but were repelled by rockfall and moved around to the south of the mountain. The 'tooth' that is Holtanna is not intact and has a large gap to the southeast. One of the edges

ALEX LOWE
climbing *Snow Petrel Wall* on Rakekniven.

SNOW PETREL WALL on Rakekniven.

of this gap is the southern pillar of the peak of Holtanna itself. The team climbed straight up this pillar, grading their route ED F6b A2/3. This was the first ascent of Holtanna, as the Norwegians in 1994 had only climbed Holstinnd, the mountain's lower northern summit. The 2001 team, minus Robert, also made the second ascent of Holstinnd via the 1994 south face route, in four hours.

Hubert and Georges then embarked on a remarkable climbing spree: a 2210 m peak at the southwestern extremity of the Fenriskjeften in 12 hours via a long TD A1 ridge; the first ascent of Midgard (2345 m) in 19 hours over two days via a TD A4 route up the east face; two more peaks from inside the wolf's jaw, 2380 m by the east ridge and 2390 m by the north ridge, both five-hour climbs graded D+; peak 2430 m by 10 hours of great TD crack climbing on the east face; the second ascent of Philiptanna by a short AD route; another short D route up the east face of a small peak nearby; the second ascent of Tungespissen; the first ascent of Stetind (2558 m), done by simul-soloing a traverse at D+ in eight hours; plus another traverse, via a new route up the east ridge of Kinntanna and down the north face, over 15 hours at TD A1. The duo rappelled the face using anchors left by the 1994 first ascent team. Finally, Georges soloed an ED+ crack route on Ulvetanna.

During this time a Spanish team arrived and set up base camp not far away. The very experienced José Carlos Tamayo, with Ferrán Latorre and Mikel Zabalaza, tried a new route on the smooth west face of Holtanna but finding bad and compact rock, turned back after 12 pitches. The trio next repeated the Norwegian route on the north face of Kinntanna, summiting on January 24th. This was followed by the second ascent of Stetind, via the west face, on January 28th before Latorre and Zabalaza completed a new route on the northeast face of Holtanna. All three Spaniards then made the third ascent of Tungespissen (2277 m) and the third ascent of Mundlauga (2455 m), before exiting via Blue-1 after more than a month in the area.

In 2001 another operator entered the Antarctic logistics arena. The Russian-based Antarctic Logistics Centre International (ALCI) began operating Ilyushin-76 flights from Cape Town to a runway near Novolazarevskaya. Internal flights initially used an Antonov-2 biplane but now ski-equipped Basler DC-3 planes are in operation. The company primarily provides access and logistics

‹ THE INTERNATIONAL TEAM OF 2000 ON THE SUMMIT OF HOLTANNA
after making the first ascent, via the south ridge.

˄ GERMAN CLIMBER RALF DUJMOVITS
climbs the wind-scoured rock of Holtanna's south ridge.

CLIMBING HOLTANNA'S SOUTH RIDGE.

for the Antarctic programs of national governments that operate in the area, but it also supports a limited amount of non-government activity such as climbing, skiing and leisure groups.

During a short period over January-February 2003 a very strong and experienced team of Russians climbed five peaks at the southern end of the Petermann Ranges, in the eastern part of the Wohlthatfjella, almost 200 km east of the Fenriskjeften. Led by Valery Kuzin, a politician and Vice-President of the Russian Olympic Committee, the team included Yuriy Baikovsky, Alexander Foigt, Georgi Gatagov, Valery Pershin, Evgeny Vinogradsky, Maxim Volkov and a specialist wall team of Gleb Sokolov, Oleg Khvostenko, Piotr Kuznetsov and Nikolay Zakarov. Their main objective was the Svarthorna Peaks, with rock summits up to 2585 m. These peaks were originally named 'Schwarz Hörner' ('black peaks') by the 1938 German expedition and this has sometimes been anglicised to 'Mount Schwarz', though the Norwegian version is the official name. The team approached the mountains from Novolazarevskaya base using specialised all-

terrain vehicles being trialled by ALCI, earlier versions of which had been used to travel from Patriot Hills to the South Pole in December 1999.

The highlight of the expedition was the first ascent of the highest Svarthorna peak via a hard, wall climb up the 800 m south face. Khvostenko, Kuznetsov, Sokolov and Zakarov took eight days to climb 21 pitches, in temperatures down to -30°C. Fourteen of those pitches consumed the first five days, with climbing on poor rock up a broken buttress in the middle of the face, mostly on aid with a little free climbing and placing bolts at belay stances, before a portaledge could be set up on top of the 14th pitch. Here all four gathered and completed the route to the summit, which was on better rock, though slightly overhanging, before taking a full day to descend. The team referred to the Svarthorna summit they reached as 'Peak Valery Chkalov' and graded their route Russian 6A.

Whilst the wall team was hard at work, the rest of the team made ascents of four other peaks in the area. On January 29th Foigt, Pershin and Vinogradsky spent 11 hours climbing and descending the northern ridge of a 2180 m peak, given moderate mixed terrain, the summit of which they named 'Peak Georgy Zhukov'. Three days later Baikovsky, Gatagov, Pershin and Vinogradsky climbed the southern ridge of a 2355 m peak that they named 'Peak of St. Boris and Gleb'. The 1000 m Alpine route had a few pitches of Russian 3B and was completed in marginal weather conditions. Unfortunately, with blatant disregard for modern accepted environmental practice in Antarctica, the team left a religious ornament – a Russian Orthodox crucifix – on the summit.

On February 3rd Foigt, Pershin and Vinogradsky drove one of the vehicles close to a nearby

ALAIN HUBERT AND ANDRÉ GEORGES
looking southeast to Hel, Kinntanna and the twin summits of Holstinnd and Holtanna.

CAMP BENEATH MIDGARD.

2239 m peak, northwest of 'Georgy Zhukov'. They then climbed a steep 600 m ridge of ice with two rock pitches of 4B beneath the summit, which they named 'Peak Vladimir'. The last climb completed was easier, on a 2060 m peak they named 'Geser Peak'. Baikovsky, Gatagov, Kuzin, Vinogradsky and Volkov reached the summit on February 5th, climbing a few pitches of 3B on loose rock near the top. The team left the area using ALCI's vehicles, one of which broke down in the process, amid various other logistical problems. Vinogradsky and Sokolov (who placed third behind Alex Lowe and Conrad Anker in the 1993 race up and down the 6995 m Khan Tengri in Kyrgyzstan) would go on to climb new routes on both the north face of Everest in 2004 and the west face of K2 in 2006.

Two American climbers, Mike Libecki and Josh Helling, arrived on the ice in December 2003, flying in on ALCI's Ilyushin-76 then transferring to an old Antonov II biplane to reach their base camp near Ulvetanna. Over 16 days they climbed a new 600 m line up the centre of the pyramidal west face of a 2680 m peak in the western wall (lower 'jaw') of the Fenriskjeften. The route was A4 right off the ground, with freeclimbing up to 5.10. After fixing the first 200 m they committed to the wall, spending the next 13 days in a portaledge, moving up capsule-style. Between roofs and off-widths, they rained down a hail of loose rock, squeezed up frigid chimneys and reached the tiny summit on January 14th, before descending in 14 rappels.

Clearly undeterred by the choss and the cold, Mike Libecki returned two years later but this time alone. In the search for new terrain, Libecki set off in the first days of November to do the first climbing in the Gruvletindane massif in the northern Holtedahlfjella. His first attempt

THE NORTH FACE OF ULVETANNA.

was on a steep wall on the end of the Andersnuten Massif that he likened to a ship's prow. In extremely cold and windy conditions he fixed three pitches, but in removing two loose flakes, he set off an enormous rockfall only metres from where he stood. His intended route fell down past him, huge chunks of stone crashing in a cacophony of noise, dust and heat as he cowered in fear. Descent was immediate.

Still wary of the rock but keen to keep exploring, Libecki spent the next day scouting a new objective: a distinctive slender spire in the centre of the Gruvletindane Massif. Sixteen days were spent inching up the tower, with ropes fixed and only one portaledge camp used, all the time buffeted by the cold winds that sculpt the rock and give the ground its trademark scoured look. On the sixteenth day the fear turned to joy as Libecki pulled over the top of what he would come to call the 'Windmill Spire', his route of ascent tellingly named *Frozen Tears* (460 m, 9 pitches, VI 5.10 A3). Soon after, understandably feeling somewhat happier, he skied to one end of the Andersnuten Massif and climbed up and along to the tip of the ship's prow, via what he named the *Dragon Back Ridge* (760 m of vertical, 5.5).

In November 2006 Tollefsen and Caspersen returned, this time with Stein-Ivar Gravdal and Trond Hilde, to settle an old score with the awesome north face of Ulvetanna. They climbed capsule-style up a line around 150 m to the left of where Hilde and Cosgriff had retreated in 1994, finding delicate aid moves up flaky rock, placing 40 bolts on belays and needing 25 bat-hook moves in the route's 21 pitches. The Norwegians graded the 960 m route at 5.10 A4 and were pleasantly surprised at the quality of the rock, considering their previous climbs in the area. They felt that this was a harder and cleaner line than that of the 1994 attempt, more difficult in the lower section and with better rock up high. Tollefsen has commented that it would obviously be better to use no bolts at all on these peaks and has tried to limit their use to belays only, with bat-hook placements in between. The problem on such uniformly steep towers is the descent, as abseil anchors must be safe and at suitable distances, hence the bolted belays. Tollefsen believes the answer lies in BASE-jumping and paragliding; climbing the route without bolts, throwing the haul bags from the lip of the cliff and descending by canopy, thus eliminating the need for abseil anchors.

The four Norwegians then skied 30 km to the east, into the Holtedahlfjella, where they made the first ascent of Gruvletind (2254 m), the second ascent of Kubbestolen and, in a long traverse, the first ascent of the four c.2200 m peaks of the Vinten-Johansen Ridge which runs southeast of Kubbestolen. The four of them then took a long day trip another 30 km further to the east to make the first ascent of Sandneshatten (2200 m), an obvious high peak at the northern tip of the Conradfjella. After skiing back to the Fenriskjeften area they did some smaller climbs, including the third ascent of Stetind, via a route on the west face.

Whilst the Norwegians were battling Ulvetanna, the experienced Finnish climber Patrick Degerman and his compatriot Pekka Holma arrived to climb nearby, but got off to a very bad start. Approaching their landing site near the mountains, the ALCI Basler DC-3 touched down far too hard, broke the landing gear and ploughed into the ice. No one was hurt but the group was stranded for a short time, until an ALE Twin Otter could be flown across the continent from Patriot Hills to take them back to Novolazarevskaya. The two Finns then climbed four peaks in the next two weeks, naming one of the peaks 'Mount Finland'. Unsure of how they would get back to Novo, the duo started hauling sleds and eventually arrived at Ulvetanna base camp, where they enjoyed meeting Tollefsen's team and partaking in his cache of frozen beers, before being flown out by ALCI in a rejuvenated Basler.

November 2008 saw the arrival of the renowned French organisation the Groupe Militaire de Haute Montagne (GMHM). It was to be their first Antarctic expedition since the 1997 tragedy in the Ellsworth Mountains, where Jean-Marc Gryzka died in a sledding fall near Vinson. The team

THE 2003 HELLING-LIBECKI ROUTE
on the west face of Fenris.

LOOKING SOUTHWEST
towards the unclimbed east face of
Ulvetanna in the distance.

consisted of Lionel Albrieux, Thomas Faucher, Didier Jourdan, Dimitry Munoz, Sebastien Ratel and François Savary, who eventually climbed a new 19-pitch route on the soaring north pillar of Holstinnd, named *Pilier de Choudens Renard* (650 m A2/A3) after the two GMHM climbers killed on their 2003 Shishapangma expedition. De Choudens of course had made the third ascent of Mount Tyree, Antarctica's second-highest mountain, via a new route on the east face in 1997.

On the south side of Ulvetanna is a large, smooth-walled, flat-topped cylinder that the French referred to as 'La Bouteille' ('The Bottle'). It is a unique, and often photographed, feature in the region and had not been climbed. The French made a route up this attractive feature to its snowy flat summit, before descending back to camp. Jourdan, Munoz and Ratel returned, jugged up their fixed lines and continued climbing, in an attempt on the unclimbed south ridge of Ulvetanna, before they were forced to retreat just three pitches from the summit. Albrieux, Faucher and Savary skied over to the Filchnerfjella area, the eastern part of which around the Kvitkleven Glacier had not been visited by climbers. They made the first ascent of the peak at the eastern end of the 2780 m Klevekampen Massif, climbing mixed ground on its southeast ridge. Two days later they summited two more peaks, Klevetind (2910 m) and a smaller peak across from it, and finished with a seven pitch route up an unnamed pillar on the south side of the Kvitkleven Glacier. They started to travel toward Rakekniven for an attempt on that spire, but were defeated by the onset of bad weather.

In November 2008 the ALCI Basler DC-3 delivered the renowned German climbers Alex and Thomas Huber, with the Swiss alpinist Stefan Siegrist and cinematographer Max Reichel. Like so many before them, they admitted to having been inspired by Tollefsen's first book and, in particular, were drawn to an objective that has become almost a trademark for these mountains, the vast brown curve of Holtanna's west face. The team started in the centre of the wall, going up to a snow ledge around one-third of the way up, before veering well to the left and heading up to hit the crest some way north of the summit. The Spanish had started on a similar central line in 2001, but were rebuffed by the blank and compact rock directly above. The 2008 team used a portaledge from around half-way up, as they had reverted to capsule-style aid climbing, finding it too hard to free climb every pitch in temperatures that dropped down to around

Mike Libecki

How did you first learn of the Queen Maud Land peaks and what motivated you to go there?

I was living in Yosemite in the mid 1990s when I heard of some Norwegian climbers who had gone to an extraordinary big wall area in Antarctica. On one of my expeditions to East Greenland, Hans Christian Florian Sorensen had the book by Ivar Erik Tollefsen, *Dronning Maud Land* (the original Norwegian title of the book), so when I had the chance to read, gaze and drool at each page of Tollefsen's book it mesmerized me. I knew that some day I would go to Queen Maud Land.

In the year 2000, I really started major detailed planning for a trip to Queen Maud Land. The information on getting there was somewhat disheartening because of the price. I thought I could try to interest a movie or production company, but at the time I did not want to do that. I wanted to go on my own agenda, for the organic reasons, for adventure. I do love photography and video but I prefer to capture my adventures myself. I learned on other expeditions that having external team members who are photographers or film makers can, in some cases, kill the reason we are there in the first place: to live in the moments of now, embrace beauty, people, adventure and to climb in solitude. So, anyway, I was 100% sure I would get to Queen Maud Land, I just needed to rely on the same way I have been able to do every other expedition – simply believe in them and they will happen. The universe has not let me down yet.

That's when I found that the Russian company ALCI had just started taking people from Cape Town to Novolazarevskaya. After my initial contact I was informed that it was for government operations only, funded by different countries to get scientific workers and such down to Antarctica. I asked to speak to the owner or director of ALCI, so I could share my philosophy of life, my dream of going to climb in Queen Maud Land, and explain that they were probably the only way I was going to live this dream in the near future. I sent them emails explaining my objective, my dream of climbing in Queen Maud Land, and if it would be possible for them to help me do this. I wrote them words from my heart and soul explaining that I am a climber, that walls are my true love, and that Queen Maud Land had been love at first sight, that I must go there. Their response was amazing. If I went through the proper channels with the US State Department, the National Science Foundation (NSF) and the United States Environmental Protection Agency (EPA), they would take me to Antarctica in 2003-04. One of my best friends and climbing partners, Josh Helling, and myself committed everything we had to get on a plane for one of the most amazing journeys of our lives.

What motivated me to go? The walls. The landscapes. The 24-hour light. The call of adventure. The mystery. The beauty. The unpredictability. The inevitable suffering. The cold that would be warmed by the summer sun, hopefully. The vertical living. The moments of living in absolute now. I have a gift, natural and organic enthusiasm that is in my body and soul to go on adventures. I don't choose it; it has just become part of me in every way.

There are plenty of unclimbed walls in Asia or Baffin Island, why go to Antarctica?

Why not? Why ration passion? Pursue passion. Death and old age are coming, we must live sweet. No, the answer is because Antarctica is not Asia or Baffin, it is Antarctica. The word 'Antarctica' alone is enough for anyone that has even the slightest hint of adventure in their soul to get the giddy feelings of being a child again. Antarctica is mystery and without mystery adventure is not possible. In Queen Maud Land there are some of the most amazing and unique rock formations on the planet. Antarctica offers utter solitude, an embrace of wilderness with almost no possibility of rescue, especially on a huge wall. Antarctica is Antarctica and I know no other place on Earth that looks, feels, smells, or tastes like it.

There is something amazing I must share. There are two views of rock mountains I have seen in my life that are more brilliant, more intense, more overpowering, more grand, more Godlike, more ominous, more down-right beautiful and impressive than anything else. They are Ulvetanna in Queen Maud Land and the Polar Sun Spire in Baffin Island.

You came across some pretty bad rock, was it all like that?

I have to say that one of the most intense experiences of my entire life was from a rock fall in Queen Maud Land. When solo in 2005, moving some loose hanging flakes, I caused the most powerful rock fall I have ever witnessed. It was unbelievable, the raw power and energy, the smell of heat and destruction, the truckloads of rock I saw crash down was not only life-changing, but a gift of reality. It was frightening, but an experience I would not change. All I could do was go into the fetal position hanging in a harness. I even peed my pants a little.

While scoping routes with Josh, using spotting scopes, we eventually decided against two of the routes we had initially considered because of how bad the rock looked. I have heard from others who have been in the area that they felt the same way: shitty rock for the most part, scary, but also some good rock as well. It is pretty evident with a good spotting scope of how bad the rock is.

One of your trips was solo — why? Can you describe how it felt to be in such a place all alone? Did it affect your decision-making and climbing?

It is really what I truly love to do on expeditions. It is my way of defining utter solitude. You have to do everything, climb, clean pitches, haul, cook, work, belay, endure everything that hap-

pens. There is no help, only you. You have to be able to rescue yourself. It is a situation I have put myself in all over the world and I absolutely love it. It is a challenge that makes me give everything I have physically, mentally and spiritually. Particularly when solo I learn so much and my entire outlook on life changes with a greater appreciation for every single moment.

Being in Queen Maud Land alone was an amazing experience; it doesn't compare to anything else in my life. I don't force myself to go alone, I love it. I am naturally enthusiastic about it; I need it, dream of it, and hope this obsession never leaves me. I could never force myself to go alone, it is too much work. Too lonely, too committing, it is a gift of life that I love to go alone. It always affects my decision-making and climbing choices, being alone to climb it is obvious. I have to make sure every variable in the huge equation of going solo is precise and correct, to make sure the final outcome is successful and I come home alive. The summit is icing on the cake. I am a father, a full-time stay-at-home dad when not traveling and my daughter is very much a 'daddy's girl'. So in some ways I am not solo out there on my solo trips; she is with me in mind and spirit. I have to come home.

Antarctic expeditions take a lot of time, effort and money that can make people very single-minded. Have you felt this?

No, I cannot say I can describe a feeling of single-mindedness. I have a very balanced life as a father and expedition climber. I travel a few months a year, to go on at least two expeditions a

year, if not more. But when I am home, I am focused on being a dad, on my work, on my friends and family, my pets, social life, etc. Then when I start planning and packing for an expedition, I start to change back into expedition mode. I cannot find one negative consequence to the expedition lifestyle. Though I must say, it is because I have the support of so many people when I am gone. My daughter's mother and her family take care of our daughter, friends take care of my home and pets, so it is an amazing amount of work on their part to have my life at home looked after when I am gone. Without the help of so many people I would never have gone on one expedition. This is very important for me to point out. It is never just me making it happen, it is through the major support of family, friends and many other people in the equation that it is possible. When I stand on a summit by myself or with a partner, I am standing there with and because of many, many people. I have all of them to thank, especially the mother of our daughter.

Have your climbs in Antarctica affected the way you think about or approach other areas of your life? Any regrets?

I do not have regrets in life. I embrace every moment I can learn from, and appreciate them greatly. Regret is a waste of time; optimism and learning is what we can take from mistakes, they make us better people. All of my experiences in Antarctica, on every expedition I have been on, correlate to my everyday life. I believe I am stronger because of my climbing expeditions and the other exploratory trips I do. Each expedition, especially the ones to Queen Maud Land, seemed to be such big undertakings at the time of planning and being out there, but they just turned into more training, more learning, more experience for the next trip to come. I learn new things every time I am out there.

Do you have any plans to go back?

Yes, of course. I have two areas that I want to go back to in Queen Maud Land. HUGE WALLS UNTOUCHED! I will be back.

'Antarctica is mystery and without mystery adventure is not possible'

-40°C. The line followed increasingly thin cracks on often brittle rock and the team was forced to haul 50 kg of snow up the route to melt for drinking water. The resulting 750 m 24 pitch 5.11 A4 route - the first ascent of the west face of Holtanna - is one of the hardest yet done in Antarctica and was named *Ice Age*. So Alex Lowe's dream line remains undone, the apex of the curve untouched. But if this smooth brown sea of rock can only be climbed using bolts - and it is admirable that this has been avoided by teams so far - then maybe it should remain unclimbed until it can be done in better style.

Several days later, the German-Swiss team made the first ascent of the narrow north buttress of Holtanna - a route that had been approached by Tollefsen and Cosgriff in 1994 but not actually touched - which they aptly named *Skywalk* (450 m, 10 pitches). This was also the first free ascent of Holtanna. To finish, they completed the first ascent of Ulvetanna's long northwest buttress by *Sound of Silence* (5.11 A2) - a major achievement in its own right - which takes an outstanding natural line up Antarctica's most impressive peak.

In the second half of November 2009, the experienced polar guide Christoph Höbenreich led fellow Austrians Karl Pichler and Paul Koller up a total of 15 summits during a two-week ski journey around the northern Holtedahlfjella. They began with the fourth ascent of Tungespissen (2277 m), then the fourth ascent of Mundlauga (2455 m). Over the next 10 days they climbed 12 first ascents on minor peaks and nunataks, as well as making the second ascent of the 2280 m east summit of Sandneshatten. Most of the peaks were non-technical alpine scrambles, though Tiroler Spitze required some technical rock climbing up to UIAA IV. The other peaks were given names which have since been officially accepted – Österreichspitze, Steirerturm, Gipfel der Stille, Kamelbuckel, Turtschinspitze and Galileoberg.

The spires and walls of Queen Maud Land will continue to attract those seeking the extreme. Not just extreme climbing, but the extremes of space and light, and of beautiful brown rock against an endless icy horizon, swept by extremes of sun and wind, together with the personal extremes to which climbers must go to realise their dreams in this Antarctic wonderland.

124

⌃ CLIMBING THE HELLING-LIBECKI ROUTE
FROZEN TEARS
on the west face of Fenris in 2003.

⌃ MIKE LIBECKI in the Gruvletindane massif.

› MIKE LIBECKI SKIS PAST THE
SOUTHWEST SIDE OF ULVETANNA.
The 1993 Norwegian route of first ascent took the mixed
face on the left. The 2008 French GMHM team climbed the
smooth walls of 'La Bouteille' (The Bottle) on the right.

1. Queen Maud Mountains
2. Queen Alexandra Range
3. Royal Society Range
4. Admiralty Mountains

TRANS-ANTARCTIC
MOUNTAINS

The Transantarctic Mountains stretch over 3500 km across the continent and divide it into East and West Antarctica. Consisting of many smaller ranges and mountains, the Transantarctics contain some of Antarctica's highest mountains and potentially some of its most difficult climbing. Vinson's stream of Seven Summits climbers provide the financial base for the logistical operation into the Sentinel Range. Without such a desirable commodity, however, the Transantarctics have no such customers and hence no established operation. It can be done, but it costs.

Nonetheless, the Transantarctics are certainly not 'unexplored', as government scientists and their support personnel from the New Zealand and US programs based at Ross Island have been working in many locations along the range for decades. A number of these scientific parties have travelled to, and within, the range by helicopter, enabling access to very remote locations and often the helicopters have been used to land high on the mountains themselves. Before the advent of helicopters, teams travelled into the nearby ranges by dogsled. As elsewhere on the continent, such work occasionally involves climbing and a number of peaks in the range have been ascended in the course of surveying, geological studies and other scientific work. In addition, the aircrew working in support of the science programs have reportedly made a number of ascents, but owing to the authorities' attitude to such activity details of these climbs are scarce.

While the range is treated as a single feature in this chapter, prospective visitors may find it easier to think of the range in two sections:

NORTHERN TRANSANTARCTICS: the ranges north of 78° South that border the Ross Sea – essentially the mountains of Victoria Land. This area includes a large number of mountains over 3000 m, the rock walls of the Dry Valleys, the Ross Island area, most notably Mount Erebus, and the higher and steeper peaks in the Admiralty Mountains to the north.

SOUTHERN TRANSANTARCTICS: the ranges south of 78° South that border the western edge of the Ross Ice Shelf and extend beyond to the Weddell Sea. The northernmost of these mountains are the Royal Society Range, where New Zealanders have been very active in over 50 years of operations from Scott Base. The central part of this section, just north of the Beardmore Glacier, contains some of Antarctica's highest and least explored mountains, particularly around the Queen Alexandra Range. South of the Beardmore Glacier are the Queen Maud Mountains.

AN AERIAL VIEW FROM THE WEST OF MOUNT ELIZABETH, the highest unclimbed mountain in Antarctica. In the background is the Beardmore Glacier.

This area contains some high mountains – many are really highpoints along the edge of the polar escarpment – and also includes the steeper and more technically demanding peaks around the Scott Glacier. The Transantarctic Mountains continue past here, heading north once again to include the Horlick Mountains, Thiel Mountains and Pensacola Mountains before dying out in the Shackleton Range, but these are minor mountain areas and little in the way of significant mountaineering has been done in them.

MOUNT EREBUS ON ROSS ISLAND.
Erebus was the first big Antarctic mountain to be climbed, by Shackleton's expedition in 1908.

CLIMBING HISTORY

This history of human activity on the ground in the Transantarctics is long and rich, but climbing for its own sake has been rare. Scott, Shackleton and Wilson tried for the Pole in November 1902 but turned back around 82° South. They had seen Mount Markham and other peaks to the west but at the time were not able to appreciate the size of the range as a whole. In October 1903 Scott led a team up the Ferrar Glacier and onto the icecap, the first humans to ever reach this vast expanse. Later Shackleton and his men became the first to realise that the Transantarctics were indeed a very long and high range, as his team passed by some of its highest mountains while ascending the Beardmore Glacier and heading for the Pole in December 1908.

In March of that year Shackleton's men achieved the first ascent of Mount Erebus (3794 m), the giant volcano on Ross Island that is for many people, even to this day, a symbol of Antarctica. The summit party, which included renowned geologist Tannatt Edgeworth David and a young

A NEW ZEALAND DOGSLED TEAM AT WORK IN THE 1970S
with the big peaks of the Royal Society Range in the background.

Royal Society Range

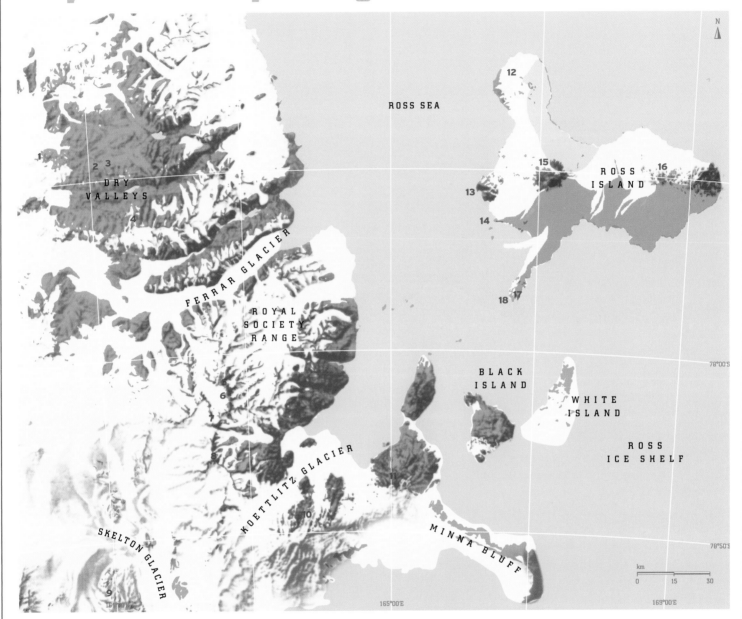

ROSS SEA

DRY VALLEYS

FERRAR GLACIER

ROYAL SOCIETY RANGE

ROSS ISLAND

BLACK ISLAND

WHITE ISLAND

ROSS ICE SHELF

KOETTLITZ GLACIER

SKELTON GLACIER

MINNA BLUFF

78°00'S

78°50'S

165°00'E

169°00'E

km
0   15   30

1.	**Shapeless Mountain** 2739 m	7.	**Mount Rücker** 3816 m	13.	**Cape Evans**
2.	**Dido** 2070 m	8.	**Mount Huggins** 3735 m	14.	**Cape Royds**
3.	**Boreas** 2180 m	9.	**Mount Harmsworth** 2765 m	15.	**Mount Erebus** 3794 m
4.	**The Obelisk** 2316 m	10.	**Mount Morning** 2723 m	16.	**Mount Terror** 3230 m
5.	**Mount Lister** 4025 m	11.	**Mount Discovery**	17.	**Scott Base**
6.	**Mount Hooker** 3785 m	12.	**Mount Bird** 1765 m	18.	**McMurdo Station**

THE BEAUTIFUL SPIRES OF THE ORGAN PIPE PEAKS FROM THE SOUTH.
The only summit to have been climbed is the highest, The Spectre, seen here in the centre. In December 1980, Ed and Mugs Stump climbed to the top via a snow couloir and ridge on the northern side.

The helicopters arrive

In 1962 seismologist George Doumani, already a veteran of expeditions in Marie Byrd Land, returned with a team and flew to the Mount Weaver area at the head of the Scott Glacier, looking for the continent's southernmost rock outcrops. They found the approach to, and climbing on, the south ridge of Mount Weaver quite difficult and turned back short of the top. Shortly after they all climbed Mount Early on November 21st 1962. They had seen this cone-shaped peak southeast of their camp from high on Weaver and approached it on snowmobiles. Skinner and Lackey left their names in Skinner's snuff box on the summit and proclaimed the peak 'Mount Doumani', but it was later named for Neal Early, a helicopter pilot.

The party finally summited Weaver on December 27th by climbing the north ridge, which they accessed via difficult crevassed terrain. On top they found a cocoa can from Byrd's second expedition that contained a sheet of lined writing paper with a note from the first ascentionists dated December 10th 1934, in which they confirmed the ascent and named the peak after Dr Charles Weaver.

This expedition marked the first use of helicopters for geological work on the mountains. Initially the helicopters dropped the men lower down and they continued on foot, sometimes climbing, but eventually the choppers flew the men directly to the summits, if necessary. As Doumani recounts:

"We finished Mount Howe, reaching the top by helicopter, to the chagrin of the mountain climbing enthusiasts, and depositing a register in a rock cairn at the peak, where the altimeter read close to 10,000ft. From its western ridge the mountain could be reached by ordinary walking, and it was only a matter of time and we could have done it. By helicopter, however, the event marked the beginning of an era of great convenience in geological exploration in Antarctica." *

During this time the party flew on to a number of peaks in the Scott Glacier area, including Mount Blackburn, although not necessarily always to the summits. The same helicopters used by Doumani's party later reached the South Pole on February 4th 1963, the first helicopters to do so.

* Doumani, George, *The Frigid Mistress: Life and Exploration in Antarctica*, American Literary Press, 1999, p.257.

Douglas Mawson, was poorly equipped and inexperienced. They had no backpacks of any kind and carried their equipment in their arms for three days, having first hauled a 250 kg sled up the lower western slopes for two days. They survived a two-day blizzard, bivouacked in the open at 3300 m, and reached the summit only after five days of toil and suffering. Erebus received a second ascent by four of the late Captain Scott's expedition team in December 1913. They climbed from the north, making it Antarctica's first 'new route'!

Erebus, often smoking and occasionally erupting, would receive many ascents over the years – and descents into the crater – almost exclusively from scientific personnel at Scott and Mc-Murdo bases. However Erebus also became the first major Antarctic mountain to receive a winter ascent, when renowned British alpinist Roger Mear completed a daring solo climb in 1985. Mear was over-wintering with Robert Swan and Gareth Wood in a private hut at Cape Evans, in order to start early on their seminal 'Footsteps of Scott' expedition. He escaped the tensions of close quarters to do some of the approach on a mountain bike, eventually reaching the summit on June 7th. Erebus received another non-government ascent in February 1991, when Antarctic veterans Mike McDowell and Colin Monteath reached the base of the mountain using a helicopter based aboard the cruise ship *Frontier Spirit* (now *Bremen*).

LOOKING NORTH ACROSS THE IMPRESSIVE ROCKY PEAKS OF THE QUEEN MAUD MOUNTAINS near the Scott Glacier. Just to the south, out of shot, is Mount Blackburn, the first big peak climbed here, in 1969, when an attempt on Zanuck East was also made. Mount Zanuck was climbed in 1987 by Paul Fitzgerald and Ed Stump. Stump had previously summited Grizzly Peak and The Spectre in 1980, with his brother Mugs. The other peaks remain unclimbed.

131

Queen Maud Mountains

1. **Supporting Party Mountain**
2. **Mount Goodale** 2570 m
3. **Patterson Peak** 1610 m
4. **Mount Hamilton** 1410 m
5. **Mount Pulitzer** 2156 m
6. **Mount Clough** 2230 m
7. **Mount Griffith** 3095 m
8. **Mount Vaughan** 3140 m
9. **Mount Astor** 3710 m
10. **Mount Crockett** 3470 m
11. **Mount Bowser** 3654 m
12. **Mount Zanuck** 2525 m
13. **Mount Danforth** 2040 m
14. **Mount Andrews** 2480 m
15. **Mount Gerdel** 2520 m
16. **Organ Pipes**
17. **Ruotolo Peak** 2490 m
18. **Beacon Dome** 3010 m
19. **Mount Borcik** 2780 m
20. **Mount Stump** 2490 m
21. **Mount Colbert** 2580 m
22. **Peak** 3470 m
23. **Peak** 3940 m
24. **Crown Mountain** 3830 m
25. **Mount Kristensen** 3460 m
26. **Mount Kendrick** 3609 m
27. **Mount Gardiner** 2479 m
28. **Mount Blackburn** 3275 m

Thus at the time of first ascent of Erebus, the rest of the Transantarctics were almost entirely unexplored and none of their peaks had been climbed. In November 1911 men from Amundsen's expedition ascended the small ridge-like Mount Betty and built a cairn on a protruding shoulder below the summit. In it they placed a large tin of paraffin, some matches and a note detailing their achievement. On Christmas Day 1929, Laurence Gould and five men from Richard Byrd's first expedition climbed to the same point on Mount Betty, where they found the cairn, paraffin and matches, and read and replaced the note. This cairn has been visited several times in the intervening years. One of this 1929 team was a young Alaskan dog-handler named Norman Vaughan. Over 60 years later Vaughan would go to great lengths to revisit these mountains and climb a peak named after him by Byrd.

Byrd's second expedition sent Quin Blackburn and two partners to these mountains once again in December 1934. In addition to the first ascents of Mount Weaver and Mount Durham, the team travelled the full length of the Scott Glacier, an area that was later to see the most climbing of any in the Queen Maud Mountains. It was Blackburn that named the Organ Pipe Peaks, a line of steep rock towers, only one of which has been climbed, which provide probably the most technical climbing in the entire range. The distant summits of the Transantarctics were then left alone for over two decades, until the return of American superpower logistics.

The 1957-58 season was a big one for Antarctica. On the continent it was the apex of the IGY, which saw Sir Edmund Hillary and friends drive converted farm tractors to the South Pole as part of the Commonwealth Trans-Antarctic Expedition. The IGY also heralded a sudden and massive increase in Antarctic activity by many nations, notably the United States. At the end of the previous season the US had flown to the South Pole and begun a base there and had also established McMurdo base on Ross Island. In conjunction with New Zealand's Scott Base, this created a centre for widespread activity that continues to this day.

The 1957-58 Commonwealth Trans-Antarctic Expedition was somewhat multi-faceted and undertook extensive surveying of the ranges to the west and south of Ross Island, with parties travel-

133

ling by dogsled and reaching numerous summits. In terms of first ascents this season was probably the most prolific in Antarctic history, although it had actually started earlier with the first ascent of Mount Harmsworth (2765 m) in February 1957. Showing that single-push ascents are not a modern invention, Bernie Gunn, Arnold Heine and Guy Warren climbed from a low base camp down on the Skelton Glacier, reaching the summit and returning to camp in a marathon 23-hour journey. They were also ahead of their time in another respect, as they manhauled their supplies along the Skelton Glacier, climbing, geologising and surveying without the aid of dogs or vehicles.

The survey parties operating during the 1957-58 season made over 30 first ascents, generally for surveying, though purely in climbing terms most were not particularly significant. Some bigger peaks were climbed, including Mount Longhurst (2796 m) by Harry Ayres, the New Zealand climbing mentor of Edmund Hillary, and there was exploration of the Dry Valleys area, where long rock climbs would be done years later. Although the southernmost survey party of George Marsh and Bob Miller did *see* Mount Kirkpatrick, Mount Miller and other peaks of the Queen Alexandra Range from a distance, and had an inkling they were very high, they could not accurately ascertain their heights. As a result, Mount Markham remained at that time the highest *verified* mountain in Antarctica.

134

above the Kent Glacier in the Queen Elizabeth Range. The rocky spurs sweep down to the Otago Glacier on the right, which flows north down to the Nimrod Glacier and the Ross Ice Shelf. The 1985 first ascent team flew in a helicopter to 2800 m, from where they used a snowmobile to 3900 m on the gently angled snow slopes to the south.

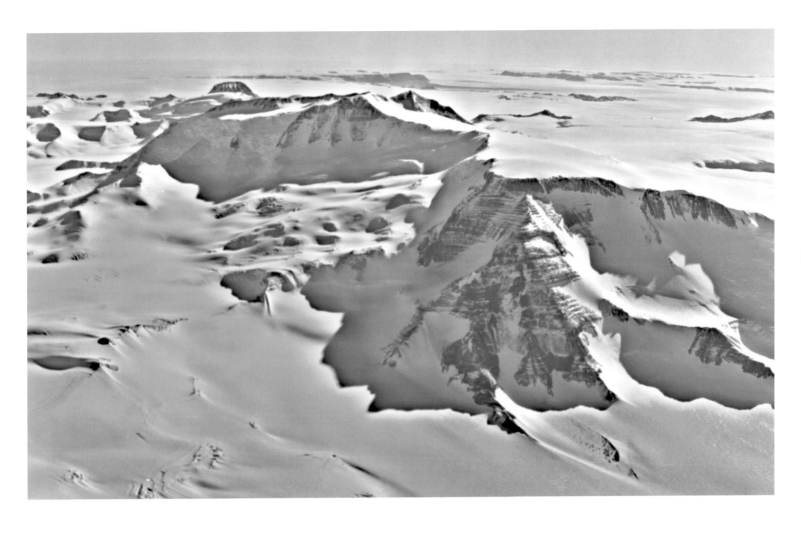

In addition to the enormous amount of glacial and mountain terrain explored and mapped by these parties, one ascent stood out, that of Mount Huggins. At 3735 m high, Huggins was regularly in view of those operating in and around the Trans-Antarctic Expedition, a number of whom were climbers, and its flanks were visible from the well-travelled route up the Skelton Glacier. Bernie Gunn and Richard Brooke had, with others, made most of the 30 first ascents mentioned above, and they climbed Huggins on January 26th 1958. Gunn had obviously planned the climb from the beginning, as he included in the team equipment a small bivouac tent specifically for Alpine climbing. Brooke had climbed in the Alps, making an ascent of Mont Blanc's famous Peuterey Ridge amongst other climbs, and was a surveyor and Lieutenant Commander in the Royal Navy. He had already climbed on the Antarctic Peninsula, making the third ascent of Jabet Peak on Wiencke Island in March 1950, yet over 40 years later Brooke felt that climbing Huggins was the highlight of his time in Antarctica and the only really significant climb he did there. Hillary, in his 1961 book *No Latitude For Error*,[8] described it as 'possibly the best piece of mountaineering yet recorded in the Antarctic'. Brooke was invited to join Ed Hillary and Griffith Pugh's 1961 'Silver Hut' expedition to the Khumbu Himalaya but declined, as doing so would require resigning from the Navy. Gunn went on to make the first ascent of Mount Lister (4025 m) in December 1962, the highest peak in the Royal Society Range and only the second Antarctic 4000er to be climbed at that time. The second ascent of Huggins was made by Simon Cox and Brenton Worley in 1989, climbing a new route

[8]   Hillary, Edmund, *No Latitude For Error*, Hodder & Stoughton, London, 1961.

from the Pipecleaner Glacier. Reaching Auster Pass they moved onto the southeast ridge, traversing around rock bluffs and following gullies to reach the summit in around eight and a half hours.

The first Antarctic 4000er also fell to New Zealanders. In January 1962 the late Wally Herbert was joined by three New Zealanders – Vic McGregor, Peter Otway and Kevin Pain – and their dog teams, and flew south from Scott Base to the southern extremity of the Ross Ice Shelf. Over the course of several weeks they made the first ascents of Mount Usher (3200 m), Mount Clarke (3210 m), Mount Mills (2955 m), Barnum Peak (2940 m), Mount Engelstad (3100 m) and another five unnamed peaks over 3300 m. But the main prize was the first ascent of Mount Fridtjof Nansen (4070 m), the southernmost 4000 m peak on the continent and the first Antarctic 4000er to be climbed. The team also retraced Amundsen's route along the Axel Heiberg Glacier and actually wanted to continue onwards to the Pole but were prevented from doing so by the US authorities, a fact which rankled with Herbert for years.

In 1967 Sir Edmund Hillary led a team to attempt the imposing Mount Herschel in the Admiralty Mountains, taking advantage of the political situation that had led to the US authorities supporting the Vinson expedition the previous summer. Hillary felt that it would be a real breakthrough in mountaineering terms to make the first ascent of a major Antarctic peak in sub-zero temperatures by a difficult face route. They planned to attempt both the north ridge and the huge east face, which rises 3000 m above the waters of Moubray Bay on the Ross Sea. Arriving at Cape Hallett by helicopter from McMurdo, they used snowmobiles to approach the mountain. However, on closer inspection they found the east face to be a vast sheet of bullet-proof green ice and settled for sending two rope teams to the summit by the north ridge. Herschel's east face remains unclimbed. Following this expedition, the US and New Zealand authorities foresaw an unmanageable and potentially unsafe demand on their logistics by private mountaineers, and took steps to ban all private mountaineering in their domain. This attitude persists to this day.

THE ELEGANT AND UNCLIMBED MOUNT SABINE IN THE ADMIRALTY MOUNTAINS seen here from the northwest. The steep rocky face drops down to the Murray Glacier and the sea ice of Moubray Bay is visible in the background.

Queen Alexandra Range

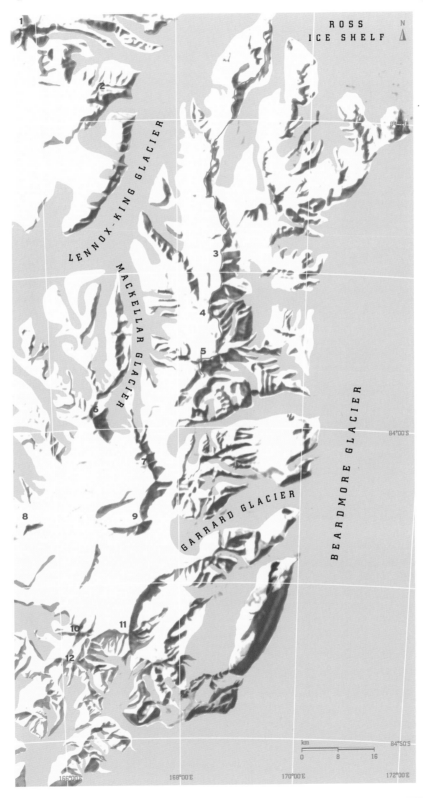

ROSS
ICE SHELF

N

LENNOX-KING GLACIER

MACKELLAR GLACIER

BEARDMORE GLACIER

GARRARD GLACIER

84°00'S

84°50'S

km
0   8   16

166°00'E   168°00'E   170°00'E   172°00'E

1. **Mount Miller** 4160 m
2. **Mount Allen Young** 2753 m
3. **Mount Bishop** 3020 m
4. **Mount Anne** 3872 m
5. **Mount Elizabeth** 4480 m
6. **Mount Mackellar** 4297 m
7. **Mount Bell** 4303 m
8. **Mount Stanley** 3220 m
9. **Mount Lockwood** 3620 m
10. **Mount Kirkpatrick** 4528 m
11. **Mount Dickerson** 4120 m
12. **Decennial Peak** 4020 m

137

Sir Wally Herbert

The British explorer, author and artist Wally Herbert is one of the great figures of polar exploration. On his first stint in Antarctica, as a FIDS surveyor from 1955-57, he traversed much of the spine of Graham Land, the northern section of the Antarctic Peninsula. However, it is his 1968-69 surface crossing of the Arctic Ocean via the North Pole for which he is probably best known. Wally claimed he was not interested in climbing for its own sake, only as a means of surveying and making maps. All the 1962 Queen Maud Mountains first ascents were from the easier plateau side, as they were travelling by dogsled, so involved little actual climbing. The team used the dogs as high as possible, up to 12,000ft (c.3660m), and one dog did die as a result of lung problems. It took them 17 hours on the summit of Mount Fritdjof Nansen to do the work required of them in poor weather conditions, which Herbert described as 'a long cold job'.

Herbert seemed to particularly enjoy retracing Amundsen's route from the Ross Ice Shelf up the Axel Heiberg Glacier to the plateau. He termed this 're-discovering', as Amundsen had made no map of his route at the time. Yet Herbert realised that in

Renowned New Zealand guide Gary Ball was part of one of the more interesting climbing episodes in Transantarctic mountaineering. In the summer of 1976-77 the famous Italian alpinist Walter Bonatti joined his country's national Antarctic program and with Ball made several significant first ascents in the Royal Society Range – Mount Hooker (3785m), Mount Giulia (3650m), Mount Rücker (3816m) and The Twins – as well as the second ascent of Mount Lister.

Another impressive piece of 'work' was Bill Atkinson and Walt Fowlie's 1981 first ascent of Mount Adam (4010m) by the east ridge. Adam, the second-highest mountain in northern Victoria Land, is an impressive rock pyramid, which required the pair to climb rock up to grade 18 and was very difficult compared with most ascents done in the name of science. A decade later, in 1991, New Zealanders Paul Fitzgerald and Charlie Hobbs made the second ascent with the American Tim Redfield and belayed over a dozen pitches for the climb. Paul Fitzgerald, a geology professor now resident in the US, has possibly made more significant first ascents in Antarctica than anyone else. These include big technical climbs in the Scott Glacier/Southern Transantarctic area with Mugs and Ed Stump in the early 1980s, an Alpine-style ascent of Vinson with Mugs and Rob Hall in 1989, and numerous first ascents in Victoria Land and elsewhere along the Transantarctics in the 80s and 90s.

doing this they were second and not first, and he felt there was 'a huge difference between first and second'. Hence he said that while it was his greatest trip up to that point, he considered later trips much more memorable. Nonetheless, it might seem somewhat ironic that on this occasion he attached so much importance to doing something at which they were the second, and so little importance to being the first, that is making first ascents! Herbert did attach great importance to being first, saying 'you can never imagine what it is like to be first, that is the magic of it', so there was no doubt that the first surface crossing of the Arctic was personally very important to him. He acknowledged that Ralph Plaisted had probably achieved the first surface journey to the North Pole, even if the rumours of a substantial mid-expedition airlift were true. Herbert actually attended a conference where Plaisted was present but never raised the question of the rumoured airlift. His reluctance to push the matter in subsequent years seemed to reflect a reluctance to engage in the kind of mudslinging that has characterised so many other expeditioners and their feats. It is hard to imaging modern day 'adventurers' showing such restraint.

Herbert was quite passionate in his disdain of most modern adventure and he described as 'pretty sickening' the media hype and associated claims, many of which are overly conditional, deliberately vague so as to flatter, or just downright false. Yet, like most great explorers, he was not without pride and a healthy ego, even if it was kept in check by an almost old-fashioned sense of integrity and decorum. He had no scientific reason to dash to the Pole in 1962, but he still very much wanted to; but then which true explorer would not? He even admitted years later in *Across The Top Of The World* that he had been 'obsessed by an ambition to reach the South Pole'. But naked personal ambition, unadorned with a weighty costume of science, has never sat well with the British polar establishment. There were rumblings that the long delay between his Arctic crossing in 1969 and receiving a knighthood in 2000 was a reaction by the establishment to what was perceived, by some at least, as an unseemly sense of entitlement for his endeavours. Some felt he hinted too hard, so they made him wait. Others said it was because his feat of reaching the Pole was eclipsed in the news by the moon landing, or because his debunking of the American Robert Peary's claim to have reached the North Pole made him unpopular in some circles.

His dismay at the US authorities' refusal for his Pole dash extended even further when they decided not to publish the map he had made of the region, as they were sending their own survey team the following season. When they did so, they used Herbert's survey stations for their work, but reached them by helicopter, a convenience not lost on Herbert as he remembered it in later years. His map, on which he worked for a year at his own expense, was included in the back of his classic book *A World Of Men*. Herbert spoke with a clear sense of pride when he recounted that the next expedition up the Axel Heiberg – Monica Kristensen's 1986-87 expedition – contacted him afterwards to tell him that his map was actually better than the US one. He felt that being on the ground gave him the ability to fine-tune the contours, something that could not be done by 'American cartographers, working from aerial photographs in Washington DC'.

These issues aside, there is no doubt that this 1962 journey through the Queen Maud Mountains was one of the most significant pieces of mountain exploration done in Antarctica, led by one of the great figures of 20th century exploration.

PRIVATE CLIMBERS IN THE TRANSANTARCTICS

The 1966-67 government-supported mountaineering expeditions to Vinson and Herschel were anomalies. Since then the official position of governments operating in Antarctica has been to provide no logistical support for private expeditions to Antarctica. This position has been occasionally adjusted, somewhat haphazardly, by a few governments on select occasions, but generally the Transantarctics have been beyond the reach of private mountaineering expeditions. There have, however, been two notable exceptions.

In early 1988 a team of Australian mountaineers set sail from Sydney to cross the Southern Ocean. Their goal was the first ascent of Mount Minto (4165 m), the highest peak in the Admiralty Mountains of North Victoria Land. The leader, Greg Mortimer, had seen Minto on previous visits to the area, whilst working as a field assistant to government scientists, and longed to return. Their boat, the *Allen & Vi Thistlethwayte*, was a 21-metre steel-hulled vessel, named after generous sponsors whose last-minute contribution enabled the expedition to happen. Team members included Lincoln Hall, who had been on the 1984 first Australian ascent of Everest, via a new route on the north face, with Mortimer, and Glenn Singleman, a doctor and film-maker

140

who would go on to pioneer BASE-jumping in the Himalaya. Also aboard was Colin Putt, who had made the first ascent of Mawson Peak (2745 m) on Heard Island's volcano, Big Ben, sailing there with the legendary Bill Tilman.

After being tossed around the Southern Ocean for nearly a month, the team arrived at a point to the north of Cape Adare. They then made their way around to Cape Hallett, the site of the abandoned Hallett Station (NZ), and went ashore at Willett Cove on the northern edge of Edisto Inlet. They had brought a snowmobile to help ferry loads up the Tucker Glacier, which they began doing in the first days of February, but the machine fell through the sea-ice in Edisto Inlet, luckily causing no harm to the people on it at the time. However, this meant they were now totally reliant on manhauling, a method for which they were not best prepared. Travelling on skis and pulling sleds, the team of six slowly made their way west up the Tucker Glacier before turning north into the Man-O-War Glacier, making a total of 12 camps and leaving depots for the return journey, before establishing a base camp on February 16th.

THE STUNNING SOUTH SPUR OF MOUNT ADAM in the Admiralty Mountains of northern Victoria Land.

THE NORTH FACE OF THE UNCLIMBED
MOUNT ASTOR,
the highest mountain in the Hays Range. In the foreground
is the Vaughan Glacier. Mount Crocket and Heinous Peak
are out of picture to the left.

Their successful February 18th ascent of Minto via the non-technical south ridge was un-eventful, if very cold, and the team started their return the next day. However, by this time they were behind schedule and the boat was having difficulties in the ice conditions for which the area is notorious. Moving too slowly and with time running out, the team elected to burn their waste and some other material in the snow to save weight. However, some team members were injured and they were still running out of time so they took the opportunity for an airlift out on a Greenpeace helicopter operating nearby, and were flown to the ship *Greenpeace*, before transferring back to the *Thistlethwayte* for another demanding voyage home. Though clearly a wise choice for safety and logistical reasons, it was far from the small, clean and independent style they had envisaged, and a somewhat disappointing end to an otherwise bold and adventurous expedition.

But the path to true adventure can never be easy, and so it was for the other private Transantarctic expedition. Norman Vaughan had visited Antarctica in 1928 as a dog-handler on Admiral Richard Byrd's first expedition. Under the leadership of Laurence Gould, his team explored the Queen Maud Mountains and surrounding area, collecting rock samples and acting as potential rescue support for Byrd's South Pole flight. They were the first to visit here since Amundsen and found Amundsen's note in the fuel can that he had left on a high shoulder of Mount Betty. They also reached around 2000m on Mount Fridtjof Nansen and did some other minor climbs, the first people to do so in the range. Afterwards Byrd proposed that a 3140m mountain in the area be named Mount Vaughan and, nearly seven decades later, Norman decided he should climb it.

In the intervening period he had led an interesting life, surviving both World War II – as a dog-musher rescuing downed pilots in Greenland – and three marriages, before ending up in Alaska at the age of 68, whereafter he proceeded to make a name for himself by completing 13 Iditarod sled-dog races. By the late 1980s ANI's operation at Patriot Hills was well established and Vaughan realised he could use it as a launching point to sled to his mountain. Dogs were to be permanently removed from Antarctica from April 1994, to comply with the 1991 Protocol on Environmental Protection to the Antarctic Treaty – the 'Madrid Protocol' – so Vaughan wanted to be one of the last to mush dogs on the continent. His first attempt, in 1993, was not well organised and his privately chartered DC-6 crashed on its approach to Patriot Hills. No one was killed, but four dogs escaped and perished. The DC-6 remains embedded in the ice to this day, with only the upper tail section showing, and is a regular day trip for visitors from the base at Patriot Hills.

Vaughan returned in 1994, this time not using dogs but with a larger team that included the Antarctic veterans Alejo Contreras and Gordon Wiltsie, ex-Vinson summiters Rob Hart, Bob Failing and Brian Berkus, a *National Geographic* film crew and Norman's wife Caroline Muegge-Vaughan. The group flew to the mountain from Patriot Hills in ANI Twin Otters. Though in good shape for his age, Vaughan was understandably very slow on the mountain. The situation was not helped by some in the team wanting to delay his summit until the day of his 89th birthday, so progress was very slow and the camps were placed very close together. There were tensions amongst various members over methods and motivations and some quite farcical activity ensued, as the first pair on the route climbed almost to the summit and back down in only a few hours, while Vaughan's own ascent was dragged out over a week.

Eventually the whole team summited Mount Vaughan on December 16th – three days before Vaughan's 89th birthday – with some of the party also climbing the slightly lower northern summit. Norman Vaughan returned home to some media acclaim, wrote an autobiography and continued as an inspirational figure to many people. Though he planned to return to Mount Vaughan for his 100th birthday on December 19th 2005, this proved unfeasible and Norman died peacefully at home a few days after reaching his one hundredth birthday.

Admiralty Mountains

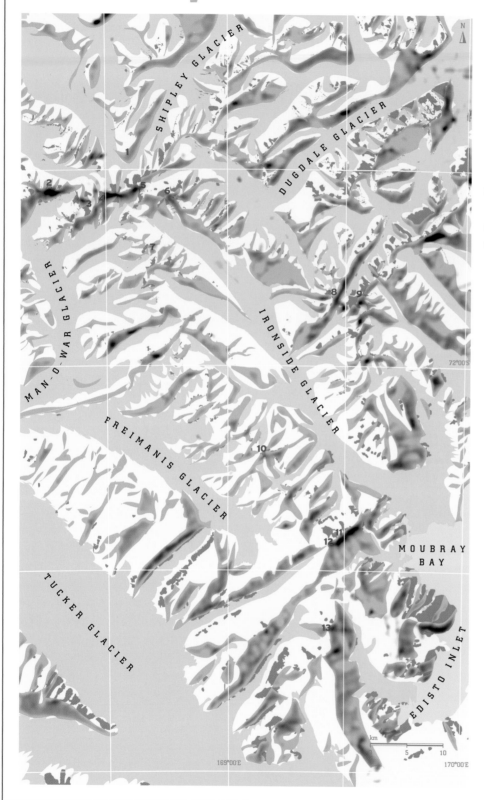

1. **Mount Faget** 3360 m
2. **Mount Black Prince** 3406 m
3. **Mount Ajax** 3770 m
4. **Mount Royalist** 3642 m
5. **Mount Adam** 4010 m
6. **Mount Minto** 4165 m
7. **Meier Peak** 3450 m
8. 3490 m
9. **Mount Sabine** 3719 m
10. **Mount Chider** 3110 m
11. **Mount Herschel** 3335 m
12. **Mount Peacock** 3210 m
13. **Mount Humphrey Lloyd** 2970 m

THE FUTURE

143

ACCESS TO THE NORTHERN TRANSANTARCTICS...

The coastal peaks of northern Victoria Land have been accessed from boats and by ship-based helicopters, but these were rare incidents. With very few exceptions, any ship large enough to carry a helicopter will have cruise passengers whose itinerary is unlikely to be flexible enough to accommodate the logistics of inserting and removing an expedition wishing to climb inland.

Yacht access gives more flexibility with time but also has serious challenges. Moving from ship to shore may not be possible in all coastal locations, so insertion points may be limited, thus potentially increasing the difficulty, time, food and fuel required for any journey inland. Those people remaining with the vessel must pass the time while the climbers are ashore and, unlike on the Antarctic Peninsula, this may not be easy or safe given the remote location and dangerous sea-ice conditions that parties have experienced there. Reaching the area requires a much longer sea journey from the north, either Australia or New Zealand, thus for most yacht charters this means either reduced climbing time or increased overall expense.

The government scientific parties active in the Transantarctics have operated out of McMurdo or Scott bases at Ross Island. No truly private mountaineering expedition (not using government logistics) has ever done so, though it is theoretically possible once the regulatory, financial and environmental difficulties are dealt with. The USAP will not permit private aircraft to land at their facilities there, though they have done so in the past for certain individuals. Sea-ice conditions prevent ship or yacht access until late December – sometimes later – and dictate departure by mid-February, which leaves a relatively narrow window in which to mount an expedition into the interior.

**THE ENORMOUS UNCLIMBED EAST FACE
OF MOUNT HERSCHEL
IN THE ADMIRALTY MOUNTAINS.**
Herschel rises over 3000 metres above the point where the
Ironside Glacier meets the sea.
The only ascent was by a NZ team in 1967, led by Sir
Edmund Hillary, which climbed the northern ridge running
down from the summit to the right. Mount Peacock at left is
unclimbed, as are the mountains behind.

...AND TO THE SOUTHERN TRANSANTARCTICS

Any non-government air access to these inner ranges will be a very expensive proposition, mainly due to the necessity of pre-placing fuel caches at some point along the great distance between the plane's base and the mountains and sustaining search and rescue coverage. It may actually be more efficient for such flights to go via the South Pole.

One method, which has not yet been tried, is to use kites to ski to the range from the South Pole, with an exit via Ross Island as several ski-traverse teams have done before. Such teams have walked or kited right past some attractive mountains but have been too focused on their distant objective to stop and climb. The winds are favourable to reach many areas of the range from the Pole. In addition, if the Pole were reached on a commercial flight via Patriot Hills or Queen Maud Land, as opposed to hauling or kiting to it from elsewhere, more time would be available to climb in the range. This would be the cheapest way currently available to climb in the innermost high ranges of the Transantarctics and certainly one of the more adventurous climbing expeditions possible.

The peaks around the Scott Glacier in the Queen Maud Mountains have been reached by Twin Otter aircraft from the private ALE base at Patriot Hills, in the southern Ellsworth Mountains, and this remains the most efficient way to place a climbing team in that area. The kiting option noted above could also be used for these mountains, particularly as the Axel Heiberg Glacier, between the plateau and the Ross Ice Shelf, has now been navigated a number of times.

Most of the major glaciers leading from the plateau down to the Ross Ice Shelf have been travelled numerous times. Several private South Pole ski expeditions in modern times have travelled either up or down both the Beardmore and Axel Heiberg Glaciers. A full traverse of the

Edmund Stump

For those who know the Antarctic mountains, there is one man whose name is always linked with the Transantarctics and particularly the southern peaks of the Queen Maud Mountains. For over 30 years Ed Stump has been a Professor in the School of Earth and Space Exploration at Arizona State University. His book *The Ross Orogen of the Transantarctic Mountains* covers both the geology and exploration of the range and is considered the major work on the area. Stump's first trip to Antarctica was as an Ohio State University grad student in the 1970-71 season, when he was drawn to gaps in the geological knowledge of the area around the Scott Glacier. He is now a veteran of 12 field seasons in Antarctica and has made over 30 first ascents in the course of his geological work. While a few of these have used helicopters and snowmobiles, many others have involved relatively technical and serious climbing.

Although Stump has made the first ascents of significant high peaks such as Mount Markham (4350 m), Mount McClintock (3492 m), Mount Early (2720 m and the world's most southerly volcano) as well as a single-push ascent of Vinson, he felt his hardest climb was the 2500 m high east face of Heinous Peak, a sub-peak of Mount Crockett (3470 m) in the Hays Mountains. The climb took 20 hours return, collecting rock samples all the way down, climbing with his

ED STUMP (LEFT), WITH HIS BROTHER MUGS in the Queen Maud Mountains.

THE EAST FACE OF HEINOUS PEAK IN THE HAYS MOUNTAINS.

MOUNT ANALOGUE (LEFT) FIRST CLIMBED IN 1978, and Phlegar Dome (right), on the Watson Escarpment.

THE NORTHEAST FACE OF MOUNT BORCIK showing the 1987 route of first ascent by Lyle Dean, Paul Fitzgerald, Ed and Mugs Stump.

brother Mugs, Lyle Dean and Paul Fitzgerald. Stump would later recall that that they had wanted to name the peak 'Janus Peak' as it had two faces – one rock and one snow – and also because Mugs knew a small boy back in Talkeetna, Alaska, by that name. However, the Advisory Committee on Antarctic Names did not accept the name and it became 'Heinous', one of the words the team had used to describe some of the climbing they did on the trip. But hardest is not always best, and Stump's best climbing memory is the December 1980 first ascent of The Spectre (2020 m) with his brother Mugs. In later seasons they would form the nucleus of teams that achieved some of the most significant climbing done in Antarctica.

Like many brothers, the relationship between Ed and Mugs was not always easy, and Mugs's untimely death on Mount McKinley in 1992 made things even harder. Mugs's big solo climbs on Tyree and Gardner in the 1989-90 season received some publicity in the broader climbing world outside Antarctica. This antagonised the authorities at NSF, who frown on such recreational climbing, and Ed was called to task for Mugs's solo accomplishments.

THE UNCLIMBED NORTHWEST FACE
OF MOUNT ADAM
with Mount Minto in the background.

Shackleton Glacier was done on snowmobiles in the early 1960s by US geologist Al Wade, who spent two seasons working there, and a team bound for the South Pole manhauled up it in 1999. The Scott Glacier was fully traversed in 1934 by dogsled, and it received much more traffic from geologists working in the area in the 1970s and 1980s.

The Shackleton Range could be reached by air from a base in Queen Maud Land, having travelled from Cape Town, South Africa. However the peaks here are of little interest to climbers and this method is unlikely to be worth the expense involved, although it could be combined with some other expedition or operation in the area.

Many of the Transantarctic peaks are not as steep and rocky as those in the Sentinel Range or Queen Maud Land and would provide excellent ski-mountaineering expeditions for those with the rare combination of time and money to visit. It also means that teams can make ascents without needing to haul great loads of technical equipment, thus facilitating lightweight approaches.

UNCLIMBED?

How about kiting from the South Pole onto the Beardmore Glacier and turning west to climb one of the great northern ridges on Mackellar before tackling Antarctica's highest unclimbed mountain, Mount Elizabeth? Or braving two weeks of seasickness across the vast Southern Ocean to land near the Admiralty Mountains, the most accessible of the Transantarctics, with their numerous aesthetic virgin peaks above 3000 m, such as Mount Sabine and Mount Royalist? Or climbing the giant 3000 m east face of Mount Herschel that defeated Hillary? For those interested in more technical climbing, the Organ Pipe Peaks contain dozens of new routes and the world's most southerly rock climbs. Some of the higher peaks here are still unclimbed, such as Crown Mountain (3830 m) and the aesthetic Mount Astor (3710 m). These are just a few suggestions, as the Transantarctic Mountains offer some of the last great mountain adventures on Earth.

SOUTH GEORGIA

Stormy, rugged, windswept, formidable; all words usually associated with the island of South Georgia, and it rarely fails to live up to such descriptions. Around 170 km long, 30 km wide, overwhelmingly mountainous and heavily glaciated, the island actually has two ranges. The higher Allardyce Range runs down the centre of the island, and the lower, rockier Salvesen Range is in the southeast of the island, the two separated by Ross Pass.

The BAS 1:200,000 topographical map shows ten peaks over 2000 m, with all but one of them in the eastern part of the island, but more modern surveying may prove some of these to be lower. However, for such a small island, in such a remote location, with such terrible weather, it has contributed a substantial amount of climbing action towards the history of mountaineering in Antarctica.

Captain James Cook saw South Georgia in 1775 and landed and took possession of it, though wayward merchants had sighted it before then. For over a century, until the 1950s, it was mainly the domain of sealers and whalers. A notable exception is the famous crossing of the island by Ernest Shackleton, Tom Crean and Frank Worsley in May 1916, after their epic 1300 km boat journey from Elephant Island, off the Antarctic Peninsula. Their 36-hour traverse from King Haakon Bay to Stromness is difficult to repeat in full now, due to changes in the terrain, but a shorter – and substantially easier – version is now commercially guided most summers. Before Shackleton, the only known climbing on the island was multiple ascents of Mount Krokisius (470 m) during the 1882-83 International Polar Year (IPY), and by various crewmembers of Nordenskjöld's *Antarctic* in May 1902. The latter climbed some way up a ridge on Mount Duse (505 m), but given the difficulty of reaching the true summit, as proven in later years, it is unlikely the Swedes went to the highest point.

These forays aside, mountaineering on South Georgia really began in the 1950s, during the four surveys led by Duncan Carse in the summers of 1951-52, 1953-54, 1955-56 and 1956-57, the latter of which he conducted alone. Carse had been on John Rymill's 1934-37 BGLE and later found a degree of fame back home in Britain as the star of popular radio program *Dick Barton - Special Agent*. But like so many who go to the poles for adventure, he seemed to have an ingrained need for recognition and acclaim. He also had a personal objective upon which he

MOUNT PAGET, THE HIGHEST MOUNTAIN ON SOUTH GEORGIA, AS SEEN FROM THE NORTH, NEAR KING EDWARD POINT.
The main summit is on the left, with the West Summit on the right. All ascents but the first have ascended lines on the north face of the main summit, either side of the obvious rock band.

South Georgia

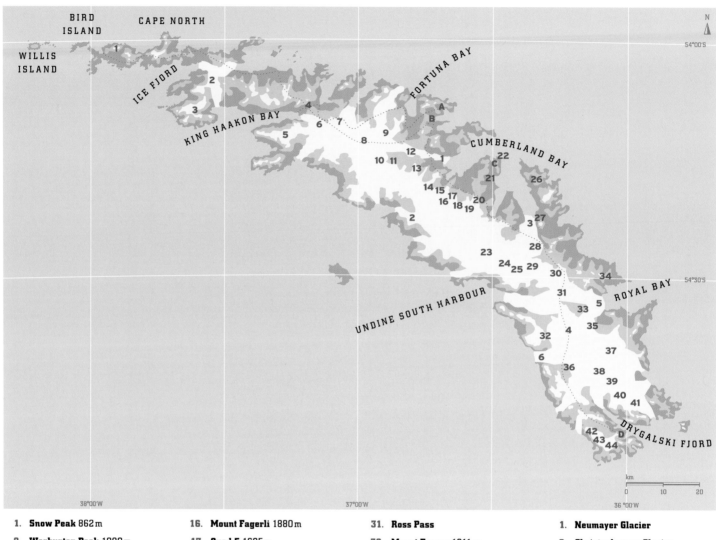

1.	**Snow Peak** 862 m	**16.**	**Mount Fagerli** 1880 m	**31.**	**Ross Pass**	
2.	**Warburton Peak** 1090 m	**17.**	**Quad 5** 1695 m	**32.**	**Mount Fraser** 1611 m	
3.	**Bomford Peak** 1141 m	**18.**	**Paulsen Peak** 1875 m	**33.**	**Vogel Peak** 1348 m	
4.	**Shackleton Gap**	**19.**	**Mount Sugartop** 2325 m	**34.**	**Mount Krokisius** 472 m	
5.	**Mount Cunningham**	**20.**	**Surprise Peak** 950 m	**35.**	**Smoky Wall** 1840 m	
6.	**Mount Worsley** 1104 m	**21.**	**Mount Duse** 505 m	**36.**	**Mount Baume** 1912 m	
7.	**The Trident**	**22.**	**King Edward Point**	**37.**	**Peak** 2089 m	
8.	**Kohl-Larsen Plateau**	**23.**	**Mount Paget** 2934 m	**38.**	**Mount Paterson** 2195 m	
9.	**Stanley Peak** 1263 m	**24.**	**Mount Roots** 2281 m	**39.**	**Mount Carse** 2325 m	
10.	**Smillie Peak** 1767 m	**25.**	**Nordenskjöld Peak** 2354 m	**40.**	**Mount Macklin** 1900 m	
11.	**Mount Spaaman** 1940 m	**26.**	**Mills Peak** 627 m	**41.**	**Douglas Crag** 1670 m	
12.	**Admiralty Peak** 945 m	**27.**	**Ellerbeck Peak** 684 m	**42.**	**Mount Sabatier** 1145 m	
13.	**The Three Brothers** 2040 m	**28.**	**Mount Sheridan** 955 m	**43.**	**Mount Senderens** 1315 m	
14.	**Larssen Peak** 1549 m	**29.**	**Mount Kling** 1842 m	**44.**	**Mount Normann** 1265 m	
15.	**Marikoppa** 1840 m	**30.**	**Mount Brooker** 1881 m			

1.	**Neumayer Glacier**
2.	**Christophersen Glacier**
3.	**Nordenskjöld Glacier**
4.	**Spenceley Glacier**
5.	**Ross Glacier**
6.	**Novosilski Glacier**
A.	**Stromness**
B.	**Husvik**
C.	**Grytviken**
D.	**Larsen Harbour**
··········	**Shackleton 1916**
··········	**Dixon / Finney / Lurcock / Watson 1999**

CLIMBERS ON THE PHILIPPI GLACIER, looking north across Drygalski Fjord to Peak 2229 in bright sunlight, with the impressive and unclimbed rocky pyramid of Mount Macklin to its right. Mount Carse is in clouds on the far left and Douglas Crag can be seen on the far right.

CLIMBING ON THE NORTH RIDGE OF MOUNT PELAGIC DURING THE FIRST ASCENT IN 2005. In the distance is the unclimbed Mount Fraser and neighbouring peaks.

hoped to build his fame. Carse wanted to succeed where Shackleton had failed, and make a surface crossing of Antarctica. When Vivian Fuchs was chosen to lead the 1957-58 Commonwealth Trans-Antarctic Expedition, Carse was reportedly crushed. In February 1961 he arrived at Undine Harbour on South Georgia to live the life of a hermit, on a piece of land for which he had paid a small sum to lease. It was to be a search for enlightenment, catharsis, and of course, fame. But a wave of unforeseen size destroyed Carse's hut, leaving him having to camp for over three months, swinging between drunken self-loathing and disciplined survival, with it all recorded in journals, Captain Scott-like, for posterity. He was rescued by a passing sealer in September and soon returned home, but the inner troubles that drove him away in the first place came back with him. He felt that his hermitage, like most of his career, had been a failure and it was to be more than 30 years before he finished writing his memoirs. It seems that no matter what heights or poles they reach, few can escape the internal perils of the ego, ambition and competition that have underpinned so much polar exploration.

The survey work led by Carse involved an enormous amount of glacier travel and quite a bit of climbing, resulting in numerous summits being reached. One of the first peaks climbed by Carse's men was the obvious Admiralty Peak (945 m) on the north side of the Neumayer Glacier, during the summer of 1951-52. John Heaney, James Roots and Kevin Walton from this group also climbed two smaller peaks above the Cook Glacier. Ascents continued to be made in the seasons that followed during exploration and surveys. On October 27th 1954 Ian Brooker, R.A Brown, George Sutton and Clive Webb climbed Sutton Crag (1489 m), a northern outlier of Mount Paget above the Paget Glacier, then in January 1955 Brooker and Webb summited Mount Brooker (1881 m), north of Ross Pass.

The next big mountain climbed was Mount Spaaman (1940 m), reached in October 1955 after a five-hour climb by Louis Baume, George Spenceley and Keith Warburton up its long west ridge that rises from the Kohl-Larsen Plateau. However, they seemed to have got more enjoyment out of making the second ascent of a minor, but spectacular, 600 m peak that overlooked the Bay of Isles. On the summit they found a note and a bottle of whisky left for them by Bernard Stone-

MOUNT PAGET NORTH FACE ROUTES:
Green: Novak et al 1994
Yellow: French variant 2007
Red: French 1980
Blue: descent traverse 1990 & 1994
Purple: Jones-Mills descent route 1990
X: Jones-Mills descent bivi
C: Novak et al Camp 3 1994

house and Nigel Bonner, who had made the first ascent in March 1954. Stonehouse would go on to become a renowned expert in Antarctic bird life and tourism, regularly visiting the Peninsula on ships into his eighth decade, while Bonner eventually became Deputy Director of the BAS from 1986-88 and founded the South Georgia Museum at Grytviken. Spaaman received a second ascent, by a team of Gurkhas in 1993. The second major peak climbed during this survey – and the highest mountain climbed on the island to that date – was Mount Paterson (2195 m), summited by John Cunningham, Stan Paterson, Tom Price and Keith Warburton in March 1956, after a climb starting from the head of the Novosilski Glacier. Paterson had already worked in the Arctic and would later author one of the most widely used texts on glaciology. Cunningham went on to make the first ascent of the Antarctic Peninsula's highest mountain, Mount Jackson (3184 m), in 1964 and would eventually become a legendary figure in Scottish climbing.

This survey team had hoped to attempt Mount Paget and cross the island from north to south via a col near Smillie Peak, but a prolonged storm damaged their tents, requiring resupply, while changes to their schedule lost them further time. After toiling across the difficult lower Neumayer Glacier, the team split: three would survey from a small nearby peak and five would reconnoitre the col. However, the col team never reached their objective and, after turning back, became lost in a severe blizzard. The situation was compounded when they all fell into a large crevasse, in which they spent the next 15 hours wet and hungry. Thinking they would die if they stayed there, and fearing for the fate of the other three, they decided to make a dash for Husvik. Travelling unroped, with no axes or crampons, and in blizzard conditions, they reversed the heavily crevassed Neumayer Glacier. Often crawling on their stomachs over crevasses, and sometimes falling in, they were led by the skill and drive of Cunningham – who climbed out of one crevasse by removing his boots and bridging up the smooth ice walls in his socks – they eventually reached Husvik. To their relief the remaining three had managed to do likewise, thus avoiding an unsuitably disastrous end to a highly successful and significant period of exploration and mountain travel. Not only had they completed a survey of the island but, in this last season alone, they had also climbed over 20 summits from the Kohl-Larsen Plateau south to the Philippi Glacier.

Skip Novak

How did you first come to know of South Georgia and what inspired you to go there?

The inspiration in voyaging to South Georgia came from reading the Shackleton stories, well before it was fashionable to do so. That created the dream, which was brought closer to reality via my Whitbread Around the World yacht-racing career. Barreling through the Southern Ocean, occasionally coming close aboard to all those rugged sub-Antarctic islands was, for an amateur climber, a big draw for the future. The way forward was obvious; sailing to climb was the thing!

When did you first visit the island and what were your first impressions?

My first visit to the island was in the winter of 1988, on our way to Cape Town after my first Antarctic season onboard the newly launched expedition vessel *Pelagic*. We had the run of the island, with no tour ships, no other yachts and little or no regulations to abide by. When the weather was foul (most of the time) we spent the days rummaging through the whaling stations and shooting reindeer for the pot. I was duly impressed and humbled during an outing when we had our tent flattened and destroyed while camped underneath Mount Senderens on the Philippi Glacier.

Now that you have been there so many times, what do you like most about the island?

In spite of things having changed dramatically with regards visitor numbers on ships and yachts, the mountaineering side today is as good as it ever was in the early days. A lot of that has do with the fact that the island is so isolated, having no airstrip and therefore no easy and quick access possible. In any given year it is likely your expedition will be the only one on the island. This coupled with the fact there is no Search and Rescue facility of any kind, in the Alpine sense, gives the island the needed edge for a real adventure. When you venture into the high ground you are really left on your own, reliant on your own skills, fitness and judgement to make it back down again. And if there is a problem the drama doesn't end at the beach, as you have to sail back to Stanley to reach an ultimate safe haven.

You made the fourth ascent of Mount Paget. Was this a long held objective, or just taking an opportunity?

My ascent of Mount Paget with a strong German team was part of a *Pelagic* charter, and I was lucky enough to be invited to participate in the climb. Many, but not all of my climbing expeditions were a consequence of finding people to mount a campaign, and planning the logistics for them, which by necessity meant chartering a sailing vessel. Voila! A niche was created.

What would you describe as your most memorable experience on the island and your best climb on the island?

No doubt standing on the top of Paget on a windless sunny day, after having completed a new route, with the whole of the island stretched out below us, was my most memorable moment. But as on all summits the time aloft was fleeting. A deeper, more satisfying experience was our 2005 traverse from Larsen Harbour to Royal Bay with my three mates; Crag Jones, Julian Freeman-Atwood and Rich Howarth, South Georgia veterans all. With 16 days on the trot this adventure had all the elements and plenty of uncertainty. The first week was navigating by compass and dodgy GPS positions in a soupy whiteout, then there was the spectacular windless camp on the Spenceley Col where we failed on Mount Baume and succeeded on the unclimbed peak that became Mount Pelagic, before arriving back at the camp in the teeth of a storm. After four days in a snow cave with food and gas running low, we bolted down the Spenceley, up and through the Ross Pass with black clouds licking our heels, making the beach at Royal Bay in a single day. *Pelagic* extracted the team in heavy surf the next afternoon.

The island is a difficult place to climb and travel. Do you think there is a certain type of person who is attracted to South Georgia?

My experience having supported many climbing expeditions over the last 20 years is that the attractions for climbers, those who can afford to go, are obvious – plenty of unclimbed summits in a remote area – and this is true both for South Georgia and the Peninsula. But unless the expedition has deep experience of going remote with no back up, given the expansive nature of the terrain and the fact that the boat is an overly comfortable base camp, quite often little is accomplished!

You have also sailed and climbed a lot on the Antarctic Peninsula. How do you compare and contrast the two places, from the points of view of both sailing and climbing?

South Georgia and the Antarctic Peninsula, although apparently similar with regards sailing to climb are in fact very different. Getting to the first shelter on the Peninsula from Cape Horn is a mere 450 nautical miles, across the wind in both directions. From Stanley to the first shelter on South Georgia is 750 miles, but the return is upwind, which not only means the total trip time must be substantially longer, but the prospect of a rough sea voyage can put many people with weak stomachs right off. With regards climbing, most interesting summits on the Peninsula are within easy reach of the shore, and there is superb boutique technical climbing right from the shore on towers, and in ice and snow couloirs. By contrast any climbing on South Georgia requires more of an expedition approach with long marches in by foot or on skis to access the big mountains. Coupled with often ferocious, tent-busting weather in the Southern Ocean storm track further north,

South Georgia is considered to be a much more challenging climbing environment.

What advice would you give to those looking to sail in Antarctic waters?

Sailing to climb in Antarctic waters is not to be underestimated and the sailing side is paramount to get right for a successful campaign in the mountains. Climbers need a reliable, safe, and mobile bolt-hole to use as a base camp, with a crew that understands their needs and desires. Many climbing expeditions have failed, or never got started, due to gear failures of the vessel, or a sailing crew lacking in confidence.

You've already attempted one of the highest unclimbed peaks on the island – do you have future climbing objectives planned?

To reveal any future climbing plans for a place like South Georgia would be a risky affair with my climbing mates – but of course, we have plans!

How do you see the future of South Georgia over the next few decades, in terms of climbing and adventure activity?

The good thing about South Georgia is that the future of the island with regards climbing and adventure activities is bright, for the few who can get there. The numbers will be self-regulating due to the cost of mounting a campaign by sea, plus the high risk factor and potential complications for Search and Rescue and evacuation. Regulations and permitting have recently been reviewed and updated, and because of the very few expeditions that actually get to the island annually, I believe little will change in terms of restrictions, at least once above the beach where the wildlife is concentrated and environmental considerations come into play. One significant factor recently implemented was to set a maximum size of 15 members on any one land-based expedition to avoid the 'Everest effect' and a minimum of four members for reasons of safety and self-rescue.

From north to south, these ascents include (all figures signify heights in metres):
- Peak 625 above the Brunonia Glacier
- Peak 620 above Cheapman Bay west of the Price Glacier
- Peak 980 summit at the head of the Crean Glacier
- Peak 1059 in the Wilckens Peaks
- Peak 922 between the Lucas and Morris Glaciers
- Mount Worsley (1104 m) and another 1010 m summit above the Murray Snowfield
- Stanley Peak (1263 m)
- Peak 861 on the Esmark Glacier, west of Mount Grant (1205 m)
- Two peaks – 1730 m and 1668 m – between Smillie Peak and Mount Spaaman
- Peak 1461 and two lower peaks – 985 m and 767 m – near the Spenceley Glacier
- Peak 707 and Peak 683 on the Novosilski Glacier
- Peak 1001 on the south side of the Novosilski Glacier
- Peak 1245, north of Starbuck Peak near the Risting Glacier, above Drygalski Fjord
- Peak 839 between the Jenkins and Philippi Glaciers
The 920 m high middle peak of the Mount Sabatier (1145 m) Massif
- Peak 904 on the south side of the Philippi Glacier, northwest of Mount Normann (1238 m)

The survey journeys, done by manhauling sledges and backpacking, established two significant routes across the island: one from Cumberland West Bay up to Ice Fjord in the extreme northwest of the island, and the other from Cumberland East Bay down to Drygalski Fjord at the southeastern tip. Carse's maps would prove invaluable during the 1982 Falklands War, for they were not bettered for 50 years. This was tangible proof of excellence and achievement, clearly contradicting Carse's own image of his life.

Mount Paget is a massive feature, dominating an already impressive line of mountains on a mountainous island. Whilst not as steep and rocky as some other peaks on the island, Paget is far bigger

TYPICAL CONDITIONS on the unclimbed east ridge of Mount Paget.

– nearly 600 m higher than the second highest mountain – and bears the full brunt of the atrocious weather that buffets the island. All early attempts on Paget were from the north, necessitating crossing difficult terrain on the approach. The first team to really get to grips with the mountain was a Royal Navy team from *HMS Protector* in December 1960. Led by Lieutenant-Commander Malcolm Burley, they approached the southern coast and were put ashore by helicopter around 15 km from the mountain. Reconnaissance began immediately whilst a base camp and then Camp 1 were being established. The top of the Henningsen Glacier was reached after the second day, but the icefall above proved impassable at the top owing to a large crevasse, and they retreated to Camp 1. The next day they attempted the next icefall to the east and reached the top but were then forced to descend to Camp 1 again by incoming bad weather. The next day was clear and Burley, with Royal Marines Stevenson and Todd, re-climbed the icefall, travelling light without tents and crossed avalanche-prone slopes to reach the southwest spur. They climbed this to the top, only to realise that this western summit was considerably lower than the main summit, which was visible over 500 m away. Given the late hour and strengthening winds, they planted a Union Jack and descended from this point.

Burley returned in 1964 leading another expedition, with John Chester, Simon Down and Tom Lynch reaching Paget's main summit on December 30th – the highlight of a very successful expedition. They became the first to retrace Shackleton's route across the island from King Haakon Bay to Stromness. They also made the first high-level traverse on the island, from Gjelsted Pass down onto the Lancing Glacier, across the Christensen and Kjerulf glaciers to the head of the Christophersen Glacier, as well as crossing the high col next to Marikoppa (1840 m) to join the Kjerulf and Geikie glaciers. Then to finish, in January 1965, Back, Peacock and Thompson made the first ascent of Mount Sugartop (2325 m), one of the highest mountains on the island.

Braving the island winter in August 1974, Terry Pye and Gerry Lawson made two attempts on Mount Roots (2281 m). They attempted the northeast ridge but were turned back around 300 m from the summit by technical difficulties.

It was 16 years before Paget had its second ascent. In 1980 the yacht *Basile* departing from Saint-Malo arrived carrying a team of French climbers: Philippe Cardis, Bertrand Dubois, Denis Ducroz, Jean-Luc Guyonneau and Firmin Mollard. They climbed from the north side, making a new route up the northwest face of Paget via a slanting ramp, mostly on snow and ice. Under severe weather conditions and threatening seracs, they made several camps during breaks to gain height and find the route. The team also made the first ascent of Smillie Peak (1767 m) on the southern side of the Kohl-Larsen Plateau. They then made the Shackleton traverse of the island and traversed from Cumberland Bay through the Kohl-Larsen plateau to Possesion Bay.

A group of New Zealand climbers had a very productive summer in 1984-85 climbing around the peninsula that runs east down to the sea east of Mount Brooker (1881 m) and forming the north side of Royal Bay. The team of B. Brown, R. Brown, D. Craw, A. Knowles, P. Johnstone and I. Turnbull climbed Mount Skittle (481 m), Mount Burley (894 m), Mount Fagan (829 m), Vogel Peak (1348 m), 'Kiwi Peak' (1500 m), Finger Peak (1520 m), Coffin Top (740 m), Mount Krokisius (472 m), Mount Brocken (692 m), the Binary Peaks (691 m) and Mount Back (652 m). All but Coffin Top and Krokisius were first ascents, the former peak having been climbed by Harry Clagg and Chris Jefferies in March 1964, leaving a beer can and an onion tin on top, the latter with a note in it for the next visitors.

1988 saw one of the boldest Antarctic climbs. French climber Christian de Marliave left the deck of the yacht *Damien II* and soloed the first ascent of Nordenskjöld Peak (2354 m) the island's second-highest mountain and one of its most impressive. Its summit has not been reached since.

On December 14th 1989 *HMS Endurance* disembarked five British climbers at Cumberland East Bay, having transported them from the Falkland Islands for one of the few private Antarctic expeditions ever to receive official government assistance purely for the purpose of mountaineering.

THE 1989-90 SOUTHERN OCEAN EXPEDITION.
From left to right: Julian Freeman-Atwood, Lindsay Griffin, Crag Jones, Stephen Venables and Kees t'Hooft.

THE UNCLIMBED MOUNT SABATIER,
with the unique hole in the ridge visible on the right

This enviable opportunity meant that Brian Davison, Julian Freeman-Atwood, Lindsay Griffin, Kees t'Hooft and Stephen Venables could spend three months on the island, a good amount of time to counter the notorious weather. They needed it. After walking to Royal Bay from Cumberland East Bay, they were then hammered by severe weather while carrying loads up the Ross Glacier to Ross Pass, where on January 4th they eventually established a base camp. Here they spent 23 days, mostly ensconced in a snow cave, often for several days at a time, but made the most of the short spells of decent weather. Davison, Freeman-Atwood, Griffin and Venables all made an ascent of Vogel Peak (1348 m), immediately southeast of Ross Pass, on January 16th, winding their way through crevasses and seracs with some steeper ice sections. The group thought they were the first to do so, but only learnt much later that the New Zealand team had climbed Vogel Peak in the 1984-85 season. Five days later Freeman-Atwood and Griffin ventured north and bagged the first ascent of Mount Kling (1842 m), climbing over a 1520 m peak on the way down after ascending the southwest ridge. At the same time, Davison and Venables skied 25 km south to Mount Carse (2325 m) – the highest un-climbed mountain on the island – made the first ascent, via the northwest ridge, and skied back to the cave, all in 31 hours. They had received advice on the journey from Carse himself, during a meeting at his home before the expedition. After moving back north to a camp near Cumberland East Bay the last three weeks were spent making three attempts on the virgin Mount Roots, but to no avail.

A young Welsh climber by the name of Caradoc 'Crag' Jones served as Harbourmaster in 1989-90, the sole civilian living at the military garrison. His job was to help re-establish civilian control of shipping and fishing activity in the area after the 1982 war, but he managed to include some climbing in his time on the island. A strong German trio of Gerhard Schmatz, Hans Engl (the third person to climb Everest without bottled oxygen) and Martin Engwander arrived to attempt Paget in 1989, part of Schmatz's project to climb the highest peaks on all the world's islands. The three arrived at the island aboard the yacht *Kotick* and were joined by Harbourmaster Jones at the last minute. They reached the head of the Paget Glacier but endured terrible conditions, with strong winds and over four metres of snowfall that buried and destroyed their tents, forcing them to retreat with some difficulty. Jones returned in 1990 with Royal Marine Ian 'Jan' Mills and spent a week making the third ascent of Mount Paget, in a long single push via the 1980 French route.

In January 1991 the South African John Moss led a team to the island aboard the yacht *Diel*. Moss, H. Davis, Paul Fatti and D. Jamieson climbed Admiralty Peak (945 m), Mount Normann (1265 m) and Mount Senderens (1315 m) but failed in their attempt at a hard new route on the east side of Mount Paget. Fatti was no stranger to bad-weather climbing, having led the 1986 first ascent of the east face of San Lorenzo (3706 m) in Patagonia. The personnel from the South Georgia Garrison continued to make ascents and in May 1993 a group comprising Dez Furness, Rupert Johnson, Mark Matthews, Billy Roy, Mark Scanlon, Harry Tymon, John Welsby and Ev Williams went up the Lyell Glacier, with only Furness summiting on a small 700 m peak that they provisionally named 'Waller Peak', after a colleague killed in Northern Ireland.

Late in 1994 another Royal Marine from the garrison, Mark Stratford, joined the German team from 1989 when they returned for another attempt at Paget, this time also climbing with the skipper of *Pelagic*, Skip Novak. The team, comprising Germans Gerhard Schmatz, Hans Engl, and Martin Engwander, the Austrian Robert Schabertsberger, with Novak and Stratford, summited on January 25th, climbing a line on the north face slightly more direct but steeper than the 1980 French line. This was the fourth ascent of Mount Paget. Mark Stratford was later killed serving in Iraq.

LOOKING NORTH ACROSS THE SECOND BROTHER, DOWN TO THE KONIG GLACIER AND FORTUNA BAY.
Shackleton crossed the glacier from left to right in 1916, around where the white ice ends. Stromness is out of picture to the right. The dark pyramidal peak at centre left is Admiralty Peak.

JULIAN FREEMAN-ATWOOD AND RICHARD HAWORTH carrying loads up from Larsen Harbour.

THE SUMMIT OF THREE BROTHERS FROM MOUNT STANLEY.
The second Brother is the rocky peak on the left. The steep rocky peak on the right is the unclimbed Sørlle Buttress. Crag Jones's route of first ascent on the highest Brother takes the left skyline and traverses all the summit tops.

FOLLOWING PAGES: SKIP NOVAK'S STUNNING PANORAMA FROM THE SUMMIT OF MOUNT PAGET, LOOKING ACROSS TO THE SALVESEN RANGE. The highest peak on the left is the formidable Nordenskjöld Peak, with the pointed snowy summit of Mount Roots in front of it. The Spenceley Glacier, on the right, runs down from three large peaks on the horizon : Peak 2089, Mount Paterson and Mount Carse. Just down to the right of Mount Carse is Mount Baume.

Pat Lurcock, a Government Officer on the island, has used his time to venture into the mountains on several occasions. In September 1996 he joined Tim Carr and Royal Marine Chris Marlow in attempting Mount Sugartop, with Marlow reaching the summit. This was the second ascent of the island's fourth highest mountain, with Paget only the second of the high peaks to have had more than one ascent. In 1999 Lurcock joined the Australian trio of Grant Dixon, Angus Finney and Jay Watson to complete an obvious challenge: the first lengthwise traverse of the island. The team used their yacht *Tooluka* to deposit three caches, at St Andrews Bay, Husvik and Salisbury Plain. Starting on October 13th from Elsehul they initially took a route along the southern coast before crossing to the northern coast. They ascended the Lucas Glacier to the Shackleton Gap and the Murray Snowfield, joined the Esmark Glacier, and crossed the Kohl-Larsen Plateau, Neumayer, Geikie, Lyell and Nordenskjöld Glaciers. They then went through Ross Pass to the Spenceley, Harmer and Philippi Glaciers to finish at Larsen Harbour on November 10th, after 270 km of walking, climbing and skiing.

At the end of the 1999-2000 summer Tim Carr and Matthew Thomas climbed a challenging 1012 m peak west of the Hamberg Glacier. Yet a big mountain problem still remained. After the ascent of Mount Carse (mentioned above), Mount Roots, a 2281 m peak to the east of Mount Paget, remained the highest unclimbed mountain on the island for over a decade. It had been attempted six times by three separate expeditions – in 1974, 1990 and 1997 – and had seen some further attempts by personnel from the garrison during the mid-1990s. In January 2001 a British military team aboard a yacht landed at King Edward Point. Using a patrol boat to shuttle around into Cumberland East Bay they spent the next three days carrying loads up the Nordenskjöld Glacier to a camp beneath the north side of Roots. Will Manners and Stuart Macdonald were selected by the leader John Bilous to make the attempt via a wandering line up the north buttress and they set off on the night of the 18th. The pair climbed quickly, left to right up sustained ground, and reached the top of the buttress after only two and a half hours. Moving past impressive rime formations and mushrooms as both the sun and the wind rose, they reached the summit in clearing mist. A climbing problem of three decades had fallen in less than five hours. Yet the descent took just

as long and proved quite demanding, as they first had to downclimb the upper buttress and then traverse west onto a very crevassed glacier that led to the flat ground of their camp.

The team then split in two. One group attempted a new route on Paget without success, encountering strong winds that blew Manners horizontally in the air, anchored only by his axes. The other team skied up the Heaney Glacier, where on January 25th Macdonald, Llinos Owen, Marcus Stutt and Clive Woodman made the first ascent of a 1400 m peak at its head, which they provisionally named 'Mount MacArthur' after the British sailor Dame Ellen MacArthur. A 450 m high snow couloir led to slightly steeper mixed ground beneath the summit, with the descent the same way.

The winter of 2001 brought little snowfall, so conditions were not ideal for the first climbing team to arrive for the summer. Americans Doug Stoup, John Griber, Rick Armstrong and Hilaree Nelson aimed to climb, ski and snowboard Mount Paget, Nordenskjöld Peak and Mount Roots, which would be filmed by a two-person crew, all travelling aboard the yacht *Golden Fleece*. On November 2nd, Griber, Armstrong and Stoup attempted Nordenskjöld but the latter two turned back after climbing 1000 m of hard 55° ice. Griber continued to the summit ridge but at around only 200 m below the summit, considering the weather had deteriorated too much, he turned to snowboard down and reached the bottom only 15 minutes later. The next day the team's tents were destroyed by winds that were measured at over 70 knots, so further forays

THE YACHT *PELAGIC* SAFELY ANCHORED IN SOUTH GOERGIA.

SOUTH GEORGIA

were limited to day trips from the yacht. On November 15th, all four climbers started from the water and ascended over 1000 m up the east face of Mount Normann (1265 m) and continued to the summit via the east ridge, before descending by ski and snowboard.

Two months later, in January 2002, Crag Jones returned to the island, this time aboard the *Pelagic*, to attempt the first ascent of The Three Brothers (2040 m), a prominent triple-summited feature that runs roughly north-south above the Neumayer Glacier. The only known attempt prior to this was the 1991 South African *Diel* expedition that retreated from a high col. Jones, Skip Novak and cameraman Alun Hughes took a week to move loads across a very dry and crevassed Neumayer Glacier in late January, finally establishing a camp beneath the western col, where they then endured seven days of traditionally bad weather in a two-man tent. Eventually only Jones climbed on, reaching the col in poor conditions and heading east toward the south ridge. Finding it too difficult, he traversed poor rock to the north ridge. This gave climbing up hard ice over two false summits to the top, which is actually a ridge around 70 m long with five small peaks. He had been climbing for eight hours but, to be sure of having reached the top, he traversed all five hoar-frosted ice peaks, sometimes climbing à cheval with a huge drop on the east side. Descent was beneath the north ridge, then a traverse to the col below which he down-climbed the face, mostly on the rocks. Jones returned to camp 15 hours after leaving, having completed one of the boldest climbs yet done in this extremely serious place.

In March 2003 the Welsh glaciologist Alun Hubbard skippered his yacht *Gambo* to Grytviken for a program of climbing and science. The team onboard split into three groups: one to attempt the unclimbed east ridge of Mount Paget, a second to attempt the other unclimbed peaks, and the third to climb the smaller peaks and carry out other activities. The second group attempted Quad 5 (1695 m), Paulsen Peak (1875 m) and Marikoppa (1840 m), all without success. Their route up the Lyell Glacier was thwarted by an icefall relatively low on the route, and their second attempt up the Geikie Glacier encountered another icefall, seracs and avalanche danger. The Paget team made their way up the Nordenskjöld Glacier to the col between Paget and Mount Roots, enduring a five-day storm, dug into a crevasse, along the way. From the col at around 1800 m, Hubbard, Tim Hall and Hamish Millar set off in good weather on the 4 km long ridge on March 25th, finding it mostly straightforward despite some cornices and hard ice. Climbing and traversing steep ice to outflank a sub-peak, they regained the ridge and saw easy ground to the summit. However, the weather had turned, and realising their seriously exposed position, they retreated from 2550 m and less than 400 m short of the summit. This proved a wise decision, as their descent was quite harrowing in the phenomenal winds and whiteout that followed and they eventually staggered back to Grytviken on March 28th, sailing away a few days later.

In November 2003 a very strong Spanish team arrived on the island bound for Mount Paget, led by veteran mountaineer Jose Carlos Tamayo. The group repeated the French northwest face route, completing the fifth ascent of the mountain. Clearly the notorious weather of the region did not upset Tamayo, as he returned in 2006, this time to the Peninsula, where his team climbed to within metres of the summit of the elusive Wandel Peak on Booth Island.

In January 2005 Skip Novak, Crag Jones, Julian Freeman-Atwood and Richard Haworth were dropped at Larsen Harbour and made their way up onto the Philippi Glacier. Their target was the steep and rocky Mount Baume, which at 1912 m is the highest unclimbed *named* mountain on the island. After crossing the Novosilski Glacier they established a camp at the head of the Spenceley Glacier, beneath the east side of Baume. In a short period of good weather they attempted to climb Baume but turned back half-way up a line beside the north face, having climbed nine pitches of difficult ice and mixed ground. They did summit a smaller 1731 m peak (5680 on the old map) just to the northwest of Baume, via the north ridge, which was later officially named Mount Pelagic. After four days stormbound in an ice cave they took just one day for the long

161

CRAG JONES AND RICH HAWORTH
climbing on Mount Pelagic.

ROMOLO NOTTARIS, CARLO SPINELLI AND ANNA MATTEI
nearing the summit of Stanley Peak. The Three Brothers are in the distance to the southeast. On the right is Mount Spaaman, with its impressive and unclimbed north spur clearly visible.

descent down the Spenceley and Ross Glaciers to Royal Bay, where they were picked up by the *Pelagic* itself.

Showing the kind of admirably short memory without which nothing hard would ever get climbed, Hubbard and Hall were back aboard *Gambo* two years later for another round with the east ridge of Paget, in March 2005. But 14 days spent attempting the unclimbed ridge were not enough and they retreated once again, though not before summiting the relatively prominent 2135 m peak on the ridge that they named 'Buzen Point'. The new team was again unsuccessful in their forays onto the unclimbed Quad 5 (1695 m), Paulsen Peak (1875 m) and an attempted third ascent of Mount Spaaman, yet they did make a successful ascent of Admiralty Peak.

2007 marked the 25th anniversary of the Falklands war, so some ascents were made of peaks named after prominent figures in the conflict. The first of the four veterans' peaks fell when Skip Novak led a team of three Italian climbers – Anna Mattei, Romolo Nottaris and Carlo Spinelli – on the second ascent of Stanley Peak (1263 m), summiting on October 23rd. Later in the season a British Schools Exploring Society (BSES) group made an ascent of the 602 m high Best Peak, overlooking Fortuna Bay.

Mount Paget also received its sixth ascent in November 2007. A strong team of French alpinists arrived aboard the yacht *Ada II,* skippered by Isabelle Autissier. They planned to make a lengthwise traverse of the island, climbing along the way, but eventually did the trip in short sections, meeting the yacht at different points for supplies and repositioning. Paget was their first summit, climbed by a variant on the northwest face route on November 12th by Philippe Batoux, Emmanuel Cauchy and Lionel Daudet. Soon after they made the first ascent of Mount Sheridan (955 m), named after Major Guy Sheridan of the Royal Marines who had countersigned the Argentine surrender on April 25th 1982. Sheridan had unsuccessfully attempted the summit himself in August 1999. The French made good time, despite many difficulties traversing the glaciers on the southern side of the Allardyce Range, and also made the second ascent of Mount Worsley (1104 m), by a new route from the south along a long ridge rising out of the

THE STEEP AND UNCLIMBED SOUTHEAST FACE of Nordenskjöld Peak.

LOOKING SOUTH ACROSS THE WATERS OF KING EDWARD COVE, with the buildings at King Edward Point in the foreground. Mount Paget is at the extreme left, the prominent pyramidal peak in the centre is Mount Sugartop and right of that is the unclimbed Paulsen Peak.

Esmark Glacier. Then on November 18th they climbed a smaller peak around 950 m high known as 'Surprise Peak', by a 900 m mixed route. After finishing the traverse in only 11 travelling days, the team ended the trip with an unsuccessful attempt on Mount Sugartop.

Mills Peak, named after another South Georgia war veteran, Keith Mills, is a 627 m summit at the northern end of the Barff Peninsula and was climbed by a party from the garrison at King Edward Point in November of the same year. The 684 m Ellerbeck Peak was the last of the unclimbed veterans' peaks, when on December 8th Andrew Chase and Anjali Pande made the first ascent from a base camp near the snout of the Nordenskjöld Glacier.

The perennial pair of Crag Jones and Skip Novak got the 2009-10 season off to an early start, arriving in October to attempt Nordenskjöld Peak with Julian Freeman-Atwood. The approach took longer than they had anticipated, and a typically unforecasted change in the weather forced them back from the upper reaches of the north face. Before leaving, Jones and Novak did manage the first ascent of Mount Ashley (1145 m), an attractive peak in the northwestern section of the island. *Pelagic Australis* dropped them ashore at Salisbury Plain and early the next morning they were skinning up the Grace Glacier. After reaching a col to the west of the peak they ascended to the southeast, eventually climbing both the highest and second highest points of this small massif, before following their GPS waypoints all the way back down to the waiting yacht.

UNCLIMBED

The highest *named* mountain on the island that is unclimbed seems to be Mount Baume (1925 m), which has had only one serious attempt. That said, there are some higher *unnamed* points that remain virgin, such as the peak marked on the map as 2229 m, which is north-northwest of Mount Macklin and is steep to the south and southwest. Macklin itself is also unclimbed and, at 1900 m, is only slightly lower than Baume and probably harder, given its steep and rocky appearance from the south. Macklin and its neighbour Douglas Crag (1670 m) form a nice pair of virgin peaks, probably best visited from the Twitcher or Salomon Glaciers that drain the far southeastern end of the range. Not too far away, north of Mount Paterson, sits an unclimbed 1900 m high pyramidal snow peak, topping a ridge that rises out of the Hindle Glacier. Mount Fraser is another sub-Antarctic island climb that sweeps up from the coast, this time rising over 1500 m to a sharp summit, although it is undoubtedly easier to reach that point from the inland north.

Moving from the Salvesen Range back up to the Allardyce Range, you come to Sørlle Buttress, a steep rocky peak of around 1370 m between Spaaman and Three Brothers. The north side above Neumayer Glacier is very steep, while the south side from Christensen Glacier may be easier. Between Three Brothers and Sugartop lie four unclimbed mountains: Larssen Peak (1549 m), Marikoppa (1840 m), Mount Fagerli (1880 m) and Paulsen Peak (1875 m). Once again, they are steeper to the north and probably easier from the south, but this would require a committing journey from either coast up into the head of the Kjerulf Glacier. The South Georgia weather makes such extended journeys to unclimbed peaks an extremely serious affair, far out of all proportion to the altitude and distances involved.

AN UNCLIMBED 1247 M PEAK
seen from Camp 1 on the Shackleton Traverse.

1. Kerguelen Islands
2. Heard Island
3. Framnes Mountains
4. Marie Byrd Land
5. Peter I Island
6. Balleny Islands

OTHER AREAS

KERGUELEN ISLANDS

The 'Îles Kerguelen' is a windswept archipelago in the far south of the Indian Ocean, with only the even bleaker Heard Island between them and Antarctica. There are around 300 islands in total, but most of them are very small, with only a single main one and barely a dozen of any significant size. The only settlement is Port-aux-Français, on the main island, La Grande Terre, which is around 150 km wide and 120 km long. The islands are French sovereign territory, with up to 100 scientists and support personnel working on them, in addition to which there is also a satellite tracking station in the vicinity. The island is supplied by a French commercial shipping company, which operates the *Marion Dufresne II.*

GRAND ROSS ON KERGUELEN.
The unclimbed southwest face.

ICE CLIFFS GUARD THE MASSIVE UNCLIMBED RIDGES rising out of the sea on Peter I Island.

The main peaks are on Grande Terre, concentrated in two areas: the Rallier du Baty Peninsula in the southwest and the Gallieni Peninsula in the central section of the southern coast. Mount Ross (1849 m), the highest peak of the archipelago, is on the latter. Mount Ross is a ridge-like massif with two main summits, Grand Ross (1849 m) and Petit Ross (1721 m). Grand Ross forms the bulky centre of the ridge and rises up like a gothic castle of steep, dark rock, rimed with ice and topped by curling snow mushrooms. It is not an easy mountain. Offset to the east from the main ridge is the Pic du Cratère (1181 m), a squat tower of dark rock.

TRAVERSING THE SUMMIT RIDGE OF THE ROSS MASSIF IN 2006.

HISTORY

The islands were discovered by the French explorer and naval officer Yves Joseph de Kerguelen de Trémarec in February 1772, as part of a voyage in two ships, seeking the rumoured great southern lands. However, Kerguelen himself never actually landed on what he thought to be the Austral continent. The disastrous weather and rough seas prevented him from getting ashore and left his vessel *La Fortune* wallowing far from shore in the mist, while François

Alesno de Saint-Allouarn, captain of his expedition's second ship, *Le Gros Ventre*, launched a jolly-boat carrying his second in command Charles de Boisguehenneuc. He got ashore through dangerous waves and landed at what is known today as Gros Ventre Cove and claimed the territory for his King. Kerguelen left before knowing this, quickly making his way to Mauritius and to Brest where he was received as a new Christopher Columbus. His fantastic reports to the King (Louis XV) of a bountiful and friendly new continent that he named *La France Australe* and which he described as a southern paradise of riches, won him the rank of Captain and he was made Chevalier de Saint-Louis. Upon retrieving the jolly-boat and his men, but finding *La Fortune* gone, Saint-Allouarn had sailed on to Australia, thinking *La Fortune* had done likewise. Some months later Saint-Allouarn died and by the time *Le Gros Ventre* reached Mauritius in September 1772, the fantasies of Kerguelen had become accepted in France as fact. He was unknowingly setting a precedent for numerous future polar adventurers, in demonstrating the power of being first to the media with his story, regardless of the truth that often struggles to catch up. Unfortunately, Kerguelen's tales of riches meant he was expected to return to exploit those riches, and when the truth of the islands was revealed his luck started to run short. The failure of his second voyage, severe disputes with his officers complaining of his behaviour, the death of Louis XV and the loss of his protectors resulted in a court-martial of all the officers. A number of them were admonished and two discharged from the Navy. As a result of this, and other charges, Kerguelen was also court-martialled and spent some years in prison

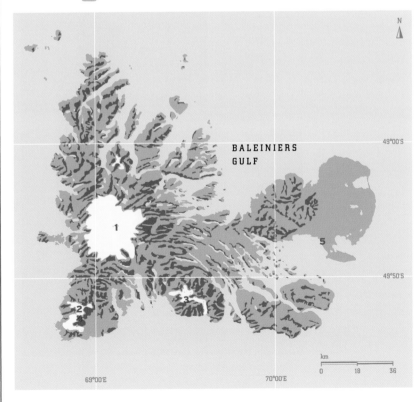

Kerguelen Islands

1. **Cook Glacier & Dome** 1049 m
2. **Mount Henri** 1262 m
3. **Grand Ross (Mount Ross)** 1849 m
4. **Mount Raymond**
5. **Port-aux-Français**

BALEINIERS GULF

Grand Ross

Base camp

THE NORTHEAST FACE OF GRAND ROSS
climbed by the French team in 2006.

before being restored to his rank, and later promoted to Commodore during the French Revolution. It was eventually Captain James Cook who named the archipelago the Kerguelen Islands. The Kerguelen archipelago was no longer of any interest to France and Britain and for more than a century afterwards it was mainly visited by sealers, only officially becoming French territory in 1893. Occasionally other vessels visited the islands, including: *HMS Challenger* in 1873, British, German, and US observers of the 1874 Transit of Venus, and a German warship in 1940. Concerns during WWII that the Nazis could use the many anchorages as a supply base caused *HMAS Australia* to visit the area in 1941 and lay mines, which remain in the waters to this day. From January 1951 onwards the main island has been occupied permanently by France and administered as part of the *Terres australes et antarctiques françaises* (TAAF).

CLIMBING ON KERGUELEN

In January 1960 Bill Tilman visited the nearby Crozet Islands, a place he would describe as '... remote and inaccessible, both desirable features'.[9] With Welshman Roger Tufft, Tilman braved the rain and mist to climb the three highest peaks on the Crozet Islands, but found them rather unimpressive after such a long journey to get there, so they headed southeast to Kerguelen. They reached Christmas Harbour in seven days, sailing aboard *Mischief,* and made plans whilst waiting on the weather. Though they knew of Grand Ross, and that it was unclimbed, they felt that it was not realistic for their team and they opted for a first crossing of the Cook Glacier, a domed icecap on the western side of the main island. They sailed around into the

[9] 'Mountains of the Crozet Islands', *Alpine Journal*, May 1961 p. 52-57.

Baleiniers Gulf, after which Tilman and Tufft took ten days food, climbed up to the icecap and crossed it to the west, sighting Grand Ross and two other high peaks on the way. They returned back across the icecap and followed up with a visit to the French base at Port-aux-Français on the shores of the Morbihan Gulf. After two days of indulging in the local cuisine, they departed Kerguelen and reached Cape Town on March 15th. Tufft had already spent several seasons in the Antarctic, on the peninsula at Hope Bay with the FIDS, where he met a young Wally Herbert. Tufft later travelled to the Arctic with Tilman for further adventures, visiting Spitsbergen and crossing Greenland on skis, and becoming one of the most accomplished, but least well known, polar men of his generation.

In February 1962 Georges Polian made the first attempt on Grand Ross, via the south face, but was unsuccessful. The mountain, and Petit Ross, saw further attempts during the 1960s and into the 1970s. Bill Tilman returned in 1965 for a reconnaissance, while his team mates were making the first ascent of Big Ben over on Heard Island, but did no real climbing. In 1975 a very strong French team arrived on the island. On January 5th, Jean Afanassieff and Patrick Cordier, two of France's leading alpinists, made the first ascent of Grand Ross by the long southeast ridge. A week later their team mates repeated the route for the second ascent, with Patrice Bodin, Denis Ducroz and Georges

Lionel Daudet

What are the mountains of Kerguelen like?

Mountains like Grand Ross, an old volcano, are unique on Earth and it looks like a strange castle: complex, with many towers... Ice structures can change very quickly with warm weather.

How was the experience of Kerguelen for you?

It is difficult to explain how great this experience was: magical, wonderful, enthusiastic... And not easy! It is a very remote place, with that extraordinary ambience of the sub-Antarctic islands.

What about the weather and snow conditions?

The weather belongs amongst the worst on Earth. Patagonia is an arid desert compared to Kerguelen, but you can have spells of good weather, with no wind. Strong winds are very common – you do not have any trees on the island – and you can experience the four seasons in just one day! It can snow a lot, but as the faces are very steep, the avalanche risk is limited. Humidity is maximal, due to the proximity of the ocean.

Do you have advice for others who might wish to climb on Kerguelen?

Climbing there is very special; you need great experience of very fast, very lightweight, but also very committing climbing. By far the most important factor is mental. Always stay motivated and patient, despite the harsh conditions. Learn to climb safely in bad weather, with strong winds. Always be on fire – try and try and try! Achieving success on technical routes on Kerguelen is much more difficult than in other places on Earth. There are some great routes that remain, but they are very dangerous. There is great ice climbing on the east and west faces, but it doesn't matter to me if they remain unclimbed!

Polian reaching the summit. Ducroz would return to the southern regions in later years to climb on the Antarctic Peninsula, putting up a particularly bold new route on the beautiful Mount William, on Anvers Island. In November 2001 France's legendary GMHM sent an equally strong team, which comprised Thierry Bolo, Antoine Cayrol, Vasken Koutoudjian, Laurent Miston, Grégory Muffat-Joly, Philippe Renard and François Savary. They repeated the 1975 route, for the third ascent of Grand Ross, with some of the team climbing a variation on the north side of the upper ridge.

November 2006 saw yet another wave of French super-alpinists arrive, aboard the supply ship *Marion Dufresne*. Emmanuel Cauchy, Lionel Daudet, Sébastien Foissac and Philippe Pellet started off with the first ascent of Pic du Cratère, taking seven hours to climb a 400m mixed route they graded TD- and named *The Ross Panther*.

They soon turned their attention to Grand Ross, where Daudet, Foissac and Pellet made the fourth ascent, by a steep new route on the northeast face that they named *Destin du Criquet*, after the veteran polar adventurer Christian 'Criquet' de Marliave. Typically poor weather and sickness becalmed the team over the following days, and an attempt on Petit Ross was foiled only 50m from the summit. With time running out, on December 6th Daudet and Cauchy chanced their luck against a poor forecast and set off for the main object of the expedition: a grand traverse of the massif, over both Grand and Petit Ross. The return journey took around 30 hours and was named *Traversée de la Lune*, graded ED+. The whole team then left their base camp in the crater and spent four days walking back to Port-aux-Français, from where they departed.

THE MASSIVE VOLCANO OF BIG BEN rises out of the sea on Heard Island.

HEARD ISLAND

Heard Island is dominated by a massive, currently active, volcano named Big Ben, which is certainly a contender for the world's most isolated mountain. Stranded far out in the Southern Ocean, 4350 km southwest of Western Australia, 4850 km southeast of South Africa and 1650 km north of the Antarctic coast, the mountain is difficult to reach and far from easy to climb. Though the slopes leading to the highest summit, Mawson Peak (2745 m), are neither steep nor difficult, the massif is heavily glaciated, crevassed, and known for its terrible weather, a function of its position in the path of the 'Furious Fifties' and south of the Antarctic Convergence. Big Ben's relatively steep rise above the surface of the ocean and the extensive ice cover also affect the island's climate, and the summit is often shrouded in fog and cloud.

Big Ben is only a mildly active volcano, but eruptions have been witnessed at various times, most recently in the 2004-05 summer. The main mass of the island is roughly circular, around 20 km across, with the narrow Laurens Peninsula extending to the northwest and a long spit to the southeast. Heard Island is approximately 70% covered by glacial ice, with some of the glaciers coming down to the sea. However, the ice mass has been rapidly shrinking in recent times, with some glaciers retreating by around 2 m per year. The Laurens Peninsula, which is also rapidly losing ice cover, has two peaks, Mount Olsen and Mount Dixon (706 m), and the latter is the summit of a second smaller inactive volcano, distinct from Big Ben.

Climbers trying to gain access to Big Ben are confronted by the compromise between the best place to land and the best route to climb. The western side of the island bears the brunt of the Furious Fifties, so the eastern side is often less windy, making routes on that side better for camping and climbing. However, the best place to get ashore is at Atlas Cove, which is on the western side of the island. Hence, for the best chance of success in both landing and climbing, aspiring climbers probably need to land at Atlas Cove and then traverse to the east-

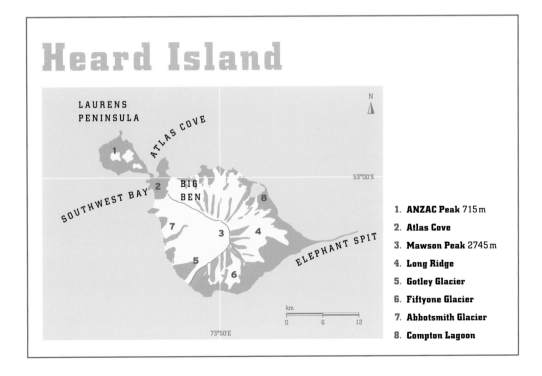

1. **ANZAC Peak** 715 m
2. **Atlas Cove**
3. **Mawson Peak** 2745 m
4. **Long Ridge**
5. **Gotley Glacier**
6. **Fiftyone Glacier**
7. **Abbotsmith Glacier**
8. **Compton Lagoon**

ern side of the island, necessitating the crossing of glaciers, ridges and other terrain, usually done in bad weather. Two of the three successful ascents to date have required such traverses. Given the generally moderate angle and non-technical nature of the climbing on Big Ben, the greatest challenge by far to any potential summiters is one of access and actually getting on the route!

HISTORY & MANAGEMENT

The first recorded landing on Heard Island was in 1855, by Erasmus Rogers aboard *Corinthian*, although the island had been sighted two years before that by John Heard aboard *Oriental*, in November 1853. The island was formally annexed by Britain in 1907 and sovereignty was transferred to Australia in 1947. From 1947 to 1955 the Australian National Antarctic Research Expedition (ANARE) operated a station near Atlas Cove. During this time expeditioners explored the island, surveying the topography but also conducting various other kinds of scientific research, both terrestrial and marine. This period also served as a preparation for later Australian Antarctic expeditions, with personnel training dog teams and developing the skills and experience that would enable safe and successful operations on the Antarctic continent in future years. Since 1955 the island has seen occasional summer visits, one winter stay by a team from the United States, sporadic visits by tourist ships and other vessels, and only five known climbing expeditions. The first complete topographic map of the island was not published until 1964.

HIGH ON MAWSON PEAK, during the third ascent.

Unlike most of the Antarctic, Heard Island is sovereign Australian territory, just as South Georgia is sovereign British territory and Kerguelen French. Therefore all legislation governing visitors to Australia also applies to anyone visiting Heard Island. It also means that Mawson Peak is the highest peak on Australia's sovereign territory, and it is often referred to as 'Australia's highest mountain'. The Transantarctic peak of Mount McClintock (3492 m) is the highest mountain in territories claimed by Australia, but such Antarctic territorial claims that divide the Antarctic mainland are not formally recognised by most nations, and remain in abeyance under the 1959 Antarctic Treaty. The highest surface in Australia's claimed territory is actually the rather indeterminate 'summit' of Dome Argus, an immense ice plateau reaching an altitude of approximately 4030 m near the centre of East Antarctica.

The Australian government administers Heard Island, through the Australian Antarctic Division (AAD), which operates the Heard Island Management Plan. All visitors must obtain a permit from the AAD. There are stringent criteria that must be satisfied regarding environmental impact, particularly for the import of materials and associated waste removal. Expeditions are required to produce evidence that they have sufficient safety measures for operating safely on the island, including provision for rescue, and evidence of appropriate insurance. Under the Management Plan a maximum of only 60 persons are allowed on the island at any one time, more a consideration for visiting cruise ships than climbing expeditions. Unlike another of Australia's sub-Antarctic islands, Macquarie Island, Heard Island has not had problems with introduced species. To preserve this situation, rigorous quarantine procedures must be followed before going ashore.

Cooperative surveillance policies between the Australian and French governments mean that vessels from the defence forces from both nations operate in the area. They detect any illegal activity, enforce fishing regulations and sometimes visit the island, occasionally going ashore. Like many of the remote islands, Heard Island is a prized base for ham radio (DX) operators. One such group of enthusiasts set up a base camp in 1997, from which they made 80,673 contacts in 17 days.

PRIVATE CLIMBING EXPEDITIONS

The first known attempt on Big Ben was in the summer of 1963-64 by an Australian team that had arrived aboard the supply ship *Nella Dan*. Led by Graham Budd, the expedition spent six weeks on the island but could not reach the summit of Mawson Peak. One member, Warwick Deacock, would return. The legendary mountain explorer Bill Tilman had wanted to climb Big Ben as early as the summer of 1959-60. During that time he discovered that Heard Island had no good anchorage for a boat such as *Mischief*, so he was forced to sail on and eventually spent time that summer at Kerguelen and the Îles Crozet.

1965 – FIRST ASCENT OF BIG BEN

After the first attempt, noted above, Deacock returned with Colin Putt and Philip Temple aboard *Patanela,* skippered by Bill Tilman. They formed the Southern Indian Ocean Expedition. In attempting to get ashore their small boat capsized three times, leading them to name their eventual arrival point as 'Capsize Beach'. Putt later claimed that it was the first mountain ascent to begin *below* sea level. As Tilman had discovered some years earlier, there was no safe anchorage for *Patanela*, so he took her back to Kerguelen to wait out the climbing. The team's route was from the southeast, travelling 11 km from 'Capsize Beach', over South Barrier and across the Fiftyone Glacier. Eventually they made a 12-hour push to the summit on the January 25th. Before leaving the island the team finished some surveying and other scientific work.

Putt would eventually return for another Antarctic ascent, as engineer on the *Allen & Vi Thistlethwayte,* the vessel that carried the team for the 1988 first ascent of Mount Minto, in the northern Transantarctics. Temple had already made the 1962 first ascent of Carstenz Pyramid in New Guinea, in what is now Indonesian West Papua, with the famous Austrian climber Heinrich Harrer, and would go on to be a chronicler of mountaineering in New Zealand and the Antarctic.

1983 – SUCCESS & FAILURE

Two expeditions sailed to Heard Island in 1983, both with the intention of climbing Big Ben. On the maxi-yacht *Anaconda II* was the Australian team of Bill Blunt, Jonathan Chester, Pauline English, Martin Hendy, Meg Thornton and Ross Vining. The team climbed a new route on the mountain via Long Ridge to the northeast. Four years later Chester, clearly undeterred by Southern Ocean sailing, joined Colin Putt in journeying to Mount Minto.

The other team, aboard the *Cheynes II,* planned various activities on the island, such as scientific observations and amateur radio transmissions, and a small Austrian contingent amongst them were certainly aiming to climb Big Ben. In this they were unsuccessful, attempting to climb from the northwest. Allegedly relations between the two teams were not good, but there was some cooperation later, when *Cheynes II* needed to be towed by the Australian Navy for the last section to return to Fremantle harbour.

2000 – THE AUSTRALIAN ARMY EXPEDITION

In the first weeks of the new millennium the Australian climbers Robb Clifton, Tim Curtis, Stuart Davies and Matt Rogerson made the third ascent of Mawson Peak. The team flew to Mauritius and on November 20th boarded an Australian fishing ship, *Southern Champion*, on which they were soon put to work processing fish. The team was landed at Atlas Cove at

dawn on the January 1st 2000. They established a base camp here, before setting an advanced base camp 300 m higher, near Walsh Bluff. On January 8th a further camp was placed around 1950 m, but bad weather forced them back down to 1450 m where they camped on the Abbot-smith Glacier. It took another two days to get back up to their Camp 2 at 1950 m, due to rain and very soggy conditions on the glacier, including collapsing snow bridges. After climbing somewhat higher, a stormy night was spent in a disintegrating tent before the weather forced them back to Camp 2.

The next day was clear, though cold and windy, and the climbers reached the summit around 8.30 am. On top they found a vent spewing sulphurous gasses and steam, strong enough to require them to cover their faces and hasten their descent. They went back to base camp in one push, reaching it that afternoon. In the remaining time they moved over to the Laurens Penin-sula, where they climbed Mount Andree, made a traverse of Mount Olsen and also climbed ANZAC Peak. The team left the island aboard *Southern Champion* on January 16th. Big Ben has not been visited since.

LOOKING NORTH TO MOUNT PARSONS FROM FANG PEAK

in the northern David Range, Framnes Mountains.

GEOFF BENNETT AND FRÉDÉRIQUE OLIVIER
climbing on Rumdoodle Peak in the Masson Range.

CLIMBERS ON THE GOLDSWORTHY RIDGE
on Mount Henderson.

FRAMNES MOUNTAINS

The Framnes Mountains are an attractive collection of rocky peaks and massifs inland from the Australian station Mawson, on the coast of Mac Robertson Land. Though neither numerous nor high, these granitic peaks have been climbed countless times by ANARE personnel for recreation and training, and so by Antarctic standards have acquired a proportionally high number of different routes, some of them relatively technical.

HISTORY

The Framnes Mountains were discovered and named in 1930-31 by Douglas Mawson, from offshore, then photographed and mapped by Christensen's 1936-37 Norwegian expedition. The first visits to the mountains were made while scouting a location to establish Mawson station in 1954. Many of these journeys were led by Phillip Law, the Director of ANARE from 1949-1966, who would become the leading figure in Australia's Antarctic activity during the second half of the 20th century. However many of the first actual summit climbs were done by parties led by John Béchervaise, a schoolteacher and active climber back in Australia, who had a profound influence on the early years of the Australian outdoor community. Before coming to the Framnes Mountains, Béchervaise had been Station Leader on Heard Island, where he unsuccessfully attempted the first ascent of Mawson Peak (2745 m) on Big Ben.

Since those early days, generations of ANARE personnel have climbed on the various peaks of the Framnes Mountains, with occasional visits further inland to the bigger Prince Charles Mountains, where much less climbing has been done. As with the BAS station Rothera on the Antarctic Peninsula, the inhabitants of Mawson have produced a basic climbing guide to the popular peaks nearby. This is available to anyone working from the station and given the negligible chances of any non-government people visiting these peaks, there is no need to reproduce such details here. Mike Woolridge started the current guide in 1994, based on an earlier collection of notes by various Field Training Officers and other personnel, but particularly Warwick Williams, who was quite a prolific climber in these peaks in the 1980s. The guide was updated in 2005 and more images were recently added.

THE MOUNTAINS

The Framnes Mountains are comprised of four smaller ranges: the Mount Henderson, Casey, Masson and David ranges.

Mount Henderson (970 m) provides the closest climbing to Mawson station, with the attractive skyline visible from the station's lounge, just 10 km away. Henderson was first climbed by Béchervaise, Hall, Law and Shaw in February 1955. The entire ridgeline is known as Goldsworthy Ridge and the north-south traverse is considered the best climbing trip in the entire Framnes Mountains. A somewhat easier south-north traverse was soloed by Warwick Williams in January 1986.

The Masson Range is in three parts – the northern, central and southern sectors – but most of the climbing has been in the northern section, around the main peaks of Rumdoodle (900 m) and Mount Ward (1030 m). Rumdoodle was first climbed by Bill Bewsher and Syd Kirkby in March 1956 and has become a relatively popular climb, despite it being more technical than most of the other Framnes summits. Most ascents are by the south face, a three-pitch traverse, for which a rope and some basic climbing skills are needed. Mount Ward is the southern culmination of a long, rocky ridge rising from the north and was another summit first climbed by a Béchervaise team, in January 1956. The ridge provides a good traverse and fine views, with a steep western face and room for more climbing.

The Northern David Range has five main peaks from north to south: Mount Parsons (1120 m), Fang Peak (1005 m), Mount Elliot (1210 m), Mount Lawrence (1120 m) and Mount Coates (1180 m). Mount Parsons is a prominent rocky peak with a steep west face and was first climbed in the busy summer of 1956 by another John Béchervaise party. The normal route is a scree slope on the southern side, reached from a col with Fang Peak. Fang Peak itself is a slightly harder climb, usually requiring a team to rope up and place protection as they reach the summit block after some ridge travel and traversing from the south around to the north. Mount Elliot is the highest peak in the David Range, with the normal route coming from the north, up easy slabs to a summit chimney.

MARIE BYRD LAND

Marie Byrd Land is a vast ice plateau in West Antarctica, with few mountains of interest to modern climbers. There are several high, mainly extinct, volcanos whose summits rise gently above the plateau, the most notable being Mount Sidley (4285 m), in the Executive Committee Range. In addition to being the highest peak in Marie Byrd Land, Mount Sidley also has an interesting place in the history of Antarctic mountaineering. Aircrew on the early flights of the US Operation Highjump often sighted the mountain and believed it was the highest on the continent, naming it 'Vinson', and a nearby peak 'Nimitz'. They did not realise that they were looking at Mount Sidley, which had already been sighted and named from the air by Admiral Byrd in November 1934. The first party to reach the area by land did so in the 1958-59 season, and included Bill Chapman, who did much of the early mapping of Antarctica's high mountains, and George Doumani. The team drove their tracked vehicles quite high on one particular mountain and Doumani, with the Scot John Pirrit, climbed up even higher. Although they did not attain the highest point, Pirrit reached a lower peak and later they both climbed some other high points in the area. Based on surveying they did at the time, Chapman calculated that they were definitely on Mount Sidley, and at the alleged location of 'Vinson' and 'Nimitz' they could see only wide-open space. Chapman later proved that the early maps had misplaced the entire Executive Committee Range, showing them around 60 km further west than their true location, which no doubt added to the early confusion surrounding these mountains.

On one of their later climbs, Doumani looked straight into the crater wall that forms the south side of the summit of Mount Sidley and recognised it as the same feature that he had seen during a flight some time before, when aircrew pointed it out to him, identifying it as 'Mount Vinson'. Doumani and Pirrit were the first people to climb high in these mountains, and though the climbing itself was not at all difficult, it did solve an important part of the unfolding enigma that was Antarctica's highest mountain. They now knew they were on Mount Sidley. They also knew that the aircrews had been looking at Mount Sidley. If there was a high peak in this part of Antarctica that might be named 'Vinson', this was not it.

The previous summer, in 1957-58, Charlie Bentley had led a long tractor traverse that sighted the Sentinel Range, but it was not realised at that time just how high these peaks were. Survey-ing and aerial photography over the next few years would eventually show that the Sentinel Range, and not Marie Byrd Land, was home to Antarctica's highest mountain. The first recorded climb to the highest point of Mount Sidley was in January 1990, by New Zealander Bill Atkin-son, working in support of a scientific team in the area. Atkinson also went to the summit of what is now Doumani Peak (2695 m), making most of the ascent by snowmobile. This summit is probably the same one that George Doumani himself climbed in February 1959, enabling him to see and recognise Mount Sidley.

THE UNCLIMBED FEATURE OF THE BILLBOARD, on Mount Rea in the Sarnoff Mountains.

^ **MIKE ROBERTS**
on the summit ridge of Mount Rea, Sarnoff Mountains.

› **AN AERIAL VIEW FROM THE WEST OF MOUNT SIDLEY,** the highest peak in Marie Byrd Land.

» **MOUNT BERLIN (3498 M) FROM THE WEST.**
The dark rock feature right of centre is
Merrem Peak (3000 m) and behind that is
the main summit of Mount Berlin.
The small dark rock feature at far left is Mefford Knoll.

Mount Berlin (3498 m) is one of the more impressive volcanic giants, an elongated massif rising over 1500 m out of the surface of the plateau, to a prominent summit crater. The first ascent of Mount Berlin was by the Americans Harold Gilmour, Charles Passel, Lawrence Warner and Loran Wells, in December 1940. Interestingly, this was the only Antarctic peak above 3000 m to be climbed in the 46 years between the second ascent of Mount Erebus (2745 m) in December 1912 and the New Zealanders Marsh and Miller's first ascent, in January 1958, of Claydon Peak (3040 m), deep in the Transantarctics. Most of the Marie Byrd Land volcanos have been the focus of study by vulcanologists, many of whom have climbed on, or to the top of, the bigger peaks such as Mount Takahe (3400 m), Toney Mountain (3595 m), Mount Waesche (3292 m) and Mount Murphy (2705 m). The latter of these was climbed at least twice in the early 1990s by international scientific teams. Another of the region's significant peaks is Mount Siple, the 3110 m high-point of Siple Island, just off the coast north of the Executive Committee Range. The mountain rises directly from the icy Amundsen Sea to the domed summit, making it one of the highest seaside peaks in the world, and it has active fumaroles near its summit.

A notable exception to the gentle volcanic domes of the region is the Sarnoff Mountains of the Ford Ranges, toward the western end of Marie Byrd Land, around 200 km in from the coast of the Ross Sea. The Ford Ranges were first visited in December 1940, when a couple of minor summits were reached, and an American flag and papers claiming the area for the USA placed on their summits. The Sarnoffs are actually a peninsula that separates the Arthur Glacier to the north from the Boyd Glacier to the south, and extends west-northwest into the Ross Sea. The southern side of the Sarnoffs features the steepest and smoothest rock walls in all of West Antarctica. The most famous feature here is The Billboard, a truncated tower sitting out to the west of the main bulk of Mount Rea, with steep rock walls rising over 300 m above the ice. The southern face of Mount Rea itself is also a broad sweep of sheer rock that would seem to be an obvious target for climbers, though the rock is reported to be of poor quality, at least on nearby features.

Mount Rea has been climbed, as have numerous other minor summits in the area, but no technical climbing has been done here and, as of 2010, all the rock walls remain unclimbed. In the 40 km length of the Sarnoffs there are other smaller faces, slabs and ridges that might provide worthwhile technical climbing, but the main problem with this area is access. Flying here would be prohibitively expensive given the nature of the peaks, and the combination of notoriously difficult sea-ice conditions off the coast, followed by a long sled journey inland, will probably deter all but the most adventurous of modern climbers.

REMOTE ANTARCTIC ISLANDS

In addition to the bigger islands discussed in the Antarctic Peninsula chapter, the Antarctic region holds a small number of smaller and more remote glaciated islands that would provide challenging expeditions for climbers so inclined. Two are included here as examples.

PETER I ISLAND

Peter I Island was the first land seen south of the Antarctic Convergence, when it was sighted in January 1821 by Bellingshausen, who named it for the Russian Czar, Peter the Great. A week later he sighted the mountains of Alexander Island. Around 400 km off the Eights Coast of Ellsworth Land, the island is heavily glaciated, with steep sides making access difficult and in recent times it has usually been reached by helicopter. The highest point is Lars Christensen Peak (1775 m), which has never been climbed but has been the objective of a few expeditions. The best attempt to date was in March 2010, when the French trio of Mathieu Cortial, Lionel Daudet and Patrick Wagnon climbed 500 m up the eastern face of the island, eventually repelled after 10 hours by many large crevasses and poor weather. Their yacht *Ada II*, skippered by Isabelle Autissier, had trouble finding a safe place to anchor and it was this that determined from which direction they climbed.

A RARE CLEAR DAY AT PETER I ISLAND. The highest point visible is the unclimbed summit of Lars Christensen Peak.

THE UNCLIMBED BROWN PEAK,
the highest point of Sturge Island, Balleny Islands.

THE BALLENY ISLANDS

The Balleny Islands lie 250km off the coast of north Victoria Land, and close enough to the mainland to be beset by the winter pack ice, accumulating the 'Balleny Pack' in most summers. Sturge Island is the largest and most southerly of the group of five, which was first sighted by Charles Wilkes in 1840. The highest point is Brown Peak (1524m), the summit of a great dome guarded on most sides by cliffs of ice and rock that are both high and steep. A team primarily made up of New Zealanders visited Sturge Island in 1964, landing by helicopter, from *USNS Glacier*. The only known access directly from the sea were brief landings by the adventurous crew of the yacht *Ice Bird* in 1978 and a tourist ship, *Kapitan Khlebnikov*, in 1993. The first ascent of Brown Peak would provide an interesting objective to any climbing team intrepid enough to sail to the big peaks of the Admiralty Mountains.

The 4000 m Mountains
& Named Sub-Peaks of Antarctica

The following list contains the officially-named mountains on the Antarctic mainland with an altitude greater than 4000 m. Altitudes for these peaks were obtained from a combination of Geographic Names of the Antarctic, the relevant USGS 1:250,000 maps and Omega Foundation surveys from 2002 to 2008. There are a number of additional summits that have an altitude greater than 4000 m but no official name. Only some of these are indicated by a spot height on maps – many are not. Owing to inaccurate measurement, a number of peaks that are shown on maps with altitudes of around 3900 m may actually be over 4000 m and vice versa.

4892 m   **Mount Vinson**, Sentinel Range

    4865 m   **Sublime Peak**, Sentinel Range

    4841 m   **Clinch Peak**, Sentinel Range

    4822 m   **Corbet Peak**, Sentinel Range

    4790 m   **Silverstein Peak**, Sentinel Range

    4743 m   **Schoening Peak**, Sentinel Range

    4729 m   **Hollister Peak**, Sentinel Range

    4677 m   **Wahlstrom Peak**, Sentinel Range

    4634 m   **Fukushima Peak**, Sentinel Range

    4551 m   **Marts Peak**, Sentinel Range

    4520 m   **Branscomb Peak**, Sentinel Range

4852 m   **Mount Tyree**, Sentinel Range

4660 m   **Mount Shinn**, Sentinel Range

4573 m   **Mount Gardner**, Sentinel Range

4528 m   **Mount Kirkpatrick**, Queen Alexandra Range

4508 m   **Mount Epperly**, Sentinel Range
(true rock summit 4m higher?)

c.4500 m **Peak 4500**, Sentinel Range,
(aka 'Peak of Kindness', 'Peak Loretan')

4480 m   **Mount Elizabeth**, Queen Alexandra Range
(unclimbed)

4477 m   **Mount Rutford**, Sentinel Range

    4401 m   **Rada Peak**, Sentinel Range

    c.4400 m **Bugueño Pinnacle**, Sentinel Range

4368 m   **Mount Craddock**, Sentinel Range

4350 m   **Mount Markham**, Queen Elizabeth Range

4303 m   **Mount Bell**, Queen Alexandra Range
(unclimbed)

4297 m   **Mount Mackellar**, Queen Alexandra Range
(unclimbed)

4285 m   **Mount Sidley**, Executive Committee Range

4230 m   **Mount Kaplan**, Hughes Range
(unclimbed)

4165 m   **Mount Minto**, Admiralty Mountains

4160 m   **Mount Miller**, Holland Range (unclimbed)

4144 m   **Mount Anderson**, Sentinel Range

4137 m   **Mount Bentley**, Sentinel Range

4120 m   **Mount Dickerson**, Queen Alexandra Range
(unclimbed)

4111 m   **Peak 4111**, Sentinel Range

4085 m   **Flat Top**, Commonwealth Range (unclimbed)

4085 m   **Mount Ostenso**, Sentinel Range

4085 m   **Mount Wade**, Prince Olav Mountains (unclimbed)

4080 m   **Mount Fisher**, Prince Olav Mountains (unclimbed)

4074 m   **Mount Giovinetto**, Sentinel Range

4070 m   **Mount Fridtjof Nansen**, Herbert Range
(southernmost 4000er)

4070 m   **Centennial Peak**, Prince Olav Mountains
(unclimbed)

4059 m   **Long Gables**, Sentinel Range

4050 m   **Mount Shear**, Sentinel Range

c.4050 m **Peak 4050**, Sentinel Range
(aka 'Sisu Peak')

4025 m   **Mount Lister,** Royal Society Range

4025 m   **Mount Wexler,** Hughes Range
(unclimbed)

4020 m   **Decennial Peak**, Queen Alexandra Range
(unclimbed)

4010 m   **Mount Adam**, Admiralty Mountains
(northernmost 4000er)

4000 m   **Mount Korsch,** Queen Elizabeth Range

Antarctic Feature Names

Antarctic mountains and other geographical features are generally named after a person who has some established connection to the area, either through work in the area itself or through scientific achievement in a related field. Older names sometimes refer to the visual appearance of the feature, as they originated from the explorers and scientists who first visited the areas, and such names often aid in navigation and chronicling an area's history. Most modern names originate from the scientific or support personnel from national Antarctic programs, although occasionally exceptions are made.

The naming of features after sponsors or other commercial supporters occurred sporadically in the earlier years of Antarctic exploration, but this has largely ceased in the modern era, reflecting the predominantly scientific nature of Antarctic activity. Such commercial naming is now considered inappropriate, and such suggestions are unlikely to gain acceptance as official names. Some areas or features may seem to have two or more names, depending on the map or publication in view. This may be due to historical errors with regard to unwittingly assigning names to previously named features, or deliberately re-naming features for political purposes - the latter is a problem in some areas of the Antarctic Peninsula. A gazetteer of Antarctic place-names is now managed by the Australian Antarctic Division on behalf of the Scientific Committee on Antarctic Research (SCAR) and may be searched online. It is a comprehensive collection of more than 36,000 names for more than 18,000 features that have been approved and submitted by 31 nations over the last two decades. Several countries also publish gazetteers of Antarctic place-names.

Recently in some locations - most notably in the South Shetland Islands - there has been a proliferation of new names for relatively minor features, with the political intention of demonstrating national presence in the area. Some names refer to people or places of the nation in question that have no connection with Antarctica. A multitude of geographically irrelevant names has been imposed on relatively small areas, even though the protagonists have negligible history in the area and undertake minimal activity there. Whilst generally considered undesirable, such overzealous naming continues due to its promulgation by recognised national Antarctic place-name committees, whose scientific communities are members of SCAR. However, though such politically motivated naming may lie within the letter of the SCAR recommended guidelines, it is very much against the spirit of Antarctic science and cooperation. This crass nationalism reflects poorly upon the protagonists, generates ill will in the Antarctic community and, paradoxically, only serves to emphasise their lack of genuine scientific and operational activity in the Antarctic region.

Index

People's names are listed in a separate index on page 188.

4111, Peak, 28, 182

Abbotsmith Glacier, 173, 176
Ada II (yacht), 58, 65, 66, 70, 75, 76, 86, 162, 180
Adam, Mount, 138, 140, 142, 145, 182
Adare, Cape, 140
Adelaide Island, 81, 85, 86, 87, 89, 92
Admiralty Bay, 53
Admiralty Mountains, 127, 136, 139, 140, 142, 145, 181, 182
Admiralty Peak, 148, 150, 156, 162
Adventure Network International (ANI), 21, 22, 23, 24, 32, 43, 45, 57, 85, 110, 114, 141,
Akademik Federov (icebreaker), 104
Akademik Shuleykin (cruise ship), 62
Alexander Island, 7, 49, 72, 81, 85, 87, 89, 94, 96, 180
Alf, Mount, 38
Allardyce Range, 147, 162, 164
Allen & Vi Thistlethwayte (yacht), 139, 141, 175
Allen, Mount, 12, 38
Alpine Journal, 92, 170
American Alpine Club, 15
Amundsen Sea, 179
Anaconda II (yacht), 175
Analogue, Mount, 144
Andersnuten Massif, 105, 120
Anderson Massif (Sentinel Range), 29, 42
Anderson Massif (Heritage Range), 45
Anderson, Mount, 8, 11, 12, 14, 29, 30, 34, 39, 182, 191
Andree, Mount, 176
Andvord Bay, 62, 63, 64
Antarctic (ship), 47, 147
Antarctic Convergence, 173, 180
Antarctic Logistics and Expeditions (ALE), 32, 43, 45, 57, 94, 95, 120, 143
Antarctic Logistics Centre International (ALCI), 116, 118, 119, 120, 121, 122
Antarctic Treaty, 17, 19, 56, 141, 174
Antarctica, East, 99, 127, 174
Antarctica, West, 13, 127, 178, 179
Anvers Island, 60, 64-68, 172
ANZAC Peak, 173, 176
Arctowski Peninsula, 60, 62
Ariel, Mount, 95
Arronax, Mount, 85, 86
Arrowsmith Peninsula, 50, 83, 85
Arthur Glacier, 179
Ashley, Mount, 164
Astor, Mount, 132, 141, 145
Asturias Peak, 24, 25, 30
Atkinson, Mount, 34
Atlas Cove, 173-175
Aurora Expeditions, 64
Auster Pass, 136
Australian National Antarctic Research Expedition (ANARE), 174, 177
Avery Plateau, 83
Axel Heiberg Glacier, 136, 138, 139

Back, Mount, 154
Bagshawe, Mount, 50, 94, 96
Balch, Mount, 80, 81
Baleiniers Gulf, 171
Balleny Islands, 167, 181
Barff Peninsula, 164
Barnum Peak, 136
Barré, Mount, 89, 92
Bartok Glacier, 95
Base T, 87-90, 92
Basile (yacht), 77, 154
Bastien Range, 7
Batterbee Mountains, 93, 96
Baume, Mount, 148, 152, 157, 161, 164
Bautaen, 114
Beardmore Glacier, 127, 128, 143, 145
Bearskin, Mount, 12, 24, 27
Beascochea Bay, 60, 82
Beaufoy Ridge, 51
Behrendt Mountains, 97
Beitzel Peak, 42, 45
Belgica (ship), 47, 65, 66, 72
Belgica Glacier, 82
Belgica Mountains, 102
Bellingshausen expedition, 93, 180
Bender Glacier, 7, 23, 33, 34
Bentley, Mount, 12, 29, 30, 182
Berlin, Mount, 179
Best Peak, 162
Betty, Mount, 133, 141
Big Ben, 140, 171, 173-177
Bigo, Mount, 50, 81, 83
Billboard, The, 178, 179
Billie Peak, 67
Binary Peaks, 154
Bingham Peak, 44
Blackburn, Mount, 130-132
Blaiklock Island, 85
Blanchard Ridge, 79
Blanchard Point, 79
Blue-1, 103, 110, 111, 114, 116
Bone Bay, 59
Booth Island, 60, 61, 73, 75, 76, 78, 161
Borg Massif, 99
Bouvetøya, 101, 102
Bouvier, Mount, 89
Bouvier-Reeves group, 87
Bowles, Mount, 50, 54, 55
Boyce Ridge, 27, 37
Boyd Glacier, 179
Brabant Island, 52, 62, 63, 64-66
Branscomb Glacier, 16, 20, 21, 23, 24, 25, 27, 39
Branscomb Peak, 20, 23, 25, 182
Bransfield House, 72
Brattnipane Massif, 104
Breccia Crags, 51
Brialmont Cove, 59, 61
Britannia, Mount, 62
British Antarctic Survey (BAS), 44, 48, 49, 54, 57, 78-80, 82-83, 85, 87-90, 94, 95, 97, 99, 147, 151, 177
British Antarctic Territory, 51

British Graham Land Expedition (BGLE), 47, 87, 89, 90, 95, 147
British Joint Services Expedition (BJSE) 1976-77, 52
British Joint Services Expedition (BJSE) 1984-85, 64-65
British Schools Exploring Society (BSES), 162
Brocken, Mount, 154
Brooker, Mount, 148, 150, 154
Brown Peak, 181
Bruce Plateau, 83
Brunonia Glacier, 153
Brunow Bay, 54
Bugueño Pinnacle, 182
Bull Ridge, 66, 67
Burley, Mount, 154
Bursik, Mount, 42, 43, 44
Bussey Glacier, 79, 81
Buzen Point, 162
Byrd Station, 14, 16
Byrd Peak, 114

Cadbury, Mount, 93
Calais, Mount, 50, 94
Calley Glacier, 59
Camp Gould, 43
Cap Gemini, 114
Cape Renard Tower, 69, 72, 73, 75
Cape Town, 102, 104, 114, 116, 122, 145, 152, 171
Cape Tuxen, 80, 81
Capsize Beach, 175
Carasole Peak, 114
Carse, Mount, 148, 149, 155, 157
Carstenz Pyramid, 21, 175
Casey, Mount, 177
Castle Peak, 83
Catherine James, Mount, 57
Catwalk, The, 59
Celsus Peak, 65
Chaigneau Peak, 80
Channel Glacier, 68
Charity, Mount, 50, 95-96
Charlotte Bay, 59, 60
Chavez Island, 78, 80, 83
Cheapman Bay, 153
Cheynes II (yacht), 175
Chilean Air Force (FACH), 52
Christchurch, New Zealand, 16
Christensen Glacier, 164
Christensen Nunatak, 47
Christi, Mount, 58
Christmas Harbour, 170
Christophersen Glacier, 148, 154
Citadel Bastion, 95
Clarence Island, 52
Clarke Glacier, 96
Clarke, Mount, 136
Claydon Peak, 179
Cléry Peak, 75
Climbers' Club, 90-91
Coal Nunatak, 95

Coates, Mount, 178
Coffin Top, 154
Colbert Mountains, 50, 95
Colbert, Mount, 132
Collins Bay, 82
Commonwealth Trans-Antarctic Expedition 1955-58, 94
Commonwealth Trans-Antarctic Expedition 1957-58, 133, 150
Conradfjella, 99, 108, 120
Cook Glacier (South Georgia), 150
Cook Glacier (Kerguelen), 169, 170
Copper Peak, 67
Corinthian (ship), 174
Coronation Islands, 48, 50, 51
Courtauld, Mount, 50, 96
Craddock Massif, 11, 33-35
Craddock, Mount, 12, 23, 33-35, 38, 40, 182
Cragsman Peaks, 51
Cratère, Pic du, 168, 172
Creagh Dhu Mountaineering Club, 91-92, 96-97
Crean Glacier, 153
Crockett, Mount, 132, 144
Crosswell Glacier, 37, 38
Crown Mountain, 132, 145
Crown Peak, 50
Crozet Islands, 57, 170, 175
Crutch Peaks, 54
Cumberland East Bay, 153-155, 157
Cumberland West Bay, 153
Cunningham, Mount, 148
Cunningham Peak, 42, 45
Cupola, Mount, 94
Cuverville Island, 61, 62

Dalrymple, Mount, 12, 38
Damien II (yacht), 86, 154
Danco (base), 61
Danco Coast, 64, 72
Dater Glacier, 30, 37, 40
David Range, 176-178
Davies Top, 50, 96
Davis, Mount, 29
Debenham Islands, 89, 90
Debussy Heights, 95
Deception Island, 48, 52, 54, 56
Demaria, Mount, 60, 67, 78, 80-81
Dents (Les), 72
Deschanel Peak, 93
Desko Mountains, 95
Detroit Plateau, 58, 59, 61
Devil's Peak, 51
Dewey, Mount, 83
Diel (yacht), 156, 161
Discovery II (ship), 51
Discovery, Mount, 129
Ditte, Mount, 87, 89
Divide Peaks, 51
Dixon, Mount, 173
Dolence, Mount, 42, 44, 45
Dome Argus, 174
Douglas Crag, 148, 149, 164

184

Douglas Peaks, 45
Douglas Range, 93, 95
Doumer Hill, 72
Doumer Island, 72
Downfall, The, 60, 61
Drake Passage, 67, 82
Dry Valleys, 127, 134
Drygalski Fjord, 149, 153
Dundee Island, 95
Durham, Mount, 133
Duse, Mount, 147, 148

Early, Mount, 130, 144
East Base, 89-90
Edisto Inlet, 140
Edred, Mount, 50, 94
Eduardo Frei (base), 52
Edwards Island, 78, 83
Eights Coast, 180
Eklund Islands, 94
Elephant Island, 50, 52, 64, 147
Elephant Point, 54
Eley Peak, 44
Elizabeth, Mount, 126, 134, 145
Ellen Glacier, 191
Ellerbeck Peak, 148, 164
Elliot, Mount, 178
Ellsworth Land, 13, 14, 180
Ellsworth Mountains, 11-45
Elvers Peak, 42, 44
Elvia Peak, 114
Embree Glacier, 8, 30, 34, 37, 38
En Avant (yacht), 57
Endurance, HMS, 95, 154
Engelstad, Mount, 136
Enigma Peak, 95
Enterprise Hills, 43
Epperly, Mount, 11, 12, 20, 23, 24, 28-30, 34-35, 40, 182
Erebus, Mount, 71, 127-129, 131, 133, 179
Errera Channel, 61, 62
Esmark Glacier, 153, 157, 164
España, Monte, 24
Eternity Range, 93, 95, 97
Ethelred, Mount, 94
Ethelwulf, Mount, 94
Evans Peak, 27, 29
Evans, Cape, 129, 131
Everest, Mount, 15, 16, 27, 92, 119, 139, 153, 156
Evohe (yacht), 62, 80, 83
Executive Committee Range, 13, 14, 178-179, 182

Fagan, Mount, 154
Fagerli, Mount, 148, 164
Faith, Mount, 50, 95, 96
Falkland Islands, 57, 72, 86, 87, 154
Falkland Islands Dependency Survey (FIDS), 48, 49, 51, 53, 58, 59, 61, 66, 67, 69, 71, 72, 77, 78, 83, 87, 90, 93, 94, 138, 171
Falklands War, 153, 162

False Bay, 54
False Cape Renard, 71, 72, 74, 75
Fang Peak, 178
Faraday (base), 77, 78, 79, 81, 83
Fenriskjeften, 99, 101, 109, 110, 116, 117, 119, 120
Ferrar Glacier, 128
Fief (Sierra du) Mountains, 69, 70
Fiftyone Glacier, 173, 175
Filchnerfjella, 111, 121
Fildes Peninsula, 52
Finger Peak, 154
Finsterwalder Glacier, 83
Flower Hills, 30
Footsteps of Scott expedition, 131
Ford Ranges, 179
Fordel, Mount, 42, 45
Forel Glacier, 83
Fortuna Bay, 148, 162
Fossil Bluff base, 50, 87, 94
Foster Plateau, 59
Foster, Mount, 56-58, 66
Framnes Mountains, 177-178
Français, Mount, 50, 60, 64, 66-67, 81
Fraser, Mount, 148, 149, 164
Fridtjof Nansen, Mount, 136, 141, 182
Friesland, Mount, 50, 52, 54-55
Frontier Spirit now Bremen (cruise ship), 131
Fuchs Ice Piedmont, 87
Fukushima, Mount, 104
Fukushima Peak, 20, 25, 182

Galindez Island, 78
Gallieni Peninsula, 168
Gambo (yacht), 61-63, 69-70, 161-162
Gardner, Mount, 12-15, 17, 20, 23, 26, 29, 30, 32-33, 35, 37-41, 85, 144, 182
Gaudry, Mount, 50, 87-89
Gaudry-Mangin-Liotard group, 87
Geikie Glacier, 154, 157, 161
George VI Sound, 89, 93, 94, 97
George's Bay, 53
Georgy Zhukov, Peak, 118, 119
Gerlache Strait, 60, 61-64
Geser Peak, 119
Gessnertind, 99, 105, 108
Gildea Glacier, 23, 34
Giovinetto, Mount, 12, 14, 18, 27, 28, 30, 34, 40, 41, 182
Giulia, Mount, 138
Gjelsted Pass, 154
Glacier, USNS, 181
Gliozzi Peak, 42, 44, 45
Glossopteris, Mount, 16
Golden Fleece (yacht), 160
Goldsworthy Ridge, 177
Goldthwait, Mount, 12, 38
Goodge Col, 16, 20, 23, 25, 37
Goudier Island, 72
Gough Island, 101
Graham (yacht), 85, 90
Graham Land, 58-92, 138
Grand Ross, 167-172

Grande Terre, 167, 168
Grant, Mount, 153
Greenpeace (ship), 141
Greenwich Island, 53, 54
Grigory Mikheev (cruise ship), 62
Gros Ventre (ship), 169
Groupe Militaire de Haute Montagne (GMHM), 26-27, 120-121, 124, 172
Gruvletind, 105, 120
Gruvletindane Massif, 106, 119, 120, 124
Grytviken, 148, 151, 161
Guarcello Peak, 42, 45
Gurkhas, 151

Hale, Mount, 12, 30
Hallett (station), 140
Hallett, Cape, 136, 140
Hamberg Glacier, 157
Hammer Col, 37
Hansen Glacier, 30
Harmer Glacier, 157
Harmsworth, Mount, 129, 134
Harris Peak, 61, 67
Harvard Mountaineering Club, 91
Hauberg Mountains, 97
Havener, Mount, 25, 30
Havre Mountains, 95
Hays Mountains, 141, 144
Heaney Glacier, 160
Heard Island, 140, 167, 171, 173-176, 177
Heimefrontfjella, 99
Heinous Peak, 141, 144
Helmet Peak, 55
Henderson, Mount, 177
Henningsen Glacier, 154
Herbert Plateau, 59
Heritage Range, 11, 42-45
Herschel, Mount, 136, 139, 142, 143, 145
Hessler Peak, 42, 44
Hiddleston Peak, 62
Highjump, Operation, 13, 178
Hindle Glacier, 164
Hinkley Glacier, 39
Hoegh, Mount, 60, 63
Hollister Peak, 20, 25, 182
Holstinnd, 100, 105, 109, 110, 111, 114, 116, 118, 121
Holtanna, 100, 103, 105, 109, 110, 111, 114, 116-118, 121, 124
Holtedahlfjella, 99, 111, 114, 119, 120, 124
Hooker, Mount, 129, 133, 138
Hope Bay, 48, 50, 58, 59, 61, 171
Hope Bay (base), 48, 59
Hope, Mount, 50, 95
Horlick Mountains, 128
Horseshoe Valley, 42, 44, 45
Howard Nunataks, 14
Huckle, Mount, 94
Huggins, Mount, 129, 135
Humphries Heights, 73, 75
Huntington, Mount, 16
Husvik, 148, 151, 157

Ice Bird (yacht), 181
Ice Fjord, 153
Independence Hills, 43
International Geophysical Year (1957-58), 104
International Polar Year (1882-3), 100, 147
International Transantarctic Expedition (1989-90), 59
Irving, Mount, 52
Israeli-Palestinian Friendship, Mountain of, 83

Jabet Peak, 60, 65, 71, 81, 135
Jaca, Pico, 24
Jackson, Mount, 50, 92, 94-97, 151
Janssen Peak, 70
Japanese Antarctic Research Expedition (JARE), 104
Jenkins Glacier, 153
John Laing (yacht), 63
John Peaks, 51
Johnston, Mount, 50, 60, 61, 67
Jøkulkyrkja, 99, 104, 105
Jones Sound, 85
Juan Carlos (station), 54, 55
Jumper, Mount, 12, 24, 27

Kapitan Khlebnikov (ship), 181
Keller Peninsula, 53
Kerguelen Islands, 57, 167-172, 174, 175
King Edward Point, 148, 157, 163, 164
King George Island, 52-54, 71
King Haakon Bay, 147, 148, 154
King Island, 82
King, Mount, 95
Kinntanna, 100, 103, 105, 109, 110, 111, 116, 118
Kirkpatrick, Mount, 134, 135, 137, 182
Kiwi Peak, 154
Kjerulf Glacier, 154, 161, 164
Klement-Ohridski (base), 55
Klevekampen Massif, 121
Klevetind, 105, 121
Kling, Mount, 148, 155
Knutzen Peak, 24, 25
Kohl-Larsen Plateau, 148, 150 ,151, 154, 157
Kosciuszko, Mount, 21
Kotick (yacht), 156
Kristen-Julie Peak, 30
Krokisius, Mount, 147, 148, 154
Kubbestolen, 105, 106, 114, 120
Kubus Mountain, 105, 111
Kurze Mountains, 114
Kvitkleven Glacier, 121
Kyrkjeskipet Peak, 99

Lacroix, Mount, 75, 76
Lancing Glacier, 154
Landmark Peak, 43
Larrouy Island, 83
Lars Christensen Peak, 180
Larsen Harbour, 148, 152, 156, 157, 161

185

Larssen Peak, 148, 164
Laurens Peninsula, 173, 176
Laurie Island, 48, 51
Laussedat Heights, 62, 63
Lavoisier Island, 83
Lawrence, Mount, 178
Laws Glacier, 51
Leay Glacier, 77, 78
Lecco Spiders, 68
Lemaire Channel, 70, 72, 74-78
Lemaire Island, 64
LeMay Range, 95
Leroux Bay, 81, 83
Lester Peak, 44
Levski Peak, 55
Liberty Hills, 43
Linder Peak, 42, 45
Liptak, Mount, 38
Lister Cove, 55
Lister, Mount, 129, 135, 138, 182
Little America (base), 95
Little Thumb, 90, 91
Livingston Island, 52, 53, 54-56
Logan, Mount, 15, 16
Long Gables, 11, 12, 17, 18, 28, 29, 40, 182
Longhurst, Mount, 134
Loretan, Peak, 24, 29, 182
Lucas Glacier, 157
Luigi Peak, 70
Lumière Peak, 79
Lunckeryggen Massif, 104
Lyaskovets Peak, 55
Lyell Glacier, 156, 157, 161

Mac Robertson Land, 7, 177
MacArthur, Mount, 160
Macklin, Mount, 148, 149, 164
Madrid Protocol, 141
Magnier Peaks, 60, 81, 83
Man-O-War Glacier, 140, 142
Mangin, Mount, 50, 89
Marguerite Bay, 85-90, 93, 94, 96, 97
Marie Byrd Land, 13, 95, 130, 178-179
Marikoppa, 148, 154, 161, 164
Marion Dufresne II (supply ship), 167, 172
Markham, Mount, 128, 134, 144, 182
Masherbrum, 15
Masson Range, 177
Matterhorn, 27, 28, 104
Matthews Peak, 85, 86
Maudheim (base), 103
Mawson (station), 177
Mawson Peak, 140, 173-175, 177
McClary Glacier, 90, 93
McClintock, Mount, 144, 174
McCollum Peak, 60, 82
McKinley, Mount, 16, 23, 47, 92, 144
McMurdo (base), 7, 15, 16, 52, 129, 133, 136, 143
Media Peak, 111
Melchior Islands, 57, 65
Melville Peak, 53
Melville, Cape, 53

Mhire Spur, 44
Midgard, 103, 105, 114, 116
Mill, Mount, 78-81
Miller Heights, 83
Miller, Mount, 134, 137, 182
Millerand Island, 90
Mills Peak, 148, 164
Mills, Mount, 136
Mimas Peak, 95
Minaret Peak, 42, 45
Minaret, The, 68
Minnesota Glacier, 11, 12, 14, 15, 18, 42, 43, 45
Minto, Mount, 139, 141, 142, 145, 175, 182
Minya Konka, 27
Mirny (station), 59
Mirny Peak, 95
Mischief (yacht), 57, 170 ,175
Mohl, Mount, 12, 30
Molar Peak, 66
Morbihan Gulf, 171
Morris Glacier, 153
Morris, Mount, 34
Moubray Bay, 136
Mühlig-Hofmann Mountains, 99, 105, 108
Mundlauga, 105, 114, 116, 124
Murphy, Mount, 179
Murray Glacier, 136
Murray Snowfield, 153, 157

Napier, Mount, 51
Natalie Peak, 30
National Geographic, 19, 111, 141
National Science Foundation (NSF), 23, 122, 144
Needles, The, 50, 72
Neko Harbour, 64
Nella Dan, supply ship, 175
Nemesis, Mount, 90, 92
Nemo Peak, 68, 71
Neny Fjord, 50, 88, 89-91
Neny Island, 90, 92, 93
Neny Matterhorn, 90, 91
Neumayer Channel, 64, 67, 71
Neumayer Glacie,r 148, 150, 151, 157, 161, 164
Neuschwabenland, 102
Newcomer Glacier, 12, 30, 38
Nimitz Glacier, 7, 34, 38
Nimitz, Mount, 13, 178
Nipple Peak, 68, 71
Nivea, Mount, 51
Noble Peak, 65, 70, 71
Nonplus Crag, 95
Nordenskjöld Peak, 86, 148, 151, 154, 157, 160, 163, 164
Nordenskjöld Glacier, 148, 157, 161, 164
Normann, Mount, 148, 153, 156, 161
Norse (ship), 103
Norsk Polarinstitutt, 104
North Pole, 47, 92, 138, 139
Northanger (yacht), 57, 58, 67, 69, 72, 73, 74, 139

Northeast Glacier, 90, 93
Northwest Passage, 57
Norwegian-British-Swedish Antarctic Expedition (NBSAE) 1949-52, 103, 104
Novolazarevskaya (base), 104, 108, 110, 114, 116, 117, 120, 122
Novosilski Glacier, 148, 151, 153, 161

Ohio Range, 7,16
Olreg Ridge, 95
Olsen, Mount, 173, 176
Omega Foundation, 30, 32, 35, 54, 182
Orcadas (station), 51
Orel Ice Fringe, 61
Organ Pipe Peaks, 132, 133, 145
Oriental (ship), 174
Orpheus Pass, 54
Orvinfjella, 99, 100, 104, 108, 114,
Ostenso, Mount, 12, 18, 30, 39, 182

Paget Glacier, 150, 156
Paget, Mount, 148, 150, 151, 152, 153, 156, 157, 160, 161, 162, 163
Palmer Land, 94, 95-97
Paradise Bay, 64, 81
Paradise Harbour, 60, 64
Pardue Peak, 44
Paris, Mount, 50, 94
Parrish Peak, 42, 44
Parry, Mount, 60, 64-66
Parsons, Mount, 178
Patagonia, 67, 156, 171
Patanela (yacht), 175
Paterson, Mount, 148, 151, 157, 164
Patriot Hills, 27, 29, 30, 32, 37, 42, 43, 45, 57, 92, 94, 103, 118, 120, 141, 143
Patton Glacier, 24, 26, 27, 29, 33, 34, 37, 40
Paulsen Peak, 148, 161, 162, 163, 164
Pavie Ridge, 93
Peary, Mount, 60, 79, 80, 81
Pelagic (yacht), 65, 67, 69, 70, 72, 73, 77, 83, 86, 152-153, 156, 160, 161, 162, 164
Pelagic Australis (yacht), 83, 164
Pelagic, Mount, 152, 161
Pendragon, Mount, 52
Penola Strait, 47, 78, 81
Pensacola Mountains, 128
Perchot, Mount, 81, 83
Perez Peninsula, 78
Perez Point, 83
Perez, Cape, 82
Perplex Ridge, 86
Perunika Glacier, 54, 55
Peter I Island, 167, 180
Petermann Island, 81
Petermann Ranges, 117
Philippi Glacier, 151, 152, 153, 157, 161
Philiptanna, 116
Phlegar Dome, 144
Pilcher Peak, 59, 60, 61
Pilot Peak, 83
Piloto Pardo (ship), 65
Pioneer Heights, 43

Pipecleaner Glacier, 136
Pisgah, Mount, 58
Plymouth, Mount, 54
Podorange (yacht), 62, 65, 80
Pond, Mount, 56
Port Lockroy (base), 48, 50, 60, 68, 69, 71, 72,
Portal Point, 61
Port-aux-Français, 167, 169, 171, 172
Pourquoi Pas Island, 85-86, 87, 90
Powell Island, 51
Presidente Gonzalez Videla (station), 60, 63
Press, Mount, 12, 34
Price Glacier, 153
Prince Charles Mountains, 177
Princess Elizabeth Land, 101
Principe de Asturias, Pico, 24
Professor Molchanov (cruise ship), 67
Prospect Point, 62, 83, 85
Protector, HMS, 88, 154
Protocol on Environmental Protection to the Antarctic Treaty ('Madrid Protocol'), 141
Puerto Williams, 82
Pulfrich Peak, 62
Pulpit Mountain, 51
Punta Arenas, 19, 52, 54, 85, 87
Pyramid Peak, 53
Quad 5, 148, 161, 162
Queen Alexandra Range, 127, 134, 137, 182
Queen Fabiola Mountains, 99
Queen Maud Land, 7, 99-125, 143, 145
Queen Maud Mountains, 127, 132, 133, 138, 139, 141, 143, 144
Rakekniven, 105, 111-114, 121
Rallier du Baty Peninsula, 168
Rasmussen Island, 80
Rea, Mount, 178, 179
Reclus Peninsula, 59, 61, 67
Red Rock Ridge, 90
Reeves, Mount, 50, 89
Renard, Cape, 60, 69, 72-75
Renaud Island, 80, 83
Renier Point, 55
Reptile Ridge, 89
Rio Branco, Mount, 78, 83
Risting Glacier, 153
Robertson Island, 47
Roman Four Promontory, 91, 92
Rondespiret, 114
Rongé Island, 60, 62
Ronne Ice Shelf, 128
Roots, Mount, 148, 151, 154, 155, 157, 160, 161
Rosenthal, Mount, 44
Ross Glacier, 148, 155, 162
Ross Ice Shelf, 95, 127, 131, 134, 136, 138, 143
Ross Island, 7, 16, 52, 127, 128, 133, 143
Ross, Grand, 167-172
Ross, Petit, 168, 171, 172
Ross Pass, 147, 148, 150, 152, 155, 157
Ross Sea, 127, 136, 179
Rothera (station), 87-90, 94, 177

186

Rothera Point, 87
Rothschild Island, 95
Rouen Mountains, 94, 95
Royal Bay, 152, 154, 155, 162
Royal Geographical Society (RGS), 85
Royal Marines, 88, 154, 156, 157, 162
Royal Navy, 135, 154
Royal Society Range, 127-129, 133, 135, 138, 182
Royalist, Mount, 142, 145
Rücker, Mount, 129, 138
Rumdoodle, 177
Rutford Ice Stream, 30
Rutford, Mount, 12, 34, 37, 182
Ryder Bay 88

Sabatier, Mount, 148, 153, 155
Sabine, Mount, 136, 142, 145
Salisbury Plain, 157, 164
Salomon Glacier, 164
Salvesen Range, 147, 164
Sam's Col, 16, 18, 35, 39
San Martín (station), 50, 90, 92
Sanctuary Pinnacle, 91
Sandefjord Peaks, 51
Sandeggtind, 108
Sandneshatten, 120, 124
Santa Maria (yacht), 73
Sarnoff Mountains, 7, 178-179
Savoia Peak, 60, 69, 70, 75
Scarlatti Peak, 94
Scheimpflug Nunatak, 62
Schoek Peak, 44
Schoening Peak, 20, 25, 39, 182
Schokalsky Bay, 94
Schwarz Hörner, 117
Scientific Committee of Antarctic Research (SCAR), 54, 183
Scotia (ship), 51
Scott (base), 16, 127, 129, 133, 136, 143
Scott Glacier, 128, 130, 131, 133, 138, 143, 144, 145
Scott, Mount, 50, 60, 67, 76-78, 81
Segers, Mount, 30, 37
Senderens, Mount, 148, 152, 156
Sentinel Range, 11-41, 95, 99, 127, 145, 178, 182
Seven Sisters of Fief, 70
Seven Summits, 19, 21, 22, 85, 92, 104, 127
Severinghaus Glacier, 11, 23, 40
Shackleton Gap, 148, 157
Shackleton Glacier, 145
Shackleton Range, 128, 145
Shackleton, Mount, 60, 78-80
Shambles Glacier, 89
Sharp Peak, 83, 84
Sharp, Mount, 12, 38
Shear, Mount, 27, 182
Sheridan, Mount, 148, 162
Shinn, Mount, 11, 12, 13, 14, 16, 17, 20, 23, 24, 25, 29, 30, 34, 35, 37, 39, 40, 182
Shirreff, Cape, 54
Sidley, Mount, 13, 14, 178-179, 182
Sierra du Fief, 69, 70

Signy Island, 48, 51
Signy Island (base), 48, 51
Signynbreen Glacier, 114
Silverstein Peak, 20, 23, 24, 25, 30, 182
Simmons, Mount, 42, 45
Siple Island, 179
Siple, Mount, 179
Sirius Knoll, 58
Sisu Peak, 29, 182
Skelly Peak, 44
Skelton Glacier, 134, 135
Skittle, Mount, 154
Sky Blu, 87
Sky-Hi Nunataks, 50, 87
Slaughter, Mount, 30, 34
Slessor Peak, 50, 83
Sloman Glacier, 89
Smillie Peak, 148, 151, 153, 154
Smith Island, 52, 56-58
Snow Hill Island, 47
Soglio Peak, 114
Soholt Peaks, 43
Sør Rondane Mountains, 99, 102, 104, 114
Sørlle Buttress, 157, 164
South Barrier, 175
South Bay, 54, 55
South Georgia, 7, 52, 86, 92, 146-165, 174
South Orkneys, 48, 51
South Pole, 11, 16, 27, 85, 94, 118, 130, 133, 135, 141, 143, 145
South Shetlands, 48, 51, 52-58, 183
Southern Champion (ship), 175-176
Southern Ocean, 51, 139, 140, 145, 152, 173, 175
Southwick, Mount, 12, 38
Spaaman, Mount, 148, 150, 151, 153, 162, 164
Spectre, The, 130, 131, 144
Spenceley Glacier, 148, 153, 157, 161
Spire, The, 90, 91
Spirit of Sydney (yacht), 64, 67, 79, 83
Spivey, Mount, 94
Splettstoesser Glacier, 43, 45
Spörli, Mount, 42, 44, 45
Springer Peak, 42, 44
Square Bay, 85
St. Andrews Bay, 157
St. Boris and Gleb, Peak, 118
Staccato Peaks, 50, 95
Stanley, Mount, 137
Stanley, Peak, 148, 153, 162
Starbuck Peak, 153
Statham, Mount, 86
Station E (base), 90
Stefansson Strait, 95
Steinskaregga, 105, 106, 114
Stephenson Nunatak, 50, 94, 95
Stephenson, Mount, 50, 94
Stetind, 105, 116, 120
Stokkantoppen, 108
Stolze Peak, 62
Stonington (base), 83, 85, 89-96
Stonington Island, 50
Stromness, 147, 148, 154, 156

Strybing, Mount, 38
Sturge Island, 181
Sublime Peak, 19, 20, 182
Sugartop, Mount, 148, 154, 157, 163, 164
Sullivan, Mount, 96
Sunshine Glacier, 51
Sutton Crag, 150
Svarthorna Peaks, 117, 118
Sweeney Mountains, 50, 97
Swine Hill, 94
Syowa (station), 104

Tabarin, Operation, 48, 71
Takahe, Mount, 179
Tangra Range, 54, 55
Tärnet, 114
Tekubi, Mount, 104
Tennant, Mount, 62
Ternyck Needle, 53
Thiel Mountains, 128
Thomas Glacier, 30
Three Brothers, 148, 157, 161, 162, 164
Thunder Glacier, 69
Tiama (yacht), 59, 61
Toney Mountain, 179
Tooluka (yacht), 157
Tottanfjella, 99
Tower, The, 53
Trinity Peninsula, 48, 58-61
Triune Peaks, 93
Trollslottet, 105, 111
Tucker Glacier, 140
Tungespissen, 105, 116, 124
Twin Hummock Island, 64
Twins, The, 138
Twiss, Mount, 42, 44
Twitcher Glacier, 164
Tyndall Mountains, 83
Tyree, Mount, 11-18, 20, 23, 24, 26, 27, 29, 32-35, 37-39, 45, 85, 121, 144, 182

Ulmer, Mount, 12, 13
Ulvetanna, 99, 103-110, 116, 119-121, 123, 124
Una's Tits, 72
Undine Harbour, 150
Union Glacier, 43-45
United States Antarctic Program (USAP), 35, 143
US Geological Survey Advisory Committee on Antarctic Names (USGS ACAN), 11, 35
Usher, Mount, 136
Ushuaia, 21, 51, 57, 82

Valery Chkalov, Peak, 118
Valiente Peak, 82
Vernadsky (base), 60, 78, 81
Verne, Mount, 85, 86
Victoria Land, 127, 138-140, 143, 181
Viets, Mount, 24, 27, 29
Vikinghögda, 104
Vinson Massif, 11, 18, 24, 27, 35, 85
Vinson, Mount, 11-37
Vinten-Johansen Ridge, 105, 120

Virginia, Mount, 44
Vladimir, Peak, 119
Vogel Peak, 148, 154, 155

Waddington Bay, 67, 80, 81
Waesche, Mount, 179
Waist, The, 59
Wakefield Highland, 89, 95, 96
Walker, Mount, 60, 61
Wall Range, 65, 68, 69, 71, 72
Waller Peak, 156
Walsh Bluff, 176
Walton Mountains, 94
Walton Peak, 93
Wandel Peak, 69, 73, 74, 76, 79, 161
Ward, Mount, 177
Waterboat Point, 63
Wave Peak, 51
Weaver, Mount, 130, 133
Weddell Sea, 127
Welcome Nunatak, 44
Widerøefjellet, 104
Wiencke Island, 48, 62, 67, 68-72, 81, 135
Wiggins Glacier, 78, 79, 80
Wilckens Peaks, 153
Wilcox, Mount, 85, 90, 95
Wilkes Land, 101
Willett Cove, 140
William Glacier, 66
William, Mount, 60, 67, 68, 83, 172
Wiltsie's Peak, 59, 61
Window Buttress, 89
Wohlthat Massif, 99, 102, 108
Wordie Ice Shelf, 93
Worsley, Mount, 148, 153, 162
Wright Peninsula, 87
Wyatt Earp, Mount, 12, 14
Wyatt Earp (ship), 101

Yamato Mountains, 99, 104
Yankee Harbour, 54

Zavis Peak, 45
Zebra Ridge, 95
Zeiss Needle, 62
Zerua Peak, 74
Zinsmeister Ridge, 39
Zograf Peak, 55

Index (people)

Aastorp, Aslak, 114
Abrahams, Simon, 88
Adams, David, 67
Adie, Ray 94
Afanassieff, Jean, 171
Albert, Kurt, 73
Albrieux, Lionel, 121
Alesno de Saint-Allouarn, François, 169
Alvaro, Sebastian, 79
Amundsen, Roald, 47, 109, 133, 136, 138, 141
Anderson, Robert, 23, 32
Anker, Conrad, 18, 23, 25, 29, 30, 32, 33, 40, 45, 110, 111, 119
Armstrong, Rick, 160
Arnold, Alwin, 65
Atkinson, Bill, 138, 178
Austin, Mike, 88
Autissier, Isabelle, 58, 162, 180
Ayres, Harry, 134

Baikovsky, Yuriy, 117, 118, 119
Ball, Gary, 138
Bass, Dick, 19, 21, 85
Bastien, Trevor, 14
Bath, John, 54
Batoux, Philippe, 162
Baud, Anselme, 29
Baume, Louis, 150
Bayly, Maurice, 59, 61
Béchervaise, John, 177, 178
Benitez, Luis, 62
Bentley, Charlie, 178
Berg, Wally, 30
Berkus, Brian, 141
Bernard, François, 27
Bewsher, Bill, 177
Bilous, John, 157
Bird, Patrick, 37
Birkitt, Dave, 97
Birnbacher, Ed, 71
Biscoe, John, 87
Blackburn, Joseph, 23
Blackburn, Quin, 133
Blackley, Peter, 81
Blunt, Bill, 175
Bodin, Patrice, 171
Boisguehenneuc, Charles de, 169
Bolo, Thierry, 27, 172
Bonatti, Walter, 138
Bonington, Chris, 19
Bonner, Nigel, 151
Brooke, Richard, 56, 71, 92, 135
Brooker, Ian, 150
Brown, B., 154
Brown, Jed, 8, 25, 34
Brown, R., 154
Brown, R.A., 150
Bruce, William Speirs, 51
Budd, Graham, 175
Buggisch, Werner, 18
Bugueño, Manuel, 33
Bull, John, 67
Bushell, 79, 96
Burley, Malcolm, 88, 154
Burns, Mike, 94, 96, 97
Butson, Arthur, 90, 91, 92
Byrd, Richard, 13, 89, 130, 133, 141, 178

Cardis, Philippe, 85, 90, 154
Care, Bernard, 95
Carr, Tim, 157
Carse, Duncan, 92, 147, 150, 153, 155
Casassa, Gino, 67
Caspersen, Robert, 108, 109, 114, 120
Castros Sotos, Vicente, 62
Cauchy, Emmanuel, 162, 172
Cayrol, Antoine, 27, 172
Challéat, Ludovic, 62, 65, 80
Chambers, 88
Chaplin, Stephen, 33, 34
Chapman, Bill, 178
Charcot, Jean-Baptiste, 47, 66, 69, 70, 72, 76, 77, 78, 81, 82, 85, 87, 89, 94
Chase, Andrew, 164
Chester, John, 154
Chester, Jonathan, 175
Choudens, Antoine de, 27, 121
Chouinard, Yvon, 22, 25
Christensen, Jytte, 63, 79, 83
Christensen, Lars, 99, 101, 177
Clagg, Harry, 154
Cleland, Robyn, 59
Clifton, Robb, 175
Clinch, Nicholas, 15
Clutterbuck, Peter, 44
Collister, 85
Condon, Jia, 69, 72, 73
Contreras, Alejo, 22, 85, 141
Cook, Bob, 51
Cook, James, 147, 170
Cook, Frederick, 47
Corbet, Barry, 16, 17, 18, 23, 25, 26, 32
Cordier, Patrick, 171
Cortial, Mathieu, 58, 65, 70, 75, 76, 86, 180
Cosgriff, Tom, 108, 109, 120, 124
Cotter, Guy, 30, 62
Cousins, Mike, 89, 92, 95
Cox, Simon, 135
Craddock, Lizzie, 70
Craddock, Campbell, 18, 43
Craw, D., 154
Crean, Tom, 147
Cunningham, John, 89, 92, 96, 97, 151
Curtis, Mike, 44
Curtis, Tim, 175

Daudet, Lionel, 58, 65, 66, 70, 75, 86, 162, 171, 172, 180
David, Tannatt Edgeworth, 128
Davies, Stuart, 85, 175
Davis, H., 156
Davison, Brian, 155
Day, Darrel, 63
Dayné, Pierre, 69, 70, 76
Deacock, Warwick, 175
Dean, Lyle, 144
Decamp, Erik, 24, 28
Degerman, Patrick, 29, 120
Densmore, Lisa, 23
DesLauriers, Kit, 23
Destivelle, Catherine, 24, 28, 29
Dickinson, Matt, 67
Dixon, Grant, 63, 79, 83, 148, 157
Dodson, Bob, 90, 91
Donaldson, 95
Donini, Jim, 30, 40, 45
Doubleday, Paul, 95

Doumani, George, 130, 178
Down, Simon, 154
Dowrick, Bruce, 57
Drygalski, Erich von, 100
Dubois, Bertrand, 154
Ducroz, Denis, 67, 83, 154, 171, 172
Dujmovits, Ralf, 24, 114

Early, Neal, 130
Eberhard, Stefan, 59, 61
Edwards, John, 51
Elias, Bob, 30
Eliassen, Odd, 108
Elliott, Frank, 90, 91
Ellsworth, Lincoln, 13, 95, 100
Engl, Hans, 156
English, Pauline, 175
Engwander, Martin, 156
Enrique, Jorge, 54
Erel, Doron, 67, 83
Ershler, Phil, 22
Evans, John, 14-19, 23, 26, 27, 32, 43, 59, 61
Ewer, J., 53

Failing, Bob, 141
Farman, Joe, 81
Fatti, Paul, 156
Faucher, Thomas, 121
Fica, Rodrigo, 30, 32, 54
Finney, Angus, 148, 157
Fitzgerald, Paul, 23, 43, 131, 138, 144
Foigt, Alexander, 117, 118
Foissac, Sébastien, 172, 173
Fossett, Steve, 21
Fouchier, Arnauld de, 65
Fowlie, Walt, 138
Fox, Adrian, 95, 97
Fox, Niel, 71
Franco, Michel, 86
Freeman-Atwood, Julian, 67, 69, 72, 73, 152, 154, 155, 161, 164
Fréjacques, Luc, 85
Fuchs, Vivian, 90, 94, 96, 150
Fukushima, Eiichi, 16-18
Furness, Dez, 156
Furse, Chris, 52, 64

Gardiner, Terry, 30
Gardino, Paolo, 44
Gardner, Jimmy, 92, 96
Garnier, Thierry, 65
Garrod, Simon, 44, 97
Gatagov, Georgi, 117, 118, 119
Georges, André, 114, 116, 118
Gerlache, Adrien de, 47, 61, 65, 66, 82
Giaever, John, 103
Gilbert, Di, 94
Gildea, Damien, 11, 19, 22, 25, 30, 32, 33-35, 37, 54
Gilmore, Adrian, 51
Gilmour, Harold, 179
Gizycki, Peter von, 18, 19
Glowacz, Stefan, 73
Goerlach, Ulrich, 65
Goldstrand, Patrick, 43, 44
Götz, Hans Martin, 73
Gould, Laurence, 133, 141
Gourdon, Ernest, 76
Graber, Mike, 85, 110, 111

Grant, Allan, 51
Gravdal, Stein-Ivar, 120
Green, J., 88, 89
Griber, John, 160
Griffin, Lindsay, 154, 155
Grimshaw, Edward, 77, 78
Gryzka, Jean-Marc, 27, 120
Gundersen, Jan Åge, 108, 109
Gunn, Bernie, 134, 135
Gustafsson, Veikka, 29
Guyonneau, Jean-Luc, 154

Hahn, Dave, 23, 25, 29, 30
Hall, Lincoln, 139
Hall, Rob, 23, 24, 30, 133, 138, 177
Hall, Tim, 161, 162
Hamilton, David, 37
Hardie, Norman, 16
Hardy, Peter, 51
Hargreaves, 80
Harrer, Heinrich, 15, 175
Harris, Leslie, 61
Hart, Rob, 141
Hattersley-Smith, Geoff, 53, 71
Haworth, Richard, 71, 161
Haworth, Roger, 70, 71
Heaney, John, 150
Heard, John, 174
Heine, Arnold, 134
Hélène, Julien, 65
Helling, Josh, 119, 122
Hendy, Martin, 175
Herbert, Wally, 59, 61, 136, 138-139, 171
Hiedorn, Gerhard, 73
Hilde, Trond, 108, 109, 120
Hill, 95
Hillary, Edmund, 133, 134, 135, 136, 143, 145
Hobbs, Charlie, 43, 138
Höbenreich, Christoph, 124
Hodges, Ben, 92
Hoeber, Hoger, 73
Hollister, Charles, 16, 18, 25
Holly, Chris, 59
Holma, Pekka, 120
Holmes, Keith, 95
Hoover, Mike, 85
Hope, 79
Hubbard, Alun, 161, 162
Huber, Alex, 121
Huber, Thomas, 121
Hubert, Alain, 25, 114-116, 118
Hughes, Alun, 161w
Hull, Brian, 44, 95w

Ibarra, Maria Paz 'Pachi', 25, 34, 35, 37
Ivanov, Lyubomir, 55

Jabet, Jacques, 69
Jamieson, D., 156
Jarvis, Robin, 45, 89
Jefferies, Chris, 154
Jewell, Chris, 76, 77
Johnson, Beverley, 85
Johnson, Frank, 51
Johnson, Rupert, 156
Johnstone, P., 154
Jones, Caradoc 'Crag', 69, 72, 73, 150, 152, 154, 156, 157, 161, 164

Jorgensen, Tina, 114
Jourdan, Didier, 121

Kaufmann, Andy, 15
Kemp, Anna, 57
Kerguelen de Trémarec, Yves Joseph de, 168-170
Kershaw, Giles, 19, 21, 85
Khvostenko, Oleg, 117, 118
Kimber, Peter, 77, 78, 79, 81
Kimbrey, John, 57
Kirkby, Syd, 177
Knappe, Jürgen, 73
Knowles, A., 154
Koller, Paul, 124
Kossart, Theo, 67
Koutoudjian, Vasken, 172
Krakauer, Jon, 110, 111
Kristensen, Monica, 139
Kuzin, Valery, 117, 119
Kuznetsov, Piotr, 117, 118

Laird, Hamish, 70
Lambert, 89
Landreth, Greg, 57, 67, 69, 73
Lang, Rudiger, 23, 25
Laserer, Walter, 37
Latady, William, 90, 91
Latorre, Ferrán, 116
Lawson, Gerry, 154
Lawton, Kieran, 59, 61
Lewis, Bob, 77, 78, 79, 81
Lewis, Nick, 95
Libecki, Mike, 110, 119, 120, 122-123, 124
Light, Jerry, 51
Logerot, Vincent, 65
Long, Bill, 14, 16-19, 23
Loretan, Erhard, 22, 24, 32, 35
Lowe, Alex, 29, 45, 77, 109, 110, 111, 114, 119, 124
Lukes, Cestmir, 114
Lurcock, Pat, 148, 157
Lynch, Tom, 154

Macdonald, Stuart, 157, 160
Manners, Will, 157, 160
Mannix, Dan, 57
Mannix, Veronica, 57
Mariani, Fulvio, 77
Marliave, Christian de, 86, 90, 154, 172
Marlow, Chris, 157
Marsh, George, 134, 179
Marts, Brian, 16-21
Marts, Steve, 19
Mattei, Anna, 162
Matthews, David, 83, 85
Matthews, Mark, 156
Mauduit, Chantal, 67
Mawson, Douglas, 100, 131, 177
McArthur, 85
McCallum, Gordon, 88
McDermott, Frank, 67
McDowell, Mike, 131
McGregor, Vic, 136
McKeith, Bugs, 89
McLean, Andrew, 68
McMorrin, Ian, 92, 93
Mear, Roger, 131
Mercier, Daniel, 114
Merrizi, Jacapo, 83, 86
Messner, Reinhold, 19, 22, 92
Metcalf, Bob, 90, 92
Millar, Hamish, 161

Miller, Bob, 134, 179
Mills, Ian 'Jan', 150, 156
Mills, Keith, 164
Milner, Luke, 70
Miston, Laurent, 27, 172
Mollard, Firmin, 154
Monégier du Sorbier, Brice, 65
Monteath, Colin, 25, 131, 133
Moore, Geoff, 59
Morgan, Ivor, 92, 93
Morgan, Jon, 67
Morning, Heather, 23, 94
Morris, Stuart, 67
Morrow, Pat, 21, 23
Mortimer, Greg, 25, 64, 139
Moss, John, 156
Moyes, A., 89
Muegge-Vaughan, Caroline, 141
Muffat-Joly, Grégory, 172
Mujica, Rodrigo, 30
Munoz, Dimitry, 121

Naar, Ronald, 62
Nash, Dave, 93
Nelson, Hilaree, 160
Nesheim, Sjur, 108, 109
Noble, John, 92, 96
Nordenskjöld, Otto, 47, 147
Norman, Shaun, 85, 93, 94, 97
Nott, Graeme, 89
Nottaris, Romolo, 24, 162
Novak, Skip, 67, 70, 72, 73, 77, 83, 86, 150, 152-153, 156, 161, 162, 164

Oehninger, Irene, 114
Olagne, Caroline, 65
Olagne, Hervé, 65
Olbery, Chuck, 67
Otway, Peter, 136
Owen, Llinos, 160

Pain, Kevin, 136
Palmer, Nathaniel, 51
Pande, Anjali, 164
Pashley, Mike, 88, 96, 97
Pashuk, Keri-Lee, 57, 73
Passel, Charles, 179
Paterson, Stan, 151
Pawson, Ken, 53, 56, 71, 72
Peacock, 154
Peary, Robert, 139
Pellet, Philippe, 172
Pershin, Valery, 117, 118
Petersen, Harries-Clichy 'Pete', 91
Pichler, Karl, 124
Pinder, Martin, 51
Pinfield, Steve, 45
Pirrit, John, 13, 14, 178
Plaisted, Ralph, 139
Polian, Georges, 171, 172
Poncet, Jérôme, 86, 90
Poncin, Philippe, 65
Porzak, Glen, 22
Postlethwaite, D., 93
Pou, Eneko, 74
Pou, Iker, 74
Preti, Marco, 83, 86
Price, Tom, 151
Prohaska, Rich, 69, 72, 73
Putt, Colin, 140, 175
Pye, Terry, 154

Quarti, Gian Luigi, 77
Quinteros, Jorge, 67,

Rada, Camilo, 22, 25, 28, 32-37
Ratel, Sébastien, 121
Redfield, Tim, 43, 138
Reichel, Max, 121
Renard, Philippe, 172
Richards, W., 71, 72
Richardson, Simon, 57
Ridgeway, Rick, 19, 21, 110, 111
Riiser-Larsen, Hjalmar, 100
Rinning, Dave, 51, 89
Roach, Gerry, 22
Robert, René, 114, 116
Roberts, Mike, 70, 179
Rogers, Erasmus, 174
Rogerson, Matt, 175
Roots, James, 150
Roy, Billy, 156
Rymill, John, 47, 67, 82, 85, 89, 90, 91, 95, 147
Rymill, Rob, 67

Sabadell, Esther, 79
Sàbat, Francesc, 54
Samsonov, Victor, 18, 19
Sand, Vebjørn, 110, 114
Savary, François, 121, 172
Sayre, Woodrow Wilson, 15
Scanlon, Mark, 156
Schabertsberger, Robert, 156
Schittich, Ingrid, 37
Schmatz, Gerhard, 156
Schoening, Pete, 15, 16, 18, 23
Searle, Derek, 93
Sedon, Mark, 62
Selva Serrano, Javier, 62
Shackleton, Ernest, 52, 109, 110, 128, 147, 148, 150, 152, 154, 156
Sharp, Mike, 57
Shewry, Arthur, 61, 66
Siegrist, Stefan, 121
Silverstein, Sam, 16, 18, 25
Singleman, Glenn, 139
Siple, Paul, 13
Skinner, 95, 130
Smith, Jay, 23, 25
Smith, Mark, 89
Sodergren, Elizabeth, 45
Sokolov, Gleb, 117, 118, 119
Somers, Geof, 89
Sorensen, Hans Christian Florian, 122
Speake, Terry, 88
Spenceley, George, 150
Spicer, Dominic, 45
Spinelli, Carlo, 162
Splettstoesser, John, 14
Spörli, Bernhard, 43
Stacey, 79
Stangl, Christian, 37
Staver, Håkon, 114
Steen, J., 83, 85
Stokken, Bård, 108
Stonehouse, Bernard, 150, 151
Stoup, Doug, 68, 160
Strange, John, 23
Stratford, Jo, 79
Stratford, Mark, 156
Strausz, Thomas, 37
Stump, Ed, 23, 131 ,138, 144
Stump, Mugs, 15, 23, 27, 29, 32, 33, 38, 130, 131 ,138, 144
Stutt, Marcus, 160
Styles, Julie, 59, 61
Sutton, George, 150
Swan, Robert, 131

Swithinbank, Charles, 103
Sykes, Ian, 93, 95

t'Hooft, Kees, 154, 155
Tallis, Terry, 79, 81
Tamayo, Jose Carlos, 76, 79, 116, 161
Tejas, Vern, 22, 23
Temple, Philip, 175
Thomas, Duncan, 67
Thomas, Matthew, 157
Thomas, Rick, 57, 67
Thompson, John, 67, 154
Thomson, Roger, 57
Thornton, Meg, 175
Tickell, Lance, 51
Tilman, Harold William 'Bill', 56, 57, 58, 67, 140, 170, 171, 175
Todd, Davie, 92, 96, 97, 154
Toftdahl, Jo ,108
Tollefsen, Ivar, 104, 108, 109, 110, 114, 120, 121, 122, 124
Tompkins, Doug, 22
Trihey, Lucas, 76, 77
Tufft, Roger, 170, 171
Txikón, Alex, 79
Tymon, Harry, 156
Tyrril, Jarmila, 25, 34, 35

Uemura, Naomi, 92
Usaj, Osvaldo, 54, 55

Vasilev, Doychin, 55
Vaughan, Norman, 133, 141
Venables, Stephen, 154, 155
Vining, Ross, 175
Vinogradsky, Evgeny, 117, 118, 119
Virelaude, Bernard, 27
Volkov, Maxim, 117, 119

Wagnon, Patrick, 58, 65, 66, 70, 75, 86, 180
Wahlstrom, Richard, 16, 18, 25
Walker, 80
Wallis, Ben, 83
Walton, Kevin, 90, 91, 150
Warburton, Keith, 150, 151
Warner, Lawrence, 179
Warren, Guy, 134
Watson, Jay, 148, 157
Webb, Clive, 179
Wells, Frank, 19, 21, 85
Wells, Loran, 179
Welsby, John, 156
Whitfield, 80
Wickens, Phil, 89
Wiles, James, 90
Wilkes, Charles, 181
Wilkins, Hubert, 82, 95
Willey, Lawrence, 89, 93
Williams, Ev, 156
Williams, Martyn, 21, 23
Williams, Warwick, 177
Wiltsie, Gordon, 29, 59, 61, 110 ,111, 141
Wood, Gareth, 131
Woodman, Clive, 160
Wooldridge, Mike, 177
Woperis, Anton, 70
Worley, Brenton, 135
Wormald, 95
Worsley, Frank, 147
Wright, Eliot, 51

Zabalaza, Mikel, 116
Zakarov, Nikolay, 117, 118
Zangrilli, Fabrizio, 114

Acknowledgements

A book of this scope can never truly be the work of one person. From my earliest days in the Antarctic world, through a decade spent climbing and travelling in Antarctica, to writing this book, I have been the recipient of outrageous fortune and unstinting assistance. Even solo on a summit, or working late into the night writing these words, I have never been alone. As always, from the Scott Polar Research Institute in Cambridge, Bob Headland, Peter Clarkson and Charles Swithinbank provided valuable feedback, proofreading and advice. Stories of the early days in the Ellsworth Mountains were told to me by John Splettstoesser, Nick Clinch, John Evans, Eiichi Fukushima and the rest of 1966-67 team, then Pat Morrow, Alejo Contreras, Conrad Anker, Jay Smith, Bernard Virelaude, Dave Hahn and others added to the later years. Along the mountainous Antarctic Peninsula I needed the historical guidance of many, but particularly ex-BAS men Geoff Hattersley-Smith, Keith Holmes, Bob Lewis, Nick Lewis, Ian McMorrin, Ivor Morgan, Shaun Norman and Ken Pawson. The stunning towers of Queen Maud Land and the routes on them were revealed to me by Ivar Tollefsen, Gordon Wiltsie, Mike Libecki, Christoph Höbenreich and Charles Swithinbank. Ed Stump, Paul Fitzgerald, Colin Monteath, Richard Brooke and the late Sir Wally Herbert helped add some flesh to the vast spine of the Transantarctics. Skip Novak, Crag Jones, Lindsay Griffin, Stephen Venables, Pat Lurcock, Grant Dixon, Alun Hubbard, Bob Headland and Lionel Daudet kindly shared their experiences of stormy southern islands I have not visited. Editors Eric Vola and Jo Cleere somehow wrangled my sea of words into a manageable stream so that my publisher Paul-Erik Mondron could channel it into the world. I would not be in a position to create any of this without my expedition partners over the years, to whom I owe so much - Camilo Rada, Rodrigo Fica, Jed Brown, Maria Paz Ibarra, Stephen Chaplin, Manuel Bugueño, Jarmila Tyrril, Osvald Usaj, John Bath, Mike Roberts, Doug Stoup, Walter Laserer, Christian Stangl and particularly, Bob Elias. My father George and a host of others, especially Jan Saunders, provided support along the way. I thank you all.

The photographs here are the product of half a century of mountaineering in Antarctica and many have never previously been published. They are the only views of a place that most will never visit. I cannot express enough my gratitude to all those who have generously contributed the valuable images from their collections. This book is nothing without them. They are, in alphabetical order: Simon Abrahams, Mike Austin, John Bath, Anselme Baud, Jacques Belge, Jed Brown, Jonathan Chester, Robb Clifton, Lionel Daudet, Grant Dixon, John Evans, Eiichi Fukushima, Simon Garrod, Henri de Gerlache, Lindsay Griffin, Bob Headland, Kari Herbert, Alun Hubbard, Alain Hubert, Rob Jarvis, Crag Jones, Kate Kiefer, Kieran Lawton, Bob Lewis, Mike Libecki, Pat Lurcock, Ian McMorrin, Colin Monteath, Ivor Morgan, Skip Novak, Frédérique Olivier, Roger Owen, Keri-Lee Pashuk, Camilo Rada, René Robert, Mark Sedon, Christine Siddoway, Ed Stump, Ivar Tollefsen, Lucas Trihey, Nicola Tsang and Gordon Wiltsie.

JED BROWN LOOKS EAST ACROSS THE ELLEN GLACIER, from the summit of Mount Anderson in the northern Sentinel Range.

Photo credits

Gordon Wiltsie: cover, 98, 111, 112-113, 114, 115
Damien Gildea: 6-7, 8 ,15, 18, 19, 21, 22, 26, 28 (2), 29 bottom, 30-31,
    32, 33, 34, 38, 39 bottom, 40 (2), 43, 44, 45, 52, 53, 54 top, 55, 56
    right, 64, 66, 67, 68, 69, 70 (2), 77 left, 82-83, 104 top, 190
International Polar Foundation - René Robert: 9, 100, 101, 109 bottom,
    116 (2), 117, 118 top, 119
Jed Brown: 10, 14, 36-37, 41
Camilo Rada: 13, 39 top
John Evans: 16 (2)
Eiichi Fukushima: 17 (2)
Paul-Erik Mondron: 24
USGS / Damien Gildea: 25
Anselme Baud: 29 top
Jonathan Chester: 46
Mark Sedon: 48, 78, 80, 81, 84
Mike Austin: 49, 86 (2), 87 bottom
John Bath: 54 bottom
Keri-Lee Pashuk: 56 left, 57
Kieran Lawton: 59 (2), 74
Gerlache Collection: 61, 65 right, 102 (2), 104 (middle & bottom)
Lucas Trihey: 62, 72 (2), 76 bottom, 77 right
Nicola Tsang: 63
Skip Novak: 65 left, 149 (2), 152, 154-155 top, 157, 158-159, 160,
    161 bottom, 162, 164-65
Nicola Tsang: 71, 73, 75, 79

Bob Lewis: 76 top
Simon Abrahams: 87 top
Roger Owen: 88, 91 left
Robin Jarvis: 89
Ian McMorrin: 90 (2)
Ivor Morgan: 91 right, 93 (2)
Simon Garrod: 94, 95 (3), 96
Ivar Tollefsen: 103, 106-107, 108 (2), 109 top, 118 bottom
Mike Libecki: 110, 120, 121, 122, 123, 124, 125
USGS: 126, 131, 134, 135, 136, 143, 179 centre, 179 right
Colin Monteath (Hedgehog House): 128 (2), 130 bottom, 133 top
Ed Stump: 130 top, 133 bottom, 141, 144 (4)
Wally Herbert Collection: 138
Jacques Belge: 140, 145
Pat Lurcock: 146
Lindsay Griffin: 150, 163 top
Alun Hubbard: 151, 153
Caradoc Jones: 154 bottom, 156 (2), 161 top
Grant Dixon: 163 bottom
Robert K. Headland: 166, 180, 181
Lionel Daudet: 167, 168, 170, 171
Kate Kiefer: 172
Robb Clifton: 174
Frédérique Olivier: 176, 177 (2)
Christine Siddoway: 178 (2), 179 left

Graphic design by Juliette de Patoul.
Printed and bound in Belgium by Lannoo Print, Tielt, September 2010.